Howard Mumford Jones is Abbott
Lawrence Lowell Professor of the
Humanities, Emeritus, at Harvard University,
and former Editor of the *Harvard Library
Bulletin*. He is the author of many works,
including *Ideas in America, Education and
World Tragedy, The Theory of American
Literature, O Strange New World*, and the
recent historical study *The Age of Energy*.
He is the editor of *American Prose Masters*
by W. C. Brownell (HUP 1963) and
English Traits by Ralph Waldo Emerson
(HUP 1966).
Richard M. Ludwig is Professor of English at
Princeton University. He is editor of
Aspects of American Poetry and *Letters of
Ford Madox Ford*, and co-editor of *Literary
History of the United States* and *Major
American Writers*.

Guide to
American Literature
and Its
Backgrounds
since 1890

Guide to American Literature and Its Backgrounds since 1890

HOWARD MUMFORD JONES
and RICHARD M. LUDWIG

Fourth Edition, Revised and Enlarged

HARVARD UNIVERSITY PRESS

Cambridge, Massachusetts

1972

Library of Congress Catalog Card Number 72–85143

SBN 674–36753–7

Printed in the United States of America

B Z J

hoc opus, hic labor

PREFATORY NOTE TO THE
FOURTH EDITION

In revising this manual, we have added new titles, removed obsolescent works, and, wherever possible, noted new editions of important background books and guides. The reading lists have been increased from the third edition by one new list on drama and by new titles from the sixties and early seventies wherever applicable. In addition, the information on periodicals has been brought up to date, and relevant material since 1966 has been added to the table of events and other historical sections. We have retained the original Introduction, with a few alterations, since this brief essay still indicates the general purport of our guide, even though some assertions in it have been modified by time and by the development of literary studies.

We remind all readers of this guide that our listings are suggestive, not definitive.

Howard Mumford Jones
Richard M. Ludwig

April 1972

Contents

The Backgrounds of American Literature since 1890

CONTENTS

CONTENTS

Reading Lists of American Literature since 1890

CONTENTS

xii

Guide to

American Literature

and Its

Backgrounds

since 1890

GENERAL INTRODUCTION

This guide to American literature since 1890 and its background is an attempt to impose intellectual order upon confusion. There are histories of fiction which cover this period; there are a few histories of poetry; there are excellent studies of this or that element in the history of ideas; but there is no single work that presents to the reader in understandable order the combination of intellectual and sociological (political) event and literary productivity, which is at once the peril and the exhilaration of this enterprise.

Neither the outline nor the selected bibliography here given can be thought of as definitive or complete. Whatever may be meant by either term, both completeness and definitiveness are impossible. The number of book titles appearing annually in twentieth-century America now hovers around thirty thousand. Even if one assumes that a mere tenth of this yearly product is worth examining, no human being could read so vast an incremental library, much less make up his own mind or the minds of his readers as to who or what is entitled to immortality.

The present guide faces an unanswerable question. What is American literature? Is it composed of the books that critics acclaim; and if so, what critics? Or is it composed of the books that some important part of the population reads? Were we to accept the judgment of one group of critics, only those books which display qualities of style or structure satisfactory to a small and special group of intellectuals, "sophisticates," academic writers, avant-gardists, or the like, exhibit the proper qualities of art. The special virtue of the judgment of this group is that it calls attention to values in books, especially poetry, literary criticism, and some kinds of fiction, that the hurly-burly of trade publishing ignores. This judgment often establishes qualities which a larger reading public by and by grows ready to accept. On the other hand, that larger segment of the public—one de-

1

voted to "good books," the patrons of circulating libraries, book clubs, reading circles, and, more rarely, book stores—mostly has so little interest in the judgments of the critics just discussed as in fact to ignore them.

This larger group of readers, less moved by esoteric poetry, is by no means opposed to poetry, though it wants poetry that is less difficult. It is by no means hostile to literary critcism, but it ↷wants literary criticism that makes reading easier rather than more complex. Though it is on the whole suspicious of sentimental and commercialized fiction, it demands of its favorite novelists qualities of narrative art and conceptions of character that seem to critics dangerously close to philistinism. Yet if a publisher can attract the interest of this important group, he will succeed, at least on the "good books" level. Does the taste of this group of readers constitute American literature in fact?

Alas, as Brander Matthews long ago pointed out, there are innumerable publics, and these are but two of them. A third important reading group cannot be ignored—the public for nonfictional prose, for the book of ideas, for history and biography. The avant-garde critic does not characteristically interest himself in biography unless it be biographical material within the limited range of his group. Yet books like the biographical studies of Gamaliel Bradford, or Douglas Freeman's *Lee*, or Dumas Malone's monumental *Jefferson*, not yet complete, are clearly as important landmarks in American writing as is, let us say, the prose of Henry Miller or the fiction of Truman Capote. How great has been the influence of works like Joseph Wood Krutch's *The Modern Temper* or Walter Lippmann's *Preface to Morals* we cannot tell, but obviously it has been vast. How immense the influence of the Beards' famous history, *The Rise of American Civilization!* Yet we do not think it harsh to say that most discussions of American literary development during the twentieth century minimize or ignore the place of biography, lay philosophy, the prose of public discourse, and historical writing—always excepting a few favored names like those of William James and Henry Adams. It seems clear, however, if we are to understand American thought in the period, that we cannot thus cavalierly neglect the rich development of our literature of knowledge.

INTRODUCTION

Indeed, in any generous or total scheme even subliterary work should have its place. Long ago Arthur M. Schlesinger, Sr., pointed out the desirability of considering dime novels, adventure stories, sentimental fiction, and other types of books below the literary salt. Fascinating recent studies of best sellers in America merely underline his theorem. Indeed, the impartial observer has some right to be either puzzled or amused to find the literary historian cherishing all he can discover about such sentimental trash as *The Power of Sympathy* or *Charlotte Temple*, yet declining to soil his hands with Harold Bell Wright or Gene Stratton Porter.

Considerations like these complicate a subject that is already complex. There are other considerations as well. What is literary history? Whatever its theory may be, practice has oscillated between two poles. At one extreme the literary historian, rightly fearful lest literature lose its aesthetic bloom if it be too deeply enmeshed in social history, tries to establish a canon of his own, wherein books produce books, authors succeed authors, and style follows upon style as if by some inner law. The virtue of this approach is that it insists on the aesthetic value of writing as art; it insists on the value of thought well expressed for its own sake; and it insists that artistic work of the highest import has often been produced with little or no reference to the spirit of the times. Yet the weakness of this position is also evident—a weakness following upon the failure to understand Emerson's wise injunction when he tells us that every scripture has the right to be read in the light of the times that brought it forth. Many works incontestably lose their meaning unless they are read in the context of the problem which produced them.

The other extreme reduces literature to documents in social history or the history of ideas; it seems to produce writers as it produces changes in the tariff; it satisfies itself with a catalogue of titles and names of men; and it is mostly oblivious of the historical importance in aesthetic appeal. From this point of view, for instance, *Uncle Tom's Cabin* is perpetually an antislavery novel, sentimental in tone, which somehow sold thousands of copies. This is scarcely an adequate concept of *Uncle Tom's Cabin*. The book is an antislavery novel, and it sold its thousands; these are primary facts. But raw fact is not literary

3

history; and the competent literary historian wants to probe further—to uncover (as he does) a lost fictional library on slavery, and to trace in Harriet Beecher Stowe's masterpiece the incongruous elements that make it up. In American literary history, a branch of learning in which political events have been particularly important in shaping literature, one must perpetually guard oneself against too much sociologizing, while accepting the basic truth that in no modern literature is the connection between literature and national event closer than it is in the United States.

If one shifts the angle of vision, if one asks what books have had most to do with shaping the American mind, the American imagination, the American vision of life since 1890, a kind of guiding principle appears. One cannot claim that this is the only principle, just as one cannot claim that this is the only thread through the immense labyrinth of American publishing. Yet it is a principle one finds more helpful than any other.

Books that have shaped the American mind may be of two sorts: individual books of such power that their influence will be granted by any competent student; and classes of books, which can be represented by examples. To the first type William James's *Varieties of Religious Experience* and Herbert Croly's *Promise of American Life* seem clearly to belong; whereas if one wants to study the kind of historical romance that swamped the country after the Spanish-American War and that long conditioned our general interpretation of history, any or all of a dozen representative titles will do.

There is a third consideration. Trends in writing and publishing—call them intellectual, fashionable, artistic, what you will—are also discernible. Such, for example, is the library of books presenting the social gospel; such also is the proletarian literature of the thirties. And a fourth consideration appears—that vague attribute known as importance. Waiving all such ticklish problems as "Important for what?" or "Important for whom?" one always finds titles of this sort, titles of which it can be said, not so much that importance requires inclusion, as that their inclusion in other lists establishes their importance here. If this distinction seems like hair-splitting, let us give an example. At the moment the literary importance of Henry L. Mencken is at a low ebb both among the literati and among general readers; but one can no more consider the twenties and omit Mencken than one can consider the Restoration and omit Dryden's verse.

This handbook is put together in the light of these considerations. The first half of the book is an organized compilation of titles designed to enable the student better to understand the social and intellectual setting of American literature in the years under survey. The second half is devoted to fifty-two lists that guide the reader through American literature itself since 1890. Each reading list has a separate Arabic number for quickness of reference as well as for treating any single unit in the guide independently, should this seem desirable. Both halves of the book are nowhere exhaustive. No doubt we have omitted many an important title. One can only plead with Dr. Johnson, "Ignorance, madam, sheer ignorance," and implore the reader to write in the missing title where he thinks it belongs. So rich and sudden has been the efflorescence of American literary art in the last eighty years, it would be quite possible to construct other groups of excellent titles paralleling ours and scarcely duplicating them. All we are trying to do is to offer to those who are puzzled by the embarrassment of our literary riches a scheme, a clue, an outline, a pattern that will make some sort of sense, even though it may not be at all points the right sense. The decision as to what is of permanent worth in this vast library will not be made for another hundred years, but in the meanwhile one is entitled to understand it if one can. No doubt somebody's special favorite is neglected or squeezed into a corner. Around the work of many leading authors—Henry James, Robert Frost, and William Faulkner, for example—a whole library of comment, interpretation, and biographical knowledge has been published. To attempt to list such studies, or to try to be even more inclusive and list references to magazine articles and magazine publication, would be to swell this guide to inordinate length. We have settled, therefore, on just two major divisions: the social and intellectual backgrounds, followed by the major works of American literature since 1890. All dates given for the publication of these titles are the dates of original publication, unless a revised edition has appeared.

We are indebted to Frederick Merk and Daniel Aaron of Harvard University, to Isaac Asimov of Boston University, and to William L. Howarth and A. Walton Litz of Princeton University for graciously reviewing the material; and are very grateful to Ann B. Hopkins and James E. Brogan for tirelessly checking the data and saving us from many blunders. We are also happy to record the patient and sympathetic interest of the late Thomas J. Wilson of Harvard University Press in planning the form of this work originally and in organizing and simplifying it for the greater happiness of its users.

ABBREVIATIONS USED FOR PUBLISHING COMPANIES

In order to avoid needless repetition and to save space in the bibliographical lists on pages 135–221, abbreviations are used for some of the publishing houses. Their full names are given here, with the *portion used as abbreviation* printed in *italics*. Since changes in name are common, certain houses are listed with several variations. In these instances, the basic name (in *italics*) is used as an abbreviation for all of the variations. For example, *Harcourt* stands for Harcourt, Brace & Co.; Harcourt, Brace & World, Inc.; and Harcourt Brace Jovanovich, Inc.

Abingdon Press; Abingdon-Cokesbury Press
D. *Appleton* & Co.; D. Appleton-Century Co.; Appleton-Century-Crofts
Atheneum Publishers

Bobbs-Merrill Co., Inc.
R. R. *Bowker* Co.
George *Braziller*, Inc.

Century Co.
Columbia University Press
Cornell University Press
Thomas Y. *Crowell* Co.
Crown Publishers

Dial Press
Dodd, Mead & Co., Inc.
Doubleday, Page & Co.; Doubleday, Doran & Co.; Doubleday & Co., Inc.
Dover Publications
Dryden Press

Duke University Press
E. P. *Dutton* & Co.

Farrar & Rinehart; Farrar, Straus; Farrar, Straus & Young; Farrar, Straus & Cudahy; Farrar, Straus & Giroux, Inc.
Funk & Wagnalls Co.

Harcourt, Brace & Co.; Harcourt, Brace & World, Inc.; Harcourt Brace Jovanovich, Inc.
Harper & Brothers; Harper & Row, Publishers, Inc.
Harvard University Press
Henry *Holt* & Co.; Holt, Rinehart & Winston, Inc.
Houghton Mifflin Co.

Indiana University Press
Iowa State University Press

Johns Hopkins Press
Johnson Reprint Corp.

7

PUBLISHING COMPANIES

Alfred A. *Knopf*, Inc.

J. B. *Lippincott* Co.
Little, Brown & Co.
Longmans, Green & Co.
Louisiana State University Press

M. I. T. Press
McGraw-Hill Book Co.
David *McKay* Co., Inc.
Macmillan Co.
Michigan State University Press

New York University Press
Northwestern University Press
W. W. *Norton* & Co., Inc.

Oxford University Press, New York

Pantheon Books
Penguin Books, Inc.
Frederick A. *Praeger*; Praeger Publishers, Inc.
Prentice-Hall, Inc.
Princeton University Press
G. P. *Putnam*'s Sons

Rand, McNally & Co.
Random House
Henry *Regnery* Co.
Reynal & Co.; Reynal & Hitchcock
Rinehart & Co.
Ronald Press Co.
Rutgers University Press

Charles *Scribner*'s Sons
Simon & Schuster, Inc.
Southern Illinois University Press
Southern Methodist University Press
Stanford University Press
Alan *Swallow*, Publisher; Swallow Press, Inc.
Syracuse University Press

Frederick *Ungar* Publishing Co.
University of California Press
University of Chicago Press
University of Florida Press
University of Georgia Press
University of Illinois Press
University of Michigan Press
University of Minnesota Press
University of Nebraska Press
University of New Mexico Press
University of North Carolina Press
University of Oklahoma Press
University of Pennsylvania Press
University of Texas Press
University of Wisconsin Press

Viking Press
Vintage Books

Wayne State University Press
H. W. *Wilson* Co.
World Publishing Co.

Yale University Press

8

The

Backgrounds of

American Literature

since 1890

I · GENERAL GUIDES

Oscar Handlin and others, *Harvard Guide to American History* (Cambridge, Harvard, 1954).

Donald Henry Mugridge and Blanche P. McCrum, *A Guide to the Study of the United States of America: Representative Books Reflecting the Development of American Thought and Life* (Washington, Library of Congress, 1960). Almost 1,200 pages of annotated bibliography of literary, scientific, historical, economic, religious, and other aspects of American civilization. A supplement is in preparation.

Writings on American History (Washington, U.S. Government Printing Office, 1906–). This invaluable annual bibliography has appeared regularly, except that the years 1941–1947 are not covered. It is a supplement to the *Annual Report* of the American Historical Association.

II · GENERAL REFERENCE WORKS

James Truslow Adams and others, *Album of American History*, 5 vols. (New York, Scribner, 1944–1949). An "attempt to tell the history of America through pictures made at the time history was being made." The 4th volume covers 1890–1920; the 5th volume is an index.

James Truslow Adams and others, *Dictionary of American History*, revised edition, 5 vols. (New York, Scribner, 1946). Supplement One, edited by J. G. E. Hopkins and Wayne Andrews, appeared in 1961. Under the advisory editorship of Thomas C. Cochran, *The Concise Dictionary of American History*, edited by Wayne Andrews, was published in 1962. It is a one-volume abridgment of the original six volumes.

Gorton Carruth and associates, *The Encyclopedia of American Facts and Dates*, 5th edition (New York, Crowell, 1970).

BACKGROUNDS

Edward T. James, Janet Wilson James, and Paul S. Boyer, *Notable American Women, 1607–1950: A Biographical Dictionary*, 3 vols. (Cambridge, Harvard, 1971). This work grew out of a proposal by the Advisory Board of the Women's Archives, Radcliffe College, and seeks to correct the fact that, of nearly 15,000 individuals in the *Dictionary of American Biography* (see below), only 700 are women. It includes 1,359 names and has a general historical introduction by Janet Wilson James on the roles of women in the nation's history. Some biographies in *Notable American Women* improve on similar ones in the *Dictionary of American Biography*.

Allen Johnson and others, *Dictionary of American Biography*, 20 vols. (New York, Scribner, 1928–1936). A supplementary, unnumbered index volume was published in 1937. Supplement One (Vol. XXI), covering the lives of important persons inadvertently omitted from the original edition and, more significantly, the lives of important persons whose deaths occurred between the completion of the first twenty volumes and December 31, 1935, was published in 1944 under the editorship of Harris E. Starr. A second supplement (Vol. XXII) under the editorship of Robert Livingston Schuyler and Edward T. James, covering material to December 31, 1940, was published in 1958. The *Concise Dictionary of American Biography* (Scribner, 1964), was prepared under the direction of Joseph G. E. Hopkins. It is a one-volume abridgment of all 14,780 articles in the original dictionary and supplements.

Thomas Herbert Johnson, in consultation with Harvey Wish, *The Oxford Companion to American History* (New York, Oxford, 1966).

Henrietta Melia Larson, *Guide to Business History* (Cambridge, Harvard, 1948). Vol. XII of Harvard Studies in Business History.

Richard Brandon Morris, *Encyclopedia of American History*, updated and revised edition (New York, Harper, 1970).

David Lawrence Sills, ed., *International Encyclopedia of the Social Sciences*, 17 vols. (New York, Macmillan, 1968).

III · GENERAL HISTORIES

Frederick Lewis Allen, *The Big Change: America Transforms Itself, 1900–1950* (New York, Harper, 1952).

Charles Austin Beard and Mary R. Beard, *The Rise of American Civilization*, revised and enlarged edition, 2 vols. (New York, Macmillan, 1947). *America in Mid-Passage* (New York, Macmillan, 1939) by the same authors continues this history into the 1930s. *The American Spirit* (New York, Macmillan, 1942), the fourth and last volume in the Beards' history, is "an effort to grasp the intellectual and moral qualities of the United States since 1776."

Ray Allen Billington, Bert James Loewenberg, and Samuel Hugh Brockunier, *The United States: American Democracy in World Perspective* (New York, Rinehart, 1947). Most of Part II and all of Part III deal with the twentieth century.

Ray Allen Billington and David S. Sparks, eds., *The Making of American Democracy: Readings and Documents*, revised edition, 2 vols. (New York, Holt, 1962).

Daniel Joseph Boorstin, *The Americans: The National Experience* (New York, Random, 1965).

Harry James Carman, Harold Coffin Syrett, and Bernard W. Wishy, *A History of the American People*, 3rd revised edition, 2 vols. (New York, Knopf, 1967). Vol. II begins with 1865.

Thomas Dionysius Clark, *The Emerging South* (New York, Oxford, 1961).

Dwight Lowell Dumond, *America in Our Time, 1896–1946* (New York, Holt, 1947).

Frank Burt Freidel, *America in the Twentieth Century*, 3rd edition (New York, Knopf, 1970).

Oscar Handlin, *The American People in the Twentieth Century* (Cambridge, Harvard, 1954). In the Library of Congress Series in American Civilization.

John Donald Hicks, George Edwin Mowry, and Robert E. Burke, *The American Nation*, 4th edition (Boston, Houghton Mifflin, 1963). It covers the years 1865–1962.

Richard Hofstadter, *Anti-Intellectualism in American Life* (New York, Knopf, 1963).

Richard Hofstadter, William Miller, and Daniel Aaron, *The United States: The History of a Republic* (New York, Prentice-Hall, 1957).

Howard Mumford Jones, *The Age of Energy: Varieties of American Experience, 1865–1915* (New York, Viking, 1971).

Walter Consuelo Langsam and Otis C. Mitchell, *The World Since 1919*, 8th edition (New York, Macmillan, 1971).

Christopher Lasch, *The New Radicalism in America, 1889–1963* (New York, Knopf, 1965). Focuses on "the intellectual as a social type."

Arthur Stanley Link and William Bruce Catton, *American Epoch: A History of the United States Since the 1890's* (New York, Knopf, 1963).

Samuel Eliot Morison, *The Oxford History of the American People* (New York, Oxford, 1965).

Samuel Eliot Morison, Henry Steele Commager, and William Edward Leuchtenburg, *The Growth of the American Republic*, 6th edition, revised and enlarged, 2 vols. (New York, Oxford, 1969). Vol. II covers the period since the Civil War.

Arthur Meier Schlesinger, Sr., *Political and Social Growth of the American People, 1865–1940*, 3rd edition (New York, Macmillan, 1941). In its most recent form, this work was retitled *The Rise of Modern America, 1865–1951*, 4th edition (New York, Macmillan, 1951).

David Allen Shannon, *Twentieth Century America: The United States Since the 1890s* (Chicago, Rand, McNally, 1963).

Mark Sullivan, *Our Times*, 6 vols. (New York, Scribner, 1926–1935). Vol. I. *The Turn of the Century* (to 1900); Vol. II. *America Finding Herself* (1900–1905); Vol. III. *Pre-War America* (1905–1908); Vol. IV. *The War Begins* (1909–1914); Vol. V. *Over Here* (1914–1918); Vol. VI. *The Twenties* (to 1926).

Harvey Wish, *Society and Thought in America*, 2nd edition, 2 vols. (New York, McKay, 1962). Vol. II discusses America from 1865 to the present.

GENERAL HISTORIES

Comer Vann Woodward, *Origins of the New South, 1877–1913* (Baton Rouge, Louisiana State, 1951). Vol. IX of *A History of the South*, edited by Wendell Holmes Stephenson and E. Merton Coulter, now in progress.

A · THE NINETIES

Frederick Lewis Allen, *The Lords of Creation* (New York, Harper, 1935). A study of business leadership.

Thomas Beer, *The Mauve Decade: American Life at the End of the Nineteenth Century* (New York, Knopf, 1926). A mannered cultural history.

French Ensor Chadwick, *The Relations of the United States and Spain: The Spanish-American War*, 2 vols. (New York, Scribner, 1911).

Paolo Enrico Coletta, *William Jennings Bryan*, 3 vols. (Lincoln, University of Nebraska, 1964–1969).

Herbert David Croly, *Marcus Alonzo Hanna: His Life and Work* (New York, Macmillan, 1912).

Frank Burt Freidel, *The Splendid Little War* (Boston, Little, Brown, 1958).

Ray Ginger, *Age of Excess: The United States from 1877 to 1914* (New York, Macmillan, 1965).

Ray Ginger, *Altgeld's America: The Lincoln Ideal Versus Changing Realities* (New York, Funk & Wagnalls, 1958). Illuminates the change from rural to urban America, 1892–1905.

Paul Wilbur Glad, *McKinley, Bryan, and the People* (Philadelphia, Lippincott, 1964).

John Donald Hicks, *The Populist Revolt: A History of the Farmers' Alliance and the People's Party* (Minneapolis, University of Minnesota, 1931). Reprinted in 1961 (Lincoln, University of Nebraska).

Richard Hofstadter, *The Age of Reform: From Bryan to Franklin Delano Roosevelt* (New York, Knopf, 1955).

Stewart Gall Holbrook, *The Age of the Moguls* (Garden City, Doubleday, 1953). In the Mainstream of America series.

BACKGROUNDS

Joseph Rogers Hollingsworth, *The Whirligig of Politics: The Democracy of Cleveland and Bryan* (Chicago, University of Chicago, 1963).

Arthur Mann, *Yankee Reformers in the Urban Age* (Cambridge, Harvard, 1954).

Walter Millis, *The Martial Spirit: A Study of Our War with Spain* (Boston, Houghton Mifflin, 1931).

Clifford Wheeler Patton, *The Battle for Municipal Reform: Mobilization and Attack, 1875–1900* (Washington, American Council on Public Affairs, 1940).

Norman Pollack, *The Populist Mind* (Indianapolis, Bobbs-Merrill, 1967).

Julius William Pratt, *Expansionists of 1898: The Acquisition of Hawaii and the Spanish Islands* (Baltimore, Johns Hopkins, 1936). Reprinted in New York, 1951, by Peter Smith.

James Ford Rhodes, *The History of the United States from Hayes to McKinley, 1877–1896*, new edition (New York, Macmillan, 1928). Vol. VIII of Rhodes' *History of the United States from the Compromise of 1850.*

Arthur Meier Schlesinger, Sr., *The Rise of the City, 1878–1898* (New York, Macmillan, 1933). Vol. X of the History of American Life series.

Francis Butler Simkins, *Pitchfork Ben Tillman, South Carolinian* (Baton Rouge, Louisiana State, 1944).

W. A. Swanberg, *Citizen Hearst: A Biography of William Randolph Hearst* (New York, Scribner, 1961).

Ida Minerva Tarbell, *The Nationalizing of Business, 1878–1898* (New York, Macmillan, 1936). Vol. IX of the History of American Life series.

Comer Vann Woodward, *Tom Watson: Agrarian Rebel* (New York, Macmillan, 1938).

B · THE PROGRESSIVE ERA

Howard Kennedy Beale, *Theodore Roosevelt and the Rise of America to World Power* (Baltimore, Johns Hopkins, 1956).

GENERAL HISTORIES

John Morton Blum, *The Republican Roosevelt* (Cambridge, Harvard, 1954).

Claude Gernade Bowers, *Beveridge and the Progressive Era* (Boston, Houghton Mifflin, 1932).

Nowell Fairchild Busch, Jr., *TR: The Story of Theodore Roosevelt and His Influence on Our Times* (New York, Reynal, 1963).

David Mark Chalmers, *The Social and Political Ideas of the Muckrakers* (New York, Citadel Press, 1964).

John Chamberlain, *Farewell to Reform: The Rise, Life, and Decay of the Progressive Mind of America*, 2nd edition (New York, John Day Co., 1933).

Tyler Dennett, *John Hay: From Poetry to Politics* (New York, Dodd, Mead, 1933).

Dwight Lowell Dumond, *Roosevelt to Roosevelt: The United States in the Twentieth Century* (New York, Holt, 1937).

Harold Underwood Faulkner, *The Quest for Social Injustice, 1898–1914* (New York, Macmillan, 1931). Vol. XI of the History of American Life series.

Charles Forcey, *The Crossroads of Liberalism: Croly, Weyl, Lippmann, and the Progressive Era, 1900–1925* (New York, Oxford, 1961).

Eric Frederick Goldman, *Rendezvous with Destiny. A History of American Reform* (New York, Knopf, 1952).

Samuel Gompers, *Seventy Years of Life and Labor: An Autobiography*, 2 vols. (New York, Dutton, 1925). Reprinted in one volume in 1943.

William Henry Harbaugh, *The Life and Times of Theodore Roosevelt*, revised edition (New York, Collier Books, 1963).

Richard Hofstadter, ed., *The Progressive Movement, 1900–1915* (Englewood Cliffs, Prentice-Hall, 1963). Excerpts from contemporaneous writing.

Belle Case La Follette and Fola La Follette, *Robert M. LaFollette, 1855–1925*, 2 vols. (New York, Macmillan, 1953).

Arthur Stanley Link, *Wilson* (Princeton, Princeton University, 1947–). Vol. I. *The Road to the White House*; Vol. II. *The*

New Freedom; Vol. III. *The Struggle for Neutrality, 1914–1915*; Vol. IV. *Confusions and Crises, 1915–1916*; Vol. V. *Campaigns for Progressivism and Peace, 1916–1917*.

Arthur Stanley Link, *Woodrow Wilson, A Brief Biography* (Cleveland, World, 1963).

Arthur Stanley Link, *Woodrow Wilson and the Progressive Era, 1910–1917* (New York, Harper, 1954). In the New American Nation series.

Walter Lord, *The Good Years: From 1900 to the First World War* (New York, Harper, 1960).

Ernest Richard May, *From Imperialism to Isolation, 1898–1919* (New York, Citadel Press, 1964).

Henry Farnham May, *The End of American Innocence: A Study of the First Years of Our Own Time, 1912–1917* (New York, Knopf, 1959).

Elting Elmore Morison and others, eds., *The Letters of Theodore Roosevelt*, 8 vols. (Cambridge, Harvard, 1951–1954). The volumes run: *The Years of Preparation, 1868–1900*, 2 vols.; *The Square Deal, 1901–1905*, 2 vols.; *The Big Stick, 1905–1909*, 2 vols.; and *The Days of Armageddon, 1909–1919*, 2 vols.

George Edwin Mowry, *The Era of Theodore Roosevelt, 1900–1912* (New York, Harper, 1958). In the New American Nation series.

Otis Pease, ed., *The Progressive Years: The Spirit and Achievement of American Reform* (New York, Braziller, 1962).

Amos Richards Eno Pinchot, *History of the Progressive Party, 1912–1916*, edited with an introduction by Helene Maxwell Hooker (New York, New York University, 1958).

Cornelius C. Regier, *The Era of the Muckrakers* (Chapel Hill, University of North Carolina, 1932).

James Ford Rhodes, *The McKinley and Roosevelt Administrations, 1897–1909* (New York, Macmillan, 1922). Vol. IX of Rhodes's *History of the United States from the Compromise of 1850*.

Lincoln Steffens, *Autobiography* (New York, Harcourt, 1931). An American classic, often reprinted.

GENERAL HISTORIES

Lincoln Steffens, *The Shame of the Cities* (New York, McClure, Phillips & Co., 1904). Famous not merely as muckraking but also as valuable insight into the psychology of city bosses.

Ida Minerva Tarbell, *The History of the Standard Oil Company*, 2 vols. (New York, McClure, Phillips & Co., 1904). Probably the most nearly objective of the muckraking volumes; often reprinted.

William Roscoe Thayer, *The Life and Letters of John Hay*, 2 vols. (Boston, Houghton Mifflin, 1915).

James Harfield Timberlake, *Prohibition and the Progressive Movement, 1900–1920* (Cambridge, Harvard, 1963).

Barbara W. Tuchman, *The Proud Tower: A Portrait of the World Before the War, 1890–1914* (New York, Macmillan, 1965).

Kermit Vanderbilt, *Charles Eliot Norton: Apostle of Culture in a Democracy* (Cambridge, Harvard, 1963).

Arthur Myron Weinberg and Lila Weinberg, eds., *The Muckrakers: The Era in Journalism That Moved America to Reform—The Most Significant Magazine Articles of 1902–1912* (New York, Simon & Schuster, 1961).

C · WORLD WAR I

Although virtually all the great leaders—political, military, economic, scientific, and medical—of the many nations who participated in World War I have published their memoirs or their correspondence (usually highly selective); and although hundreds of thousands of documents have issued since 1919 from hundreds of printing plants concerning every phase of this titanic struggle, it remains difficult to gain a just, impartial view of the causes, conduct, and conclusion of the conflict. Historians are still at work on primary material. The following titles are therefore suggestive only. The first group is Europe-oriented; the second is concerned with pre- and postwar America.

Frank Lee Benns, *European History Since 1870*, 4th edition (New York, Appleton, 1955). A standard text.

John Buchan, *A History of the Great War*, revised edition, 8 vols.

(Boston, Houghton Mifflin, 1922). Less a history than a day-by-day chronicle from the British point of view. It originally appeared in 24 volumes between February 1915 and July 1919 under the title *Nelson's History of the War*.

Winston Leonard Spencer Churchill, *The World Crisis*, 5 vols. (New York, Scribner, 1923–1929). Sir Winston's prose is remarkably clear. The first four volumes, devoted to the years 1911–1918, were later condensed to one volume under the same title (New York, Scribner, 1931).

Charles Loch Mowat, ed., *The Shifting Balance of World Forces, 1898–1945* (London, Cambridge University Press, 1968). The second revised edition of a volume formerly entitled *The Era of Violence*, this is perhaps the best over-all view of world history for this half-century. It is also Vol. XII of the New Cambridge Modern History.

Ellery Cory Stowell, *The Diplomacy of the War of 1914: The Beginnings of the War* (Boston, Houghton Mifflin, 1915). Written too close to events to be thorough, this is nonetheless an attempt at a fair-minded account.

Ray Stannard Baker, *Woodrow Wilson: Life and Letters*, 8 vols. (Garden City, Doubleday, 1927–1939). See also Arthur Stanley Link entries in Section B above.

Allen Churchill, *Over Here! An Informal Re-creation of the Home Front in World War I* (New York, Dodd, Mead, 1968).

Edward M. Coffman, *The War To End All Wars: The American Military Experience in World War I* (New York, Oxford, 1968).

Frank Burt Freidel, *Over There: The Story of America's First Great Overseas Crusade* (Boston, Little, Brown, 1964).

Burton Jesse Hendrick, *Life and Letters of Walter H. Page*, 3 vols. (Garden City, Doubleday, 1922–1925). Important in itself and also for the light it throws on British-American cultural ties.

Ernest Richard May, ed., *The Coming of War, 1917* (Chicago, Rand, McNally, 1963).

GENERAL HISTORIES

Walter Millis, *Road to War: America, 1914–1917* (Boston, Houghton Mifflin, 1935). An excellent instance of the revisionist history of the 1930s.

Robert Keith Murray, *Red Scare: A Study in National Hysteria, 1919–1920* (Minneapolis, University of Minnesota, 1955).

Frederic Logan Paxson, *American Democracy and the World War*, 3 vols. (Boston, Houghton Mifflin, 1936–1948). The three volumes, originally published separately, are: *Pre-War Years, 1913–1917; America at War, 1917–1918*; and *Post-War Years: Normalcy, 1918–1933*.

Horace Cornelius Peterson and Gilbert Courtland Fite, *Opponents of War, 1917–1918* (Madison, University of Wisconsin, 1957).

Charles Seymour, *American Neutrality, 1914–1917* (New Haven, Yale, 1935).

Charles Seymour, *Woodrow Wilson and the World War* (New Haven, Yale, 1921). In the Chronicles of America series.

Preston William Slosson, *The Great Crusade and After, 1914–1928* (New York, Macmillan, 1930). Vol. XII of the History of American Life series.

Charles Callan Tansill, *America Goes to War* (Boston, Little, Brown, 1938).

Barbara W. Tuchman, *The Guns of August* (New York, Macmillan, 1962).

D · THE TWENTIES

Samuel Hopkins Adams, *Incredible Era: The Life and Times of Warren Gamaliel Harding* (Boston, Houghton Mifflin, 1939). Popular in tone.

Frederick Lewis Allen, *Only Yesterday: An Informal History of the Nineteen-Twenties* (New York, Harper, 1931). Popular cultural history.

Harold Underwood Faulkner, *From Versailles to the New Deal: A Chronicle of the Harding-Coolidge Era* (New Haven, Yale, 1950). In the Chronicles of America series.

BACKGROUNDS

William Edward Leuchtenburg, *The Perils of Prosperity, 1914–1932* (Chicago, University of Chicago, 1958). In the Chicago History of American Civilization series.

Robert Staughton Lynd and Helen Merrell Lynd, *Middletown: A Study in Contemporary American Culture* (New York, Harcourt, 1929). A sociological analysis of Muncie, Indiana. It was followed in 1937 by *Middletown in Transition: A Study in Cultural Conflicts*, by the same authors. Both are available in paperback (Harvest Books, Harcourt).

Henry Farnham May, ed., *The Discontent of the Intellectuals: A Problem of the Twenties* (Chicago, Rand, McNally, 1963).

George Edwin Mowry, ed., *The Twenties: Fords, Flappers, and Fanatics* (Englewood Cliffs, Prentice-Hall, 1963). Excerpts from contemporaneous writing.

Peter H. Odegard, *Pressure Politics: The Story of the Anti-Saloon League* (New York, Columbia, 1928). How national prohibition came into being.

Kirby Page, ed., *Recent Gains in American Civilization* (New York, Harcourt, 1928). Estimates of contemporary society by fifteen specialists.

Francis Russell, *The Shadow of Blooming Grove: Warren G. Harding and His Times* (New York, McGraw-Hill, 1968).

Andrew Sinclair, *Prohibition: The Age of Excess* (Boston, Houghton Mifflin, 1962).

George Henry Soule, *Prosperity Decade: From War to Depression, 1917–1929* (New York, Rinehart, 1947).

Caroline Farrer Ware, *Greenwich Village, 1920–1930: A Comment on American Civilization in the Post-War Years* (Boston, Houghton Mifflin, 1935). With this should be read Malcolm Cowley's *Exile's Return*, published in 1934, revised in 1951 (New York, Viking).

E · THE GREAT DEPRESSION AND THE THIRTIES

Frederick Lewis Allen, *Since Yesterday: The Nineteen-Thirties in America* (New York, Harper, 1940).

GENERAL HISTORIES

Francis Beverly Biddle, *In Brief Authority* (Garden City, Doubleday, 1962).

Denis William Brogan, *The Era of Franklin D. Roosevelt: A Chronicle of the New Deal and Global War* (New Haven, Yale, 1950). In the Chronicles of America series.

James MacGregor Burns, *Roosevelt: The Lion and the Fox* (New York, Harcourt, 1956), followed by *Roosevelt: The Soldier of Freedom* (New York, Harcourt, 1970).

Malcolm Cowley, *Exile's Return*, revised edition (New York, Viking, 1951).

Milton Crane, ed., *The Roosevelt Era* (New York, Boni & Gaer, 1947). An anthology of political and literary documents.

Frank Burt Freidel, *Franklin D. Roosevelt*, 3 vols. (Boston, Little, Brown, 1953–1956). Vol. I. *The Apprenticeship*; Vol. II. *The Ordeal*; Vol. III. *The Triumph*.

Frank Burt Freidel, *The New Deal and the American People* (Englewood Cliffs, Prentice-Hall, 1964).

Leo Gurko, *The Angry Decade* (New York, Dodd, Mead, 1947).

Edwin Palmer Hoyt, *The Tempering Years* (New York, Scribner, 1963).

Harold LeClaire Ickes, *The Secret Diary*, 3 vols. (New York, Simon & Schuster, 1953–1955). Vol. I. *The First Thousand Days, 1933–1936*; Vol. II. *The Inside Struggle, 1936–1939*; Vol. III. *The Lowering Clouds, 1939–1941*.

William Henry ("Will") Irwin, *Herbert Hoover: A Reminiscent Biography* (New York, Century, 1928).

William Edward Leuchtenburg, *Franklin D. Roosevelt and the New Deal, 1932–1940* (New York, Harper, 1963).

Eugene Lyons, *Herbert Hoover: A Biography* (Garden City, Doubleday, 1964).

Dexter Perkins, *The New Age of Franklin Roosevelt, 1932–1945* Chicago, University of Chicago, 1957). In the Chicago History of American Civilization series.

Arthur Meier Schlesinger, Jr., *The Age of Roosevelt* (Boston, Houghton Mifflin, 1957–). Vol. I. *The Crisis of the Old*

Order, 1919–1933; Vol. II. *The Coming of the New Deal*; Vol. III. *The Politics of Upheaval.*

Rexford Guy Tugwell, *The Democratic Roosevelt: A Biography of Franklin D. Roosevelt* (Garden City, Doubleday, 1957).

Dixon Wecter, *The Age of the Great Depression, 1929–1941* (New York, Macmillan, 1948).

Edmund Wilson, *The American Earthquake: A Documentary of the Twenties and Thirties* (Garden City, Doubleday, 1964).

Edmund Wilson, *The American Jitters: A Year of the Slump* (New York, Scribner, 1932). A social history of the American worker from October 1930 to October 1931.

F · THE FORTIES: WORLD WAR II AND ITS AFTERMATH

An excellent short account of World War II appears in the second volume of Morison and Commager's *Growth of the American Republic*; see opening of Section III, above.

John Brooks, *The Great Leap: The Past Twenty-Five Years in America* (New York, Harper, 1970).

Basil Collier, *A Short History of the Second World War* (London, William Collins Sons & Co., 1967).

Kenneth Sydney Davis, *Experience of War: The United States in World War Two* (Garden City, Doubleday, 1965).

Dwight David Eisenhower, *Crusade in Europe* (New York, Doubleday, 1948).

Herbert Feis, *Churchill, Roosevelt, Stalin: The War They Waged and the Peace They Sought* (Princeton, Princeton University, 1957).

Herbert Feis, *The Road to Pearl Harbor: The Coming of the War Between the United States and Japan* (Princeton, Princeton University, 1950).

(Major-General) John Frederick Charles Fuller, *The Second World War, 1939–1945: A Strategical and Tactical History* (New York, Duell, Sloan & Pearce, 1949). An excellent one-volume account.

Eric Frederick Goldman, *The Crucial Decade: America, 1945–1955* (New York, Knopf, 1956).

GENERAL HISTORIES

Kent Roberts Greenfield, *American Strategy in World War II: A Reconsideration* (Baltimore, Johns Hopkins, 1963).

John Gunther, *Inside U.S.A.*, revised edition (New York, Harper, 1951).

Charles Grove Haines and Ross J. S. Hoffman, *The Origins and Background of the Second World War*, 2nd edition (New York, Oxford, 1947).

David Eli Lilienthal, *The Journals of David E. Lilienthal*, 5 vols. (New York, Harper, 1964–1971). See especially Vol. I. *The TVA Years, 1939–1945*, and Vol. II. *The Atomic Energy Years, 1945–1950*.

Richard R. Lingeman, *Don't You Know There's a War On? The American Home Front, 1941–1945* (New York, Putnam, 1970).

Walter Lord, *Day of Infamy* (New York, Holt, 1957). The attack on Pearl Harbor, December 7, 1941.

Samuel Eliot Morison, *History of U.S. Naval Operations in World War II*, 15 vols. (Boston, Little, Brown, 1947–1962). Vol. XV is a supplement and general index.

Fletcher Pratt, *War for the World: A Chronicle of Our Fighting Forces in World War II* (New Haven, Yale, 1950). In the Chronicles of America series.

Eleanor Roosevelt, *This I Remember* (New York, Harper, 1949).

Robert Emmet Sherwood, *Roosevelt and Hopkins: An Intimate History* (New York, Harper, 1950).

Henry Lewis Stimson and McGeorge Bundy, *On Active Service in Peace and War* (New York, Harper, 1948).

Harry S. Truman, *Memoirs*, 2 vols. (Garden City, Doubleday, 1955–1956). Vol. I. *Year of Decisions, 1945–1946*; Vol. II. *Years of Trial and Hope, 1946–1952*.

G · THE FIFTIES AND SIXTIES

Dean Acheson, *Present at the Creation: My Years in the State Department* (New York, Norton, 1969).

Herbert Agar, *The Price of Power: America Since 1945* (Chicago,

University of Chicago, 1960). In the Chicago History of American Civilization series.

Daniel Bell, *The End of Ideology: On the Exhaustion of Political Ideas in the Fifties* (New York, Free Press, 1962).

James MacGregor Burns, *John Kennedy: A Political Profile* (New York, Harcourt, 1960).

Robert J. Donovan, *Eisenhower: The Inside Story* (New York, Harper, 1956).

Dwight David Eisenhower, *The White House Years*, 2 vols. (Garden City, Doubleday, 1963–1965). Vol. I. *Mandate for Change, 1953–1956*; Vol. II. *Waging Peace, 1956–1961*.

T. R. Fehrenbach, *This Kind of War: A Study in Unpreparedness* (New York, Macmillan, 1963). On the Korean War, 1950–1953.

Norman A. Graebner, *The New Isolationism: A Study in Politics and Foreign Policy Since 1950* (New York, Ronald, 1956).

Andrew Hacker, *The End of the American Era* (New York, Atheneum, 1970).

Kenneth Ingram, *History of the Cold War* (New York, Philosophical Library, 1955).

Lyndon Baines Johnson, *The Vantage Point: Perspectives of the Presidency, 1963–1969* (New York, Holt, 1971).

George Frost Kennan, *Memoirs, 1925–1950* (Boston, Little, Brown, 1967).

John Fitzgerald Kennedy, *The Strategy of Peace*, ed. Allan Nevins (New York, Harper, 1960). Speeches of the then Senator Kennedy.

William Manchester, *The Death of a President: November 20–November 25, 1963* (New York, Harper, 1967). Controversial.

William L. O'Neill, *Coming Apart: An Informal History of America in the 1960s* (Chicago, Quadrangle Books, 1971).

Merlo John Pusey, *Eisenhower, the President* (New York, Macmillan, 1956).

Richard Halworth Rovere, *Affairs of State: The Eisenhower Years* (New York, Farrar, 1956).

GENERAL HISTORIES

Arthur Meier Schlesinger, Jr., *A Thousand Days: John F. Kennedy in the White House* (Boston, Houghton Mifflin, 1965).

Jean-Jacques Servan-Schreiber, *The American Challenge* (New York, Atheneum, 1968). Translated from the French by Ronald Steele.

Hugh Sidey, *John F. Kennedy, President*, new edition (New York, Atheneum, 1964).

Theodore Chaikin Sorensen, *Kennedy* (New York, Harper, 1965).

Adlai Ewing Stevenson, *Call to Greatness* (New York, Harper, 1954).

Isidor F. Stone, *The Haunted Fifties and a Glance at the Sixties* (New York, Random, 1963).

James Lloyd Sundquist, *Politics and Policy: The Eisenhower, Kennedy, and Johnson Years* (Washington, Brookings Institution, 1968).

IV · SPECIAL ASPECTS

A · SOCIAL AND ECONOMIC HISTORY AND PROBLEMS

1 · *General Social History and Discussion*

Jane Addams, *Twenty Years at Hull-House* (New York, Macmillan, 1910). Often reprinted, this classic autobiography of a settlement worker has a sequel, *The Second Twenty Years at Hull-House* (New York, Macmillan, 1930).

Frederick Lewis Allen, *The Big Change: America Transforms Itself, 1900–1950* (New York, Harper, 1952).

Ramsey Clark, *Crime in America: Observations on Its Nature, Causes, Prevention and Control* (New York, Simon & Schuster, 1970).

David Lewis Cohn, *The Good Old Days: A History of American Morals and Manners As Seen Through the Sears, Roebuck Catalogs, 1905 to the Present* (New York, Simon & Schuster, 1940).

Frederick Warren Cozens and Florence Stumpf, *Sports in American Life* (Chicago, University of Chicago, 1953).

Lewis Anthony Dexter and David Manning White, eds., *People, Society, and Mass Communications* (New York, Free Press, 1964).

Sidney Herbert Ditzion, *Marriage, Morals, and Sex in America: A History of Ideas* (New York, Bookman Associates, 1953).

Foster Rhea Dulles, *America Learns to Play: A History of Popular Recreation, 1607–1940* (New York, Appleton, 1940).

Harold Underwood Faulkner, *American Political and Social History*, 7th edition (New York, Appleton, 1957).

John Kenneth Galbraith, *The Affluent Society*, revised edition (Boston, Houghton Mifflin, 1969).

Thomas Hoag Greer, *American Social Reform Movements: The Pattern Since 1865* (New York, Prentice-Hall, 1949).

Ralph Eugene Lapp, *The New Priesthood: The Scientific Elite and the Uses of Power* (New York, Harper, 1965).

Eric Larrabee, ed., *American Panorama: Essays by Fifteen Amer-*

ican Critics on 350 Books Past and Present Which Portray the U.S. in Its Many Aspects (New York, New York University, 1957).

Max Lerner, *America as a Civilization: Life and Thought in the United States Today* (New York, Simon & Schuster, 1957).

Carl E. Lindstrom, *The Fading American Newspaper* (Garden City, Doubleday, 1960).

Walter Lippmann, *Drift and Mastery: An Attempt To Diagnose the Current Unrest* (New York, Mitchell Kennerley, 1914).

Russell Lynes, *The Domesticated Americans* (New York, Harper, 1963).

Russell Lynes, *The Tastemakers* (New York, Harper, 1954).

Elton Mayo, *The Social Problems of an Industrial Civilization* (Boston, Harvard Graduate School of Business Administration, 1945). A pioneer study of great importance.

Lloyd R. Morris, *Postscript to Yesterday: America—The Last Fifty Years* (New York, Random, 1947). Listed here rather than in Section II because of the emphasis on social and cultural history.

Frank Luther Mott, *American Journalism: A History, 1690–1960*, 3rd edition (New York, Macmillan, 1962).

David Morris Potter, *People of Plenty: Economic Abundance and the American Character* (Chicago, University of Chicago, 1954).

David Riesman, with Reuel Denney and Nathan Glazer, *The Lonely Crowd: A Study of the Changing American Character* (New Haven, Yale, 1950). An abridged version appeared as a Doubleday Anchor Book, 1953.

Bradford Smith, assisted by Marion Collins Smith, *Why We Behave Like Americans* (Philadelphia, Lippincott, 1957).

Harold Edmund Stearns, ed., *America Now: An Inquiry into Civilization in the United States by 36 Americans* (New York, Scribner, 1938).

Harold Edmund Stearns, ed., *Civilization in the United States: An Inquiry by Thirty Americans* (New York, Harcourt, 1922).

Lillian Symes and Travers Clement, *Rebel America: The Story of Social Revolt in the United States* (New York, Harper, 1934).

Dixon Wecter, *The Hero in America: A Chronicle of Hero-Worship* (New York, Scribner, 1941).

Charles Winick, *The New People: Desexualization in American Life* (New York, Pegasus, 1968).

2 · *General Economic History and Problems*

Ernest Ludlow Bogart and Donald L. Kemmerer, *Economic History of the American People*, revised edition (New York, Longmans, 1947).

Harrison Brown, James Bonner, and John Weir, *The Next Hundred Years: Man's Natural and Technological Resources* (New York, Viking, 1957).

Joseph Dorfman, *The Economic Mind in American Civilization*, 5 vols. (New York, Viking, 1946–1959). The last three volumes cover the years 1865–1933.

Joseph Dorfman, *Thorstein Veblen and His America* (New York, Viking, 1934).

Peter Ferdinand Drucker, *America's Next Twenty Years* (New York, Harper, 1957).

Harold Underwood Faulkner, *American Economic History*, 8th edition (New York, Harper, 1960).

Harold Underwood Faulkner, *The Decline of Laissez-Faire, 1897–1917* (New York, Rinehart, 1951). Vol. VII of his *Economic History of the United States.*

Sidney Fine, *Laissez Faire and the General-Welfare State: A Study of Conflict in American Thought, 1865–1901* (Ann Arbor, University of Michigan, 1956).

John Kenneth Galbraith, *American Capitalism: The Concept of Countervailing Power*, 2nd edition, revised (Boston, Houghton Mifflin, 1956).

Louis Morton Hacker, *The Triumph of American Capitalism: The Development of Forces in American History to the End of the Nineteenth Century* (New York, Columbia, 1946).

Louis Morton Hacker, *The World of Andrew Carnegie, 1865–1901* (Philadelphia, Lippincott, 1968).

SPECIAL ASPECTS

Walton Hale Hamilton, *The Politics of Industry* (New York, Knopf, 1957).

Peter d'Alroy Jones, *America's Wealth: The Economic History of an Open Society* (New York, Macmillan, 1963).

Matthew Josephson, *The Robber Barons: The Great American Capitalists* (New York, Harcourt, 1934).

Edward Chase Kirkland, *A History of American Economic Life*, 3rd edition (New York, Appleton, 1951).

Allan Nevins, *Study in Power: John D. Rockefeller, Industrialist and Philanthropist*, 2 vols. (New York, Scribner, 1953).

Allan Nevins, with the collaboration of Frank Ernest Hill, *Ford: The Times, the Man, the Company* (New York, Scribner, 1954). Nevins and Hill have also written a two-volume history of the Ford Motor Company, *Ford: Decline and Rebirth, 1933–1962* (New York, Scribner, 1963).

Paul Anthony Samuelson, *Stability and Growth in the American Economy* (Stockholm, Almqvist, 1963). Addressed to a European audience.

Fred Albert Shannon, *America's Economic Growth*, 3rd edition (New York, Macmillan, 1951).

Joseph Frazier Wall, *Andrew Carnegie* (New York, Oxford, 1970).

Bernard Allen Weisberger, *The New Industrial Society* (New York, John Wiley & Sons, 1968).

3 · General Political Problems

Alan Barth, *Government by Investigation* (New York, Viking, 1955).

Daniel Bell, ed., *The Radical Right* (Garden City, Doubleday, 1963). First appeared as *The New American Right* (New York, Criterion Books, 1955).

Alexander Mordecai Bickel, *Politics and the Warren Court* (New York, Harper, 1955).

Alexander Mordecai Bickel, *The Supreme Court and the Idea of Progress* (New York, Harper, 1970).

Eleanor Bontecou, *The Federal Loyalty-Security Program* (Ithaca, Cornell, 1953). In the Cornell Studies in Civil Liberty.

BACKGROUNDS

Paul Samuel Boyer, *Purity in Print: The Vice-Society Movement and Book Censorship in America* (New York, Scribner, 1968).

Earl Russell Browder, *Communism in the United States* (New York, International Publishers Co., 1935).

William Frank Buckley, *Up from Liberalism* (New York, McDowell, Obolensky, 1959).

Ira Harris Carmen, *Movies, Censorship, and the Law* (Ann Arbor, University of Michigan, 1966).

Zechariah Chafee, Jr., *Free Speech in the United States,* revised edition (Cambridge, Harvard, 1941). This great work has become standard, Although based on problems of censorship and suppression of speech in World War I, it is here extended to cover later issues.

William Ludlow Chenery, *Freedom of the Press* (New York, Harcourt, 1955).

Harry M. Clor, *Obscenity and Public Morality: Censorship in a Liberal Society* (Chicago, University of Chicago, 1969).

Edward Samuel Corwin and Louis W. Koenig, *The Presidency Today* (New York, New York University, 1956).

Charles Pelham Curtis, *The Oppenheimer Case: The Trial of a Security System* (New York, Simon & Schuster, 1955).

Gottfried Dietze, *America's Political Dilemma: From Limited to Unlimited Democracy* (Baltimore, Johns Hopkins, 1968).

Theodore Draper, *The Roots of American Communism* (New York, Viking, 1957). This is the first volume of a two-volume study. Draper's *American Communism and Soviet Russia: The Formative Period* (New York, Viking, 1960) is an independent, self-contained book.

Donald Drew Egbert and Stow Persons, eds., *Socialism and American Life,* 2 vols. (Princeton, Princeton University, 1952).

Herbert B. Ehrmann, *The Case That Will Not Die: Commonwealth vs. Sacco and Vanzetti* (Boston, Little, Brown, 1969).

Arthur Alphonse Ekirch, *The Decline of American Liberalism* (New York, Longmans, 1955).

Nathan Fine, *Labor and Farmer Parties in the United States, 1828–1928* (New York, Rand School of Social Research, 1928).

SPECIAL ASPECTS

Paul Abraham Freund, *The Supreme Court of the United States: Its Business, Purposes and Performance* (Cleveland, World, 1961).

Robert Jennings Harris, *The Quest for Equality: The Constitution, Congress, and the Supreme Court* (Baton Rouge, Louisiana State, 1960).

Arthur Norman Holcombe, *The Middle Class in American Politics* (Cambridge, Harvard, 1940).

Irving Howe and Lewis Coser, with the assistance of Julius Jacobson, *The American Communist Party: A Critical History, 1919–1957* (Boston, Beacon Press, 1957).

Donald Janson and Bernard Eismann, *The Far Right* (New York, McGraw-Hill, 1963).

Stanley Kelley, *Professional Public Relations and Political Power* (Baltimore, Johns Hopkins, 1956).

Vladimir Orlando Key, Jr., *Politics, Parties, and Pressure Groups*, 4th edition (New York, Crowell, 1958).

Walter Lippmann, *Essays in the Public Philosophy* (Boston, Little, Brown, 1955).

Samuel Lubell, *Revolt of the Moderates* (New York, Harper, 1956).

Reinhard Henry Luthin, *American Demagogues: Twentieth Century* (Boston, Beacon Press, 1954).

Dwight Macdonald, *Memoirs of a Revolutionist: Essays in Political Criticism* (New York, Farrar, 1957).

Alpheus Thomas Mason, *Brandeis: A Free Man's Life* (New York, Viking, 1946).

Alpheus Thomas Mason, *Security Through Freedom: American Political Thought and Practice* (Ithaca, Cornell, 1955).

Alpheus Thomas Mason and William S. Beaney, *The Supreme Court in a Free Society* (New York, Norton, 1968).

H. Wayne Morgan, ed., *American Socialism, 1900–1960* (Englewood Cliffs, Prentice-Hall, 1964).

Hans J. Morgenthau, *Politics in the 20th Century*, 3 vols. (Chicago, University of Chicago, 1962). Vol. I. *The Decline of Democratic Politics*; Vol. II. *The Impasse of American Foreign Policy*; Vol. III. *The Restoration of American Politics.*

Terence J. Murphy, *Censorship: Government and Obscenity* (Baltimore, Helicon Press, 1963).

Dexter Perkins, *The Diplomacy of a New Age: Major Issues in United States Policy Since 1945* (Bloomington, Indiana University, 1967).

Wilson Record, *Race and Radicalism: The NAACP and the Communist Party in Conflict* (Ithaca, Cornell, 1964).

Clinton Lawrence Rossiter, *Conservatism in America: The Thankless Persuasion*, 2nd edition (New York, Knopf, 1962).

Clinton Lawrence Rossiter, *Marxism: The View from America* (New York, Harcourt, 1960). Strongly anti-Communist.

David Allen Shannon, *The Decline of American Communism: A History of the Communist Party in the United States Since 1945* (New York, Harcourt, 1959).

Lewis Lichtenstein Strauss, *Men and Decisions* (Garden City, Doubleday, 1962). An autobiographical view of federal politics from 1919 to 1960.

Telford Taylor, *Grand Inquest: The Story of Congressional Investigations* (New York, Simon & Schuster, 1955).

Theodore Harold White, *The Making of the President, 1960* (New York, Atheneum, 1961). The campaign of John F. Kennedy.

Theodore Harold White, *The Making of the President, 1964* (New York, Atheneum, 1965). The campaign of Lyndon B. Johnson.

Theodore Harold White, *The Making of the President, 1968* (New York, Atheneum, 1969). The campaign of Richard M. Nixon.

4 · *Some Special Themes*

a · *Population Elements*

(1) *Immigration*

Oscar Handlin, *The Uprooted: The Epic Story of the Great Migrations That Made the American People* (Boston, Little, Brown, 1951).

34

SPECIAL ASPECTS

John Higham, *Strangers in the Land: Patterns of American Nativism, 1860–1925* (New Brunswick, Rutgers, 1955).

Maldwyn Allen Jones, *American Immigration* (Chicago, University of Chicago, 1960).

Michael Kraus, *Immigration, the American Mosaic: From Pilgrims to Modern Refugees* (Princeton, D. Van Nostrand Co., 1966).

William Carlson Smith, *Americans in the Making: The Natural History of the Assimilation of Immigrants* (New York, Appleton, 1939).

(2) *The Class Issue*

Louis Adamic, *Dynamite: The Story of Class Violence in America*, revised edition (New York, Viking, 1934). Covers a hundred years, beginning in 1830.

Robert Hamlett Bremner, *From the Depths: The Discovery of Poverty in the United States* (New York, New York University, 1956).

John C. Donovan, *The Politics of Poverty* (New York, Pegasus, 1967).

Charles Wright Mills, *White Collar: The American Middle Class* (New York, Oxford, 1951).

Dixon Wecter, *The Saga of American Society: A Record of Social Aspiration, 1607–1937* (New York, Scribner, 1937).

(3) *The Race Issue*

John H. Braccy, Jr., August Meier, and Elliott Rudwick, eds., *Black Nationalism in America* (Indianapolis, Bobbs-Merrill, 1970).

Dee Brown, *Bury My Heart at Wounded Knee: An Indian History of the American West* (New York, Holt, 1970).

Angie Debo, *A History of the Indians of the United States* (Norman, University of Oklahoma, 1970).

Samuel H. Dresner, *The Jew in American Life* (New York, Crown, 1963).

Essien Udosen Essien-Udom, *Black Nationalism: The Search for an Identity in America* (Chicago, University of Chicago, 1962).

John Hope Franklin, *From Slavery to Freedom: A History of American Negroes*, 3rd edition (New York, Knopf, 1967).

Nathan Glazer and Daniel Patrick Moynihan, *Beyond the Melting Pot: The Negroes, Puerto Ricans, Jews, Italians, and Irish of New York City*, 2nd edition (Cambridge, M.I.T. and Harvard, 1970).

Claude M. Lightfoot, *Ghetto Rebellion to Black Liberation* (New York, International Publishers Co., 1968). Leftist in sentiment.

Alain LeRoy Locke, *The New Negro: An Interpretation* (New York, Johnson Reprint Corp., 1968). This classic was originally published in 1925 (New York, Albert & Charles Boni).

Elizabeth W. Miller, comp., *The Negro in America* (Cambridge, Harvard, 1966); 2nd edition, revised and enlarged, compiled by Mary L. Fisher (Cambridge, Harvard, 1970). A bibliography of 6,500 entries.

Gunnar Myrdal, *An American Dilemma: The Negro Problem and Modern Democracy*, revised edition, 2 vols. (New York, Harper, 1962).

Comer Vann Woodward, *The Strange Career of Jim Crow*, 2nd edition (New York, Oxford, 1966).

James Yaffe, *The American Jews* (New York, Random, 1968).

(4) *Toward an Open Society*

Charles Abrams, *Forbidden Neighbors: A Study in Prejudice in Housing* (New York, Harper, 1955).

Milton Leon Barron, ed., *American Minorities* (New York, Knopf, 1957).

Adolph Burnett Benson and Naboth Hedin, *Americans from Sweden* (Philadelphia, Lippincott, 1950).

Leola Marjorie Bergmann, *Americans from Norway* (Philadelphia, Lippincott, 1950).

Albert P. Blaustein and Clarence Clyde Ferguson, Jr., *Desegregation and the Law*, 2nd revised edition (New York, Random, 1962).

SPECIAL ASPECTS

Eleanor Flexner, *Century of Struggle: The Women's Rights Movement in the United States* (Cambridge, Harvard, 1959).

Arthur William Hoglund, *Finnish Immigrants in America, 1880–1920* (Madison, University of Wisconsin, 1960).

Jacob Koppell Javits, *Discrimination—U.S.A.*, revised edition (New York, Harcourt, 1962).

Shien-Woo Kung, *Chinese in American Life: Some Aspects of Their History, Status, Problems, and Contributions* (Seattle, University of Washington, 1962).

Joseph Lopreato, *Italian Americans* (New York, Random, 1970).

Wayne Moquin and Charles Van Doren, eds., *A Documentary History of the Mexican Americans* (New York, Praeger, 1971).

Richard O'Connor, *The German-Americans* (Boston, Little, Brown, 1968).

Theodore Saloutos, *The Greeks in the United States* (Cambridge, Harvard, 1964).

Carl Wittke, *The Irish in America* (Baton Rouge, Louisiana State, 1956).

Joseph Anthony Wytrwal, *America's Polish Heritage: A Social History of the Poles in America* (Detroit, Endurance Press, 1961).

Whitney M. Young, Jr., *Beyond Racism: Building an Open Society* (New York, McGraw-Hill, 1969).

b · *Regionalism*

Lewis Eldon Atherton, *Main Street on the Middle Border* (Bloomington, Indiana University, 1954).

William Terry Couch, ed., *Culture in the South* (Chapel Hill, University of North Carolina, 1934).

Edward Everett Dale, *The Range Cattle Industry* (Norman, University of Oklahoma, 1930).

Donald Davidson, *The Attack on Leviathan: Regionalism and Nationalism in the United States* (Chapel Hill, University of North Carolina, 1938).

Wayne Edison Fuller, *RFD: The Changing Face of Rural America* (Bloomington, Indiana University, 1964).

Jean Gottmann, *Megalopolis: The Urbanized Northeastern Seaboard of the United States* (New York, Twentieth Century Fund, 1961).

Constance McLaughlin Green, *The Rise of Urban America* (New York, Harper, 1965).

Edward Counselman Higbee, *Farms and Farmers in an Urban Age* (New York, Twentieth Century Fund, 1963).

Emerson Hough, *The Story of the Cowboy* (New York, Appleton, 1897).

Emerson Hough, *The Story of the Outlaw: A Study of the Western Desperado* (New York, A. L. Burt & Co., 1907).

Jane Jacobs, *The Death and Life of Great American Cities* (New York, Random, 1961).

Jane Jacobs, *The Economy of Cities* (New York, Random, 1969).

Merrill Jensen, ed., *Regionalism in America* (Madison, University of Wisconsin, 1951).

Ralph Emerson McGill, *The South and the Southerner* (Boston, Little, Brown, 1963).

Lewis Mumford, *City Development: Studies in Disintegration and Renewal* (New York, Harcourt, 1945).

Lewis Mumford, *The Culture of Cities* (New York, Harcourt, 1938).

Lowry Nelson, *American Farm Life* (Cambridge, Harvard, 1954). In the Library of Congress Series in American Civilization.

William Hord Nicholls, *Southern Tradition and Regional Progress* (Chapel Hill, University of North Carolina, 1960).

E. Louise Peffer, *The Closing of the Public Domain: Disposal and Reservation Policies, 1900–1950* (Stanford, Stanford University, 1951).

Roy Marvin Robbins, *Our Landed Heritage: The Public Domain, 1776–1936* (Princeton, Princeton University, 1942).

Theodore Saloutos and John Donald Hicks, *Agricultural Discontent in the Middle West, 1900–1939* (Madison, University of Wisconsin, 1951).

SPECIAL ASPECTS

Wallace Earle Stegner, *Wolf Willow: A History, a Story, and a Memory of the Last Plains Frontier* (New York, Viking, 1962).

Walter Prescott Webb, *The Great Frontier*, revised edition (Austin, University of Texas, 1964).

Walter Prescott Webb, *The Great Plains* (Boston, Ginn & Co., 1931).

c · *Business and Industry*

Edward Digby Baltzell, *An American Business Aristocracy* (New York, Macmillan, 1962).

John Chamberlain, *The Enterprising Americans: A Business History of the United States* (New York, Harper, 1963).

Thomas Childs Cochran, *The American Business System: A Historical Perspective, 1900–1955* (Cambridge, Harvard, 1957). In the Library of Congress Series in American Civilization.

Thomas Childs Cochran and William Miller, *The Age of Enterprise: A Social History of Industrial America*, revised edition (New York, Harper, 1961).

Sigmund Diamond, *The Nation Transformed: The Creation of an Industrial Society* (New York, Braziller, 1963).

Sigmund Diamond, *The Reputation of the American Businessman* (Cambridge, Harvard, 1955).

Herrymon Maurer, *Great Enterprise: Growth and Behavior of the Big Corporation* (New York, Macmillan, 1955).

Charles Wright Mills, *The Power Elite* (New York, Oxford, 1956). See also Mills' *White Collar* (New York, Oxford, 1951) and *Power, Politics, and People* (New York, Oxford, 1963).

Gustavus Myers, *History of the Great American Fortunes*, 3 vols. (Chicago, C. H. Kerr & Co., 1910). More easily available in the Modern Library edition of 1936.

Michael Idvorsky Pupin, *From Immigrant to Inventor* (New York, Scribner, 1923).

Michael Daniel Reagan, *The Managed Economy* (New York,

Oxford, 1963). The activities and responsibilities of large
companies in the American power structure.

Francis Xavier Sutton and others, *The American Business Creed*
(Cambridge, Harvard, 1956).

Thorstein Veblen, *The Theory of Business Enterprise*, revised
edition (New York, Scribner, 1935).

William Hollingsworth White, *The Organization Man* (New
York, Simon & Schuster, 1956).

Irvin Gordon Wyllie, *The Self-Made Man in America: The
Myth of Rags to Riches* (New Brunswick, Rutgers, 1954).

d . *Labor*

Derek Curtis Bok and John T. Dunlop, *Labor and the American
Community* (New York, Simon & Schuster, 1970).

Neil W. Chamberlain and Jane Metzger Schilling, *The Impact
of Strikes: Their Social and Economic Costs* (New York,
Harper, 1954).

John Rogers Commons and others, *History of Labour in the
United States*, 4 vols. (New York, Macmillan, 1935–1936).
Vols. III and IV cover the years from 1896 to 1932.

Foster Rhea Dulles, *Labor in America: A History*, 3rd edition
(New York, Crowell, 1966).

Marguerite Green, *The National Civic Federation and the American Labor Movement, 1900–1925* (Washington, Catholic
University of America Press, 1956). A study mainly of industrial relations, which shows the development of labor attitudes toward nationalism and conservatism.

J. David Greenstone, *Labor and American Politics* (New York,
Knopf, 1969).

Lewis Levitski Lorwin, with the assistance of Jean Atherton
Flexner, *The American Federation of Labor: History, Policies, and Prospects* (Washington, Brookings Institution,
1933).

Carey McWilliams, *Ill Fares the Land: Migrants and Migratory
Labor in the United States* (Boston, Little, Brown, 1942).

Truman Moore, *The Slaves We Rent* (New York, Random,
1965). On migrant labor.

SPECIAL ASPECTS

Selig Perlman, *A History of Trade Unionism in the United States* (New York, Macmillan, 1922).

Philip Taft, *Organized Labor in American History* (New York, Harper, 1964).

Philip Taft, *The Structure and Government of Labor Unions* (Cambridge, Harvard, 1954).

Lloyd Ulman, *The Rise of the National Trade Union: The Development and Significance of Its Structure, Governing Institutions, and Economic Policies* (Cambridge, Harvard, 1955).

William Lloyd Warner, *American Life: Dream and Reality*, revised edition (Chicago, University of Chicago, 1962). A revision of his *Structure of American Life* (Edinburgh, Edinburgh University Press, 1952).

Leo Wolman, *The Growth of American Trade Unions, 1880–1923* (New York, National Bureau of Economic Research, 1924).

B · THE UNITED STATES IN INTERNATIONAL AFFAIRS

Yehoshua Arieli, *Individualism and Nationalism in American Ideology* (Cambridge, Harvard, 1964).

Thomas Andrew Bailey, *A Diplomatic History of the American People*, 8th edition (New York, Appleton, 1969).

Samuel Flagg Bemis, *The United States as a World Power: A Diplomatic History, 1900–1955*, revised edition (New York, Holt, 1955).

Adolf Augustus Berle, *Tides of Crisis: A Primer of Foreign Relations* (New York, Reynal, 1957).

Chester Bowles, *Ambassador's Report* (New York, Harper, 1954). On India.

Robert A. Devine, *Second Chance: The Triumph of Internationalism in America During World War II* (New York, Atheneum, 1967).

Foster Rhea Dulles, *America's Rise to World Power, 1898–1954* (New York, Harper, 1955). In the New American Nation series.

William W. Kaufmann and others, eds., *Military Policy and National Security* (Princeton, Princeton University, 1956).

George Frost Kennan, *American Diplomacy, 1900–1950* (Chicago, University of Chicago, 1951).

George Frost Kennan, *Soviet-American Relations, 1917–1920* (Princton, Princeton University, 1956–). Vol. I. *Russia Leaves the War*; Vol. II. *The Decision to Intervene.*

Hans Kohn, *American Nationalism: An Interpretative Essay* (New York, Macmillan, 1957).

William Leonard Langer and S. Everett Gleason, *The Challenge to Isolation, 1937–1940* (New York, published by Harper for the Council on Foreign Relations, 1952).

Samuel Lubell, *The Revolution in World Trade and American Economic Policy* (New York, Harper, 1955).

Julius William Pratt, *A History of United States Foreign Policy* (New York, Prentice-Hall, 1955).

Edwin Oldfather Reischauer, *Beyond Vietnam: The United States and Asia* (New York, Knopf, 1967).

Edwin Oldfather Reischauer, *Wanted: An Asian Policy* (New York, Knopf, 1955).

Frank Tannenbaum, *The American Tradition in Foreign Policy* (Norman, University of Oklahoma, 1955).

James Paul Warburg, *The United States in a Changing World: An Historical Analysis of American Foreign Policy* (New York, Putnam, 1954).

Sumner Welles and Donald Cope McKay, eds., *American Foreign Policy Library* (Cambridge, Harvard). These editors were succeeded by Crane Brinton in 1961 and, after his death in 1968, by Edwin O. Reischauer. The following titles are in print:

Crane Brinton, *The Americans and the French*, 1968.

William Norman Brown, *The United States and India and Pakistan*, revised edition, 1963.

Howard Francis Cline, *The United States and Mexico*, revised edition, 1963.

Gerald M. Craig, *The United States and Canada*, 1968.

SPECIAL ASPECTS

John King Fairbank, *The United States and China*, third edition, 1971.

Charles Frederick Gallagher, *The United States and North Africa: Morocco, Algeria, and Tunisia*, 1963.

James W. Gould, *The United States and Malaysia*, 1969.

Clinton Hartley Grattan, *The United States and the Southwest Pacific*, 1961.

Henry Stuart Hughes, *The United States and Italy*, revised edition, 1965.

Dexter Perkins, *The United States and the Caribbean*, revised edition, 1966.

William Roe Polk, *The United States and the Arab World*, revised edition, 1969.

Edwin Oldfather Reischauer, *The United States and Japan*, third edition, 1965.

Nadav Safran, *The United States and Israel*, 1963.

Arthur Preston Whitaker, *The United States and Argentina*, 1954.

Robert Lee Wolff, *The Balkans in Our Time*, 1956.

The following titles of the *American Foreign Policy Library* are no longer in print:

Crane Brinton, *The United States and Britain*, 1948.

Vera Micheles Dean, *The United States and Russia*, 1947.

Donald Cope McKay, *The United States and France*, 1951.

Franklin Daniel Scott, *The United States and Scandinavia*, 1950.

Ephraim Avigdor Speiser, *The United States and the Near East*, 1950.

Lewis Victor Thomas and Richard Nelson Frye, *The United States and Turkey and Iran*, 1951.

C · EDUCATION IN THE UNITED STATES

Jerry L. Avorn and Members of the Staff of the *Columbia Daily Spectator*, *Up Against the Ivy Wall: A History of the Co-*

lumbia Crisis (New York, Atheneum, 1969). Of all the books on student revolt, this is one of the best.

Daniel Bell and Irving Kristol, eds., *Confrontation: The Student Rebellion and the Universities* (New York, Basic Books, 1969).

Bernard Berelson, *Graduate Education in the United States* (New York, McGraw-Hill, 1960).

Rollo Walter Brown, *Harvard Yard in the Golden Age* (New York, Current Books, 1948).

James Samuel Coleman and others, *Equality of Educational Opportunity* (Washington, U.S. Government Printing Office, 1966). An important 737-page report to the U.S. Office of Education.

James Bryant Conant, *The American High School Today* (New York, McGraw-Hill, 1959).

James Bryant Conant, *The Education of American Teachers* (New York, McGraw-Hill, 1963).

Lawrence Arthur Cremin, *The Transformation of the School: Progressivism in American Education, 1876–1957* (New York, Knopf, 1961).

Merle Eugene Curti, *The Social Ideas of American Educators*, revised edition (Paterson, Pageant Books, 1960).

William Clyde De Vane, *Higher Education in Twentieth-Century America* (Cambridge, Harvard, 1965).

Paul Goodman, *The Community of Scholars* (New York, Random, 1962).

Richard Hofstadter and Walter Paul Metzger, *The Development of Academic Freedom in the United States* (New York, Columbia, 1955).

Richard Hofstadter and Wilson Smith, eds., *American Higher Education: A Documentary History*, 2 vols. (Chicago, University of Chicago, 1961). Described as "an anthology of discussion about American higher education throughout our history." The second volume concerns the years 1850 to the present.

Sidney Hook, *Academic Freedom and Academic Anarchy* (New York, Cowles Book Co., 1970).

SPECIAL ASPECTS

Howard Mumford Jones, *Education and World Tragedy* (Cambridge, Harvard, 1946). Reprinted by Greenwood Press, New York, 1967.

Howard Mumford Jones, *One Great Society: Humane Learning in the United States* (New York, Harcourt, 1959).

Clark Kerr, *The Uses of the University* (Cambridge, Harvard, 1963).

James D. Koerner, *The Miseducation of American Teachers* (Boston, Houghton Mifflin, 1963).

Edward H. Levi, *Point of View: Talks on Education* (Chicago, University of Chicago, 1969).

Fritz Machlup, *Production and Distribution of Knowledge in the United States* (Princeton, Princeton University, 1962).

Allan Nevins, *The State Universities and Democracy* (Urbana, University of Illinois, 1962). A historical approach.

Mabel Newcomer, *A Century of Higher Education for American Women* (New York, Harper, 1959).

William Kenneth Richmond, *Education in the U.S.A.: A Comparative Study* (New York, Philosophical Library, 1956).

James Ridgeway, *The Closed Corporation: American Universities in Crisis* (New York, Random, 1968).

Frederick Rudolph, *The American College and University: A History* (New York, Knopf, 1962).

Theodore W. Schultz, *The Economic Value of Education* (New York, Columbia, 1963).

Don Shoemaker, ed., *With All Deliberate Speed: Segregation-Desegregation in Southern Schools* (New York, Harper, 1957).

Russell Brown Thomas, *The Search for a Common Learning: General Education, 1800–1960* (New York, McGraw-Hill, 1962).

Thorstein Veblen, *The Higher Learning in America* (New York, Sagamore Press, 1957). Originally published by B. W. Huebsch in 1918.

Rush Welter, *Popular Education and Democratic Thought in America* (New York, Columbia, 1962).

Thomas Woody, *The History of Women's Education in the United States*, 2 vols. (New York, Octagon Books, 1966). First published in 1923, this work includes an excellent bibliography.

D · SCIENCE AND TECHNOLOGY

Roger Burlingame, *Engines of Democracy: Invention and Society in Mature America* (New York, Scribner, 1940).

Roger Burlingame, *Machines That Built America* (New York, Harcourt, 1953).

Vannevar Bush, *Modern Arms and Free Men: A Discussion of the Role of Science in Preserving Democracy* (New York, Simon & Schuster, 1949).

Nigel Calder, *Technopolis: Social Control of the Uses of Science* (New York, Simon & Schuster, 1970).

Walter Bradford Cannon, *The Way of an Investigator: A Scientist's Experiences in Medical Research* (New York, Norton, 1945).

Barry Commoner, *The Closing Circle: Nature, Man, and Technology* (New York, Knopf, 1971). An ecologist discusses the environmental crisis.

Arthur Holly Compton, *Atomic Quest: A Personal Narrative* (New York, Oxford, 1956).

Alexander Richard Crabb, *The Hybrid-Corn Makers: Prophets of Plenty* (New Brunswick, Rutgers, 1947).

Anderson Hunter Dupree, ed., *Science and the Emergence of Modern America, 1865–1916* (Chicago, Rand, McNally, 1963).

Anderson Hunter Dupree, *Science in the Federal Government: A History of Policies and Activities to 1940* (Cambridge, Harvard, 1957).

Donald Harnish Fleming, *William H. Welch and the Rise of Modern Medicine* (Boston, Little, Brown, 1954).

John Farquhar Fulton, *Harvey Cushing: A Biography* (Springfield, Charles C. Thomas, 1946).

Sigfried Giedion, *Mechanization Takes Command: A Contribu-*

tion to Anonymous History (New York, Oxford, 1948). A study of technology in industry. Reprinted in 1969 (New York, Norton).

Courtney Robert Hall, *History of American Industrial Science* (New York, Library Publishers, 1954).

Bernard Jaffe, *Men of Science in America: The Role of Science in the Growth of Our Country*, revised edition (New York, Simon & Schuster, 1958). Runs from Thomas Hariot of Virginia to the astronomer Edwin Powell Hubble.

Bessie Zaban Jones, *Lighthouse of the Skies: The Smithsonian Astrophysical Observatory, Background and History, 1846–1955* (Washington, Smithsonian Institution, 1965).

Thomas Samuel Kuhn, *The Structure of Scientific Revolutions*, 2nd edition (Chicago, University of Chicago, 1970).

Richard Gordon Lillard, *The Great Forest* (New York, Knopf, 1947). On the utilization of timber resources.

McGraw-Hill Encyclopedia of Science and Technology, 15 vols. (New York, McGraw-Hill, 1960). Annual supplements are entitled *McGraw-Hill Yearbook of Science and Technology*.

Stephen Finney Mason, *Main Currents of Scientific Thought: A History of the Sciences* (New York, Henry Schuman, 1953). Revised as *A History of the Sciences* (New York, Collier Books, 1962).

Robert Andrews Millikan, *Autobiography* (New York, Prentice-Hall, 1950). A Nobel Prize physicist, Millikan was executive head of the California Institute of Technology from 1921 until 1945. This work discusses the impact of the physical sciences on modern life.

Gardner Murphy, *Historical Introduction to Modern Psychology*, revised edition (New York, Harcourt, 1949).

Paul Henry Oehser, *Sons of Science: The Story of the Smithsonian Institution and Its Leaders* (New York, Henry Schuman, 1949).

Don Krasher Price, *Government and Science: Their Dynamic Relation in American Democracy* (New York, New York University, 1954).

47

Moody Erasmus Prior, *Science and the Humanities* (Evanston, Northwestern, 1962). Disunity in American intellectual life and its reflection in education.

Abraham Aaron Roback, *History of American Psychology* (New York, Library Publishers, 1952).

John William Navin Sullivan, *The Limitations of Science* (New York, New American Library of World Literature, 1949). Originally published in England in 1933.

Holland Thompson, *The Age of Invention: A Chronicle of Mechanical Conquest* (New Haven, Yale, 1921). In the Chronicles of America series.

Edna Yost, *Americans in Science and Technology* (New York, Dodd, Mead, 1962).

Edna Yost, *Modern American Engineers*, revised edition (Philadelphia, Lippincott, 1958).

James Harvey Young, *The Toadstool Millionaires: A Social History of Patent Medicines in America Before Federal Regulation* (Princeton, Princeton University, 1961).

E · GENERAL INTELLECTUAL HISTORY

Daniel Aaron, ed., *America in Crisis: Fourteen Crucial Episodes in American History* (New York, Knopf, 1952).

Ronald Berman, *America in the Sixties: An Intellectual History* (New York, Free Press, 1968).

Herbert Brucker, *Freedom of Information* (New York, Macmillan, 1949).

Roger Burlingame, *The American Conscience* (New York, Knopf, 1957).

Morris Raphael Cohen, *American Thought: A Critical Sketch*, edited by Felix S. Cohen (Glencoe, Free Press, 1954).

Henry Steele Commager, *The American Mind: An Interpretation of American Thought and Character Since the 1880's* (New Haven, Yale, 1950).

Kent Cooper, *The Right To Know: An Exposition of the Evils of News Suppression and Propaganda* (New York, Farrar, 1956).

SPECIAL ASPECTS

Harold L. Cross, *The People's Right To Know: Legal Access to Public Records and Proceedings* (New York, Columbia, 1953).

Merle Eugene Curti, *The Growth of American Thought*, 2nd edition (New York, Harper, 1951).

Carl N. Degler, *Out of Our Past: The Forces That Shaped Modern America* (New York, Harper, 1959).

Charles Frankel, *The Case for Modern Man* (New York, Harper, 1956).

Ralph Henry Gabriel, *The Course of American Democratic Thought: An Intellectual History Since 1815*, 2nd edition (New York, Ronald, 1956).

Reinhold Niebuhr, *The Irony of American History* (New York, Scribner, 1952).

Russel Blaine Nye, *This Almost Chosen People* (East Lansing, Michigan State, 1966). Essays on the history of American ideas.

Vernon Louis Parrington, *Main Currents in American Thought: An Interpertation of American Literature from the Beginnings to 1920*, 3 vols. (New York, Harcourt, 1927–1930). The third volume, covering the years 1860–1920, is entitled *The Beginnings of Critical Realism in America* and is incomplete, having been published posthumously (New York, 1930).

Stow Persons, ed., *Evolutionary Thought in America* (New Haven, Yale, 1950).

Robert Allen Skotheim, *American Intellectual Histories and Historians* (Princeton, Princeton University, 1966). Treats the major interpreters of our history and their methodology.

Lionel Trilling, *Freud and the Crisis of Our Culture* (Boston, Beacon Press, 1955).

John William Ward, *Red, White, and Blue: Men, Books, and Ideas in American Culture* (New York, Oxford, 1969).

1 · *Theories of Politics, History, and Political Trends*

Daniel Aaron, *Men of Good Hope: A Story of American Progressives* (New York, Oxford, 1951).

Daniel Bell, *The End of Ideology: On the Exhaustion of Political Ideas in the Fifties*, revised edition (New York, Free Press, 1962).

Robert Kenneth Carr, *The House Committee on Un-American Activities, 1945–1950* (Ithaca, Cornell, 1952). In the Cornell Studies in Civil Liberty.

Chester McArthur Destler, *American Radicalism, 1865–1901* (New London, Connecticut College Publications Dept., 1946).

Louis Filler, *The Muckrakers: Crusaders for American Liberalism*, 2nd edition (Chicago, Regnery, 1968). Published in 1961 under the title *Crusaders for American Liberalism* (Yellow Springs, Antioch Press).

Louis Hartz, *The Liberal Tradition in America: An Interpretation of American Political Thought since the Revolution* (New York, Harcourt, 1955).

Richard Hofstadter, *The American Political Tradition and the Men Who Made It* (New York, Knopf, 1948).

Robert Green McCloskey, *American Conservatism in the Age of Enterprise: A Study of William Graham Sumner, Stephen Field, and Andrew Carnegie* (Cambridge, Harvard, 1951).

Charles Allan Madison, *Critics and Crusaders: A Century of American Protest*, 2nd edition (New York, Ungar, 1959).

Russel Blaine Nye, *Midwestern Progressive Politics: A Historical Study of Its Origins and Development, 1870–1958*, revised edition (East Lansing, Michigan State, 1959).

John Homer Schaar, *Loyalty in America* (Berkeley, University of California, 1957).

Samuel Andrew Stouffer, *Communism, Conformity and Civil Liberties: A Cross-Section of the Nation Speaks Its Mind* (Garden City, Doubleday, 1955).

Benjamin Fletcher Wright, *American Interpretations of Natural Law: A Study in the History of Political Thought* (Cambridge, Harvard, 1931).

2 . *Philosophy*

Alfred Jules Ayer, *The Origins of Pragmatism* (San Francisco, Freeman, Cooper & Co., 1968).

SPECIAL ASPECTS

Robert Nelson Beck, *The Meaning of Americanism: An Essay on the Religious and Philosophical Basis of the American Mind* (New York, Philosophical Library, 1956).

Joseph Leon Blau, *Men and Movements in American Philosophy* (New York, Prentice-Hall, 1952).

Merle Eugene Curti, *American Paradox: The Conflict of Thought and Action* (New Brunswick, Rutgers, 1956).

Walter B. Gallie, *Peirce and Pragmatism* (Baltimore, Penguin, 1952).

Richard Hofstadter, *Social Darwinism in American Thought, 1860–1915* (Philadelphia, University of Pennsylvania, 1944).

Howard Mumford Jones, *The Pursuit of Happiness* (Cambridge, Harvard, 1953). Examines the history and development of an inalienable right.

Maurice Mandelbaum, *History, Man, and Reason: A Study in Nineteenth Century Thought* (Baltimore, Johns Hopkins, 1971). Invaluable as a background for the development of systematic American thought in the nineteenth and twentieth centuries.

Ralph Barton Perry, *Philosophy of the Recent Past: An Outline of European and American Philosophy Since 1860* (New York, Scribner, 1926).

Andrew J. Reck, *Recent American Philosophy: Studies of Ten Representative Thinkers* (New York, Pantheon, 1964).

David Riesman, *Thorstein Veblen: A Critical Interpretation* (New York, Scribner, 1953).

Isaac Woodbridge Riley, *American Thought from Puritanism to Pragmatism and Beyond*, 2nd edition (New York, Holt, 1923).

Herbert Wallace Schneider, *A History of American Philosophy*, 2nd edition (New York, Columbia, 1963). Valuable both as a history and as an anthology of source materials.

John Edwin Smith, ed., *Contemporary American Philosophy: Second Series* (New York, Humanities Press, 1970).

John Edwin Smith, *The Spirit of American Philosophy* (New York, Oxford, 1963).

William Henry Werkmeister, *A History of Philosophical Ideas in America* (New York, Ronald, 1949).

Morton Gabriel White, *Social Thought in America: The Revolt Against Formalism* (New York, Viking, 1949). Studies of Beard, Dewey, Holmes, Robinson, Veblen.

Robert Clifton Whittemore, *Makers of the American Mind: Three Centuries of American Thought and Thinkers* (New York, William Morrow & Co., 1964).

Philip Paul Wiener, *Evolution and the Founders of Pragmatism* (Cambridge, Harvard, 1949).

Ralph Bubrich Winn, ed., *American Philosophy* (New York, Philosophical Library, 1955).

3 · Religious History

Aaron Ignatius Abell, *American Catholicism and Social Action: A Search for Social Justice, 1865–1950* (Garden City, Doubleday, 1960).

Aaron Ignatius Abell, *The Urban Impact on American Protestantism, 1865–1900* (Cambridge, Harvard, 1943).

Mathew Ahmann, ed., *Race: Challenge to Religion* (Chicago, Regnery, 1963). Papers delivered at a national conference on race and religion.

Ursula Brumm, *American Thought and Religious Typology* (New Brunswick, Rutgers, 1970). A history of doctrines, translated from the German by John Hooglund.

Elmer Talmage Clark, *The Small Sects in America*, revised edition (New York, Abingdon, 1949).

Robert Dougherty Cross, *The Emergence of Liberal Catholicism in America* (Cambridge, Harvard, 1958).

John Tracy Ellis, *American Catholicism*, revised edition (Chicago, University of Chicago, 1969).

John Tracy Ellis, *The Life of James Cardinal Gibbons, Archbishop of Baltimore, 1834–1921* (Milwaukee, Bruce Publishing Co., 1952).

Vergilius Ture Anselm Ferm, ed., *The American Church of the Protestant Heritage* (New York, Philosophical Library, 1953). Essays by various authorities, each on a separate denomination.

SPECIAL ASPECTS

Frank Hugh Foster, *The Modern Movement in American Theology: Sketches in the History of American Protestant Thought from the Civil War to the World War* (New York, Fleming H. Revell Co., 1939).

Edward Franklin Frazier, *The Negro Church in America* (New York, Schocken Books, 1963).

Norman F. Furniss, *The Fundamentalist Controversy, 1918–1931* (New Haven, Yale, 1954).

Nathan Glazer, *American Judaism* (Chicago, University of Chicago, 1957). In the Chicago History of American Civilization series.

Clyde Amos Holbrook, *Religion, A Humanistic Field* (Englewood Cliff, Prentice-Hall, 1963). Argues the case for religion as a liberal arts study, reappraising the entire field of religious instruction and scholarship.

Charles Howard Hopkins, *History of the Y.M.C.A. in North America* (New York, Association Press, 1951).

Charles Howard Hopkins, *The Rise of the Social Gospel in American Protestantism, 1865–1915* (New Haven, Yale, 1940).

Mark DeWolfe Howe, *The Garden and the Wilderness: Religion and Government in American Constitutional History* (Chicago, University of Chicago, 1965).

Winthrop Still Hudson, *American Protestantism* (Chicago, University of Chicago, 1961).

Winthrop Still Hudson, *Religion in America* (New York, Scribner, 1965).

Howard Mumford Jones, *Belief and Disbelief in American Literature* (Chicago, University of Chicago, 1967).

Gail Kennedy, ed., *Evolution and Religion: The Conflict Between Science and Theology in Modern America* (Boston, D. C. Heath & Co., 1957).

Gerhard Emmanuel Lenski, *The Religious Factor: A Sociological Study of Religion's Impact on Politics, Economics, and Family Life* (New York, Doubleday, 1961).

Thomas Timothy McAvoy, *The Great Crisis in American Catholic History, 1895–1900* (Chicago, Regnery, 1957).

53

William Gerald McLoughlin, *Billy Sunday Was His Real Name* (Chicago, University of Chicago, 1955).

William Gerald McLoughlin, *Modern Revivalism: From Charles Grandison Finney to Billy Graham* (New York, Ronald, 1959).

Henry Farnham May, *Protestant Churches and Industrial America* (New York, Harper, 1949).

Frederick Emmanuel Mayer, *Religious Bodies of America*, 4th edition, revised by Arthur Carl Piepkorn (St. Louis, Concordia Publishing House, 1961).

Frank Spencer Mead, *Handbook of Denominations in the United States*, 5th edition (New York, Abingdon, 1970).

Ralph Luther Moellering, *Modern War and the American Churches: A Factual Study of the Christian Conscience on Trial from 1939 to the Cold War Crisis of Today* (New York, American Book Co., 1956).

Walter J. Ong, S.J., *Frontiers in American Catholicism: Essays on Ideology and Culture* (New York, Macmillan, 1957).

Ralph Lord Roy, *Apostles of Discord: A Study of Organized Bigotry and Disruption on the Fringes of Protestantism* (Boston, Beacon Press, 1953).

Herbert Wallace Schneider, *Religion in 20th Century America*, revised edition (New York, Atheneum, 1964). First published in 1952 (Cambridge, Harvard) in the Library of Congress Series in American Civilization.

Nathan A. Scott, Jr., *The Broken Center: Studies in the Theological Horizon of Modern Literature* (New Haven, Yale, 1966).

James Ward Smith and A. Leland Jamison, eds., *Religion in American Life*, 4 vols. (Princeton, Princeton University, 1961). An ambitious survey by more than twenty scholars. Vol. I. *The Shaping of American Religion*; Vol. II. *Religious Perspectives in American Culture*; Vol. III—announced but never published, to be called *Religious Thought and Economic Society*; Vol. IV. *A Critical Bibliography of Religion in American Life*, prepared by Nelson R. Burr, in 2 parts, bound separately.

SPECIAL ASPECTS

Arnold Smithline, *Natural Religion in American Literature* (New York, College & University Press, 1966).

William Learoyd Sperry, *Religion in America* (New York, Macmillan, 1946). Written for a British public, this book gives an excellent brief account of American churches and church life.

Anson Phelps Stokes, *Church and State in the United States*, 3 vols. (New York, Harper, 1950).

William Warren Sweet, *The American Churches: An Interpretation* (New York, Abingdon, 1948).

William Warren Sweet, *The Story of Religion in America*, 2nd edition (New York, Harper, 1950).

Elizabeth Gray Vining, *Friend of Life: The Biography of Rufus M. Jones* (Philadelphia, Lippincott, 1958). Concerns the Quakers.

Edward Arthur White, *Science and Religion in American Thought: The Impact of Naturalism* (Stanford, Stanford University, 1952). Vol. VIII in the Stanford University Series in History, Economics and Political Science.

4 · American Studies

Marshall William Fishwick, ed., *American Studies in Transition*, revised edition (Philadelphia, University of Pennsylvania, 1968).

Arie Nicholaas Jan den Hollander and Sigmund Skard, eds., *American Civilization: An Introduction* (Harlow, Longmans, 1968).

Joseph T. Kwait and Marcy C. Turpie, eds., *Studies in American Culture: Dominant Ideas and Images* (Minneapolis, University of Minnesota, 1960).

Tremaine McDowell, *American Studies* (Minneapolis, University of Minnesota, 1948).

Robert Meredith, ed., *American Studies: Essays on Theory and Method* (Columbus, Charles E. Merrill Publishing Co., 1968).

BACKGROUNDS

Robert Harris Walker, *American Studies in the United States: A Survey of College Programs* (Baton Rouge, Louisiana State, 1958).

F · THE FINE ARTS

John Ireland Howe Baur, *Revolution and Tradition in Modern American Art* (Cambridge, Harvard, 1951). In the Library of Congress Series in American Civilization.

Erwin Ottomar Christensen, *The Index of American Design* (New York, Macmillan, 1950).

Marshall Bowman Davidson, *Life in America*, 2 vols. (Boston, Houghton Mifflin, 1951).

Sigfried Giedion, *Space, Time and Architecture: The Growth of a New Tradition*, 5th edition (Cambridge, Harvard, 1967).

John Atlee Kouwenhoven, *Made in America: The Arts in Modern Civilization* (Garden City, Doubleday, 1948).

Suzanne La Follette, *Art in America from Colonial Times to the Present Day* (New York, Norton, 1929).

Oliver Waterman Larkin, *Art and Life in America*, revised and enlarged edition (New York, Rinehart, 1960). Valuable among other matters for its bibliography.

Marjorie Longley, Louis Silverstein, and Samuel A. Tower, eds., *America's Taste, 1851–1959* (New York, Simon & Schuster, 1960).

Roy McMullen, *Art, Affluence, and Alienation: The Fine Arts Today* (New York, Praeger, 1968).

Lewis Mumford, *The Brown Decades: A Study of the Arts in America, 1865–1895* (New York, Harcourt, 1931). Revised in 1955.

Lewis Mumford, *Sticks and Stones: A Study of American Architecture and Civilization* (New York, Boni & Liveright, 1924). On the interrelation of the arts, particularly architecture and culture. Revised in 1955.

Harold Rosenberg, *The Anxious Object: Art Today and Its Audience* (New York, Horizon Press, 1964).

56

SPECIAL ASPECTS

Aline Bernstein Saarinen, *The Proud Possessors: The Lives, Times, and Tastes of Some Adventurous Art Collectors* (New York, Random, 1958).

Ben Shahn, *The Shape of Content* (Cambridge, Harvard, 1957). The Charles Eliot Norton Lectures at Harvard University.

William Snaith, *The Irresponsible Arts* (New York, Atheneum, 1964). An attack on current tendencies in the arts and their "establishments."

1 · *Architecture*

Wayne Andrews, *Architecture, Ambition and Americans: A History of American Architecture* (New York, Harper, 1955).

Bainbridge Bunting, *Houses of Boston's Back Bay: An Architectural History, 1840–1917* (Cambridge, Harvard, 1967).

John Ely Burchard and Albert Bush-Brown, *The Architecture of America: A Social and Cultural History* (Boston, Little, Brown, 1961).

William A. Coles, ed., *Architecture and Society: Selected Essays by Henry Van Brunt* (Cambridge, Harvard, 1969).

William A. Coles and Henry Hope Reed, Jr., *Architecture in America: A Battle of Styles* (New York, Appleton, 1961).

Carl Wilbur Condit, *American Building Art: The Nineteenth Century* (New York, Oxford, 1960). A comprehensive history of structural forms and techniques, followed by a companion volume, *American Building Art: The Twentieth Century* (New York, Oxford, 1961).

Carl Wilbur Condit, *The Rise of the Skyscraper* (Chicago, University of Chicago, 1952).

Ralph Adams Cram, *My Life in Architecture* (Boston, Little, Brown, 1936).

Finis Farr, *Frank Lloyd Wright: A Biography* (New York, Scribner, 1961).

James Marston Fitch, *Architecture and the Esthetics of Plenty* (New York, Columbia, 1961).

Talbot Faulkner Hamlin, *Forms and Functions of Twentieth-Century Architecture*, 4 vols. (New York, Columbia, 1952).

John Jacobus, *Twentieth-Century Architecture: The Middle Years, 1940–1965* (New York, Praeger, 1966).

Ian McCallum, *Architecture U.S.A.* (New York, Reinhold Publishing Corp., 1959). An excellent survey of contemporary architects.

Sherman Paul, *Louis Sullivan: An Architect in American Thought* (Englewood Cliffs, Prentice-Hall, 1962).

Henry Hope Reed, Jr., *The Golden City* (Garden City, Doubleday, 1958).

John William Reps, *The Making of Urban America: A History of City Planning in the United States* (Princeton, Princeton University, 1965).

Montgomery Schuyler, *American Architecture and Other Writings*, edited by William H. Jordy and Ralph Coe, 2 vols. (Cambridge, Harvard, 1961).

"Mel" (Mellier G.) Scott, *American City Planning Since 1890* (Berkeley, University of California, 1969).

Louis Henry Sullivan, *The Autobiography of an Idea* (New York, Press of the American Institute of Architects, 1924). Republished in New York in 1949 by Peter Smith, in 1956 by Dover Publications.

Thomas Eddy Tallmadge, *The Story of Architecture in America*, new enlarged and revised edition (New York, Norton, 1936).

Christopher Tunnard and Henry Hope Reed, Jr., *American Skyline: The Growth and Form of Our Cities and Towns* (Boston, Houghton Mifflin, 1955).

Frank Lloyd Wright, *An Autobiography*, revised edition (New York, Duell, Sloan & Pearce, 1943).

2 · *Sculpture*

C. Ludwig Brumme, *Contemporary American Sculpture* (New York, Crown, 1948).

Charles Henry Caffin, *American Masters of Sculpture* (New York, Doubleday, 1903).

Wayne Craven, *Sculpture in America* (New York, Crowell, 1968).

Carola Giedion-Welcker, *Contemporary Sculpture: An Evolution in Volume and Space,* revised and enlarged edition (New York, George Wittenborn, 1960). Contains a selective bibliography by Bernard Karpel.

Sam Hunter, *Modern American Painting and Sculpture* (New York, Dell Publishing Co., 1959). A brief survey, paperbound.

Jacques Preston Schnier, *Sculpture in Modern America* (Berkeley, University of California, 1948).

Lorado Taft, *The History of American Sculpture,* new edition with supplementary chapter by Adeline Adams (New York, Macmillan, 1930).

3 · Painting

Virgil Barker, *American Painting: History and Interpretation* (New York, Macmillan, 1950).

John Ireland Howe Baur, ed., *New Art in America: Fifty Painters of the 20th Century* (New York, Praeger, 1957).

Wolfgang Born, *American Landscape Painting* (New Haven, Yale, 1948).

Wolfgang Born, *Still-Life Painting in America: An Interpretation* (New York, Oxford, 1947).

Milton Wolf Brown, *American Painting: From the Armory Show to the Depression* (Princeton, Princeton University, 1955).

Holger Cahill and Alfred Hamilton Barr, Jr., eds., *Art in America: A Complete Survey* (New York, Reynal, 1935).

Henry Geldzahler, *American Painting in the Twentieth Century* (New York, Metropolitan Museum of Art, 1965).

Lloyd Goodrich and John Ireland Howe Baur, *American Art of Our Century* (New York, Praeger, 1961).

Sadakichi Hartmann, *A History of American Art,* revised edition, 2 vols. (Boston, L. C. Page & Co., 1932).

Sam Hunter, *Modern American Painting and Sculpture* (New York, Dell Publishing Co., 1959). A brief survey, paperbound.

Daniel Marcus Mendelowitz, *A History of American Art* (New York, Holt, 1960).

Bernard B. Pearlman, *The Immortal Eight: American Painting from Eakins to the Armory Show (1870–1913)* (New York, Exposition Press, 1962).

Jules David Prown, *American Painting: From Its Beginning to the Armory Show* (Geneva, Skira, 1969).

Mary Chalmers Rathbun and Bartlett H. Hayes, Jr., *Layman's Guide to Modern Art: Painting for a Scientific Age* (New York, Oxford, 1949).

Edgar Preston Richardson, *Painting in America: From 1502 to the Present*, 2nd edition (New York, Crowell, 1965).

Andrew Carnduff Ritchie, *Abstract Painting and Sculpture in America* (New York, Museum of Modern Art, 1951).

Barbara Rose, *American Painting: The Twentieth Century* (Lausanne, Skira, 1969).

James Thrall Soby, *Modern Art and the New Past* (Norman, University of Oklahoma, 1957).

4 · *Music*

Whitney Balliett, *Dinosaurs in the Morning: 41 Pieces on Jazz* (Philadelphia, Lippincott, 1962).

Rudi Blesh, *Shining Trumpets: A History of Jazz*, 2nd edition, revised and enlarged (New York, Knopf, 1958).

Gilbert Chase, *America's Music: From the Pilgrims to the Present*, 2nd revised edition (New York, McGraw-Hill, 1966).

Harold Courlander, *Negro Folk Music, U.S.A.* (New York, Columbia, 1963).

Henry and Sidney Cowell, *Charles Ives and His Music* (New York, Oxford, 1955).

Charlie Gillett, *The Sound of the City: The Rise of Rock and Roll* (New York, Outerbridge and Dienstfrey, 1970).

Stanley Green, *The World of Musical Comedy*, revised edition (New York, A. S. Barnes & Co., 1969).

Robert S. Gold, comp., *A Jazz Lexicon* (New York, Knopf, 1964).

John Tasker Howard and George Kent Bellows, *A Short History of Music in America* (New York, Crowell, 1957).

SPECIAL ASPECTS

John Tasker Howard and Arthur Mendel, *Our Contemporary Composers: American Music in the Twentieth Century* (New York, Crowell, 1941).

Neil Leonard, *Jazz and the White Americans: The Acceptance of a New Art Form* (Chicago, University of Chicago, 1962).

Lester S. Levy, *Grace Notes in American History: Popular Sheet Music from 1820 to 1900* (Norman, University of Oklahoma, 1967).

Joseph Machlis, *An Introduction to Contemporary Music* (New York, Norton, 1961). About one-third of the book is devoted to American composers.

Edward Bennett Marks, *They All Sang: From Tony Pastor to Rudy Vallée* (New York, Viking, 1934).

John Henry Mueller, *The American Symphony Orchestra: A Social History of Musical Taste* (Bloomington, Indiana University, 1951).

Bruno Nettl, *An Introduction to Folk Music in the United States*, 2nd edition (Detroit, Wayne State, 1962).

Irving L. Sablosky, *American Music* (Chicago, University of Chicago, 1969). In the Chicago History of American Civilization series.

Eric Salzman, *Twentieth Century Music: An Introduction* (Englewood Cliffs, Prentice-Hall, 1967). In addition to giving considerable space to recent and living American composers, this book is an excellent general survey of musical trends of the period.

Winthrop Sargeant, *Jazz: A History*, revised edition (New York, McGraw Hill, 1964).

Gunther Schuller, *Early Jazz: Its Roots and Musical Development* (New York, Oxford, 1968).

Nat Shapiro and Nat Henthoff, eds., *Hear Me Talkin' to Ya: The Story of Jazz by the Men Who Made It* (New York, Dover, 1966).

Nicolas Slonimsky, *Music Since 1910*, 4th edition, revised and enlarged (New York, Scribner, 1971).

Oscar Thompson, *The American Singer: A Hundred Years of Success in Opera* (New York, Dial, 1937).

Oscar Thompson, ed., *The International Cyclopedia of Music and Musicians*, 9th edition, revised by Robert Sabin (New York, Dodd, Mead, 1964).

Virgil Thomson, *American Music Since 1910* (New York, Holt, 1971).

Barry Ulanov, *A Handbook of Jazz* (New York, Viking, 1957).

G · THE POPULAR ARTS

For books on popular music, see Music, above.

Erik Barnouw, *Mass Communication: Television, Radio, Film, Press: The Media and Their Practice in the United States of America* (New York, Rinehart, 1956).

Reuel Denney, *The Astonished Muse* (Chicago, University of Chicago, 1957). Essays on television, comic strips, and sports.

Richard Mercer Dorson, *American Folklore* (Chicago, University of Chicago, 1959). A comprehensive survey (limited to prose narrative), ranging from Colonial times to the present.

Jean Herzberg Lipman, *American Folk Art in Wood, Metal and Stone* (New York, Pantheon, 1948).

Jean Herzberg Lipman, *American Primitive Painting* (New York, Oxford, 1942).

Herbert Marshall McLuhan, *Understanding Media: The Extensions of Man* (New York, McGraw-Hill, 1964).

Russel Blaine Nye, *The Unembarrassed Muse: The Popular Arts in America* (New York, Dial, 1970).

Posters in Miniature: With an Introduction by Edward Penfield (New York, R. H. Russell & Son, 1897).

Bernard Rosenberg and David Manning White, eds., *Mass Culture: The Popular Arts in America* (Glencoe, Free Press, 1957). Contains excellent bibliographies in addition to a variety of essays.

Ellen Sabine, *American Folk Art* (Princeton, Van Nostrand-Reinhold Books, 1958).

Gilbert Vivian Seldes, *The Public Arts* (New York, Simon & Schuster, 1956).

SPECIAL ASPECTS

Gilbert Vivian Seldes, *The Seven Lively Arts* (New York, Harper, 1924). Reprinted in 1957 in New York by Thomas Yoseloff.

Geoffrey Wagner, *Parade of Pleasure: A Study of Popular Iconography in the U.S.A.* (New York, Library Publishers, 1955).

Robert Warshow, *The Immediate Experience: Movies, Comics, Theatre, and Other Aspects of Popular Culture* (Garden City, Doubleday, 1962).

Frank Weitenkampf, *American Graphic Art*, new edition, revised and enlarged (New York, Macmillan, 1924).

1 · *Photography and the Movies*

Ansel Easton Adams, *These We Inherit: The Parklands of America* (San Francisco, Sierra Club, 1962). Text and pictures.

Andreas Feininger, *Feininger on Photography* (Chicago, Ziff-Davis Publishing Co., 1949).

Waldo Frank and others, eds., *America and Alfred Stieglitz: A Collective Portrait* (New York, The Literary Guild, 1934).

Oliver Jensen, Joan Paterson Kerr, and Murray Belsky, comps., *American Album* (New York, American Heritage Publishing Co., 1968). Rare photographs collected and described by the editors of *American Heritage*. Valuable as social history.

Beaumont Newhall, *The History of Photography from 1839 to the Present*, revised edition (New York, Museum of Modern Art, 1964).

Nancy Newhall, *The Photographs of Edward Weston* (New York, Museum of Modern Art, 1946).

Edward Steichen, *A Life in Photography* (Garden City, Doubleday, 1963).

John Szarkowski, ed., *The Photographer and the American Landscape* (New York, Museum of Modern Art, 1963).

Robert Taft, *Photography and the American Scene: A Social History, 1839–1889* (New York, Dover, 1964). First published in 1938. Important as background to modern photography.

Edward Weston, *My Camera on Point Lobos: 30 Photographs*

and Excerpts from Edward Weston's Daybook (Boston, Houghton Mifflin, 1950).

James Agee, *Agee on Film: Reviews and Comments* (New York, McDowell, Obolensky, 1958). Considered to be the most perceptive critic of his time, Agee wrote for the *Nation* (1942–1948) and *Time* (1941–1948). He died in 1955.

George N. Fenin and William K. Everson, *The Western: From Silents to Cinerama* (New York, Orion Press, 1962).

Albert Rondthaler Fulton, *Motion Pictures: The Development of an Art from Silent Films to the Age of Television* (Norman, University of Oklahoma, 1960).

Robert Gessner, *The Moving Image: A Guide to Cinematic Literacy* (New York, Dutton, 1968).

Richard Griffith and Arthur Mayer, *The Movies: The Sixty-Year Story of the World of Hollywood and Its Effect on America* (New York, Simon & Schuster, 1957). Generously illustrated.

Leslie Halliwell, *The Filmgoer's Companion*, 3rd revised edition (New York, Hill & Wang, 1970).

Lewis Jacobs, *The Emergence of Film Art: The Evolution and Development of the Motion Picture as an Art, from 1900 to the Present* (New York, Hopkinson & Blake, 1969).

Arthur Knight, *The Liveliest Art: A Panoramic History of the Movies* (New York, Macmillan, 1957). A good brief survey, with a useful bibliography.

Dwight Macdonald, *Dwight Macdonald on the Movies* (Englewood Cliffs, Prentice-Hall, 1969).

Jonas Mekas, *Movie Journal: The Rise of a New American Cinema, 1959–1971* (New York, Macmillan, 1972).

Hortense Powdermaker, *Hollywood, the Dream Factory: An Anthropologist Looks at the Movie-Makers* (Boston, Little, Brown, 1950).

Andrew Sarris, *The American Cinema: Directors and Directions, 1929–1968* (New York, Dutton, 1969).

Richard Schickel, *Movies: The History of an Art and an Institution* (New York, Basic Books, 1964).

SPECIAL ASPECTS

Parker Tyler, *Magic and Myth of the Movies* (New York, Holt, 1947).

Parker Tyler, *The Three Faces of the Film*, revised edition (South Brunswick, A. S. Barnes & Co., 1967).

Parker Tyler, *Underground Film: A Critical History* (New York, Grove Press, Inc., 1969).

Martha Wolfenstein and Nathan Leites, *Movies: A Psychological Study* (Glencoe, Free Press, 1950).

2 · Radio, Television, Records

Erik Barnouw, *A History of Broadcasting in the United States*, 3 vols. (New York, Oxford, 1966–1970). Vol. I. *A Tower of Babel: to 1933*; Vol. II. *The Golden Web: 1933–1953*; Vol. III. *The Image Empire: from 1953*.

Leo Bogart, *The Age of Television: A Study of Viewing Habits and the Impact of Television on American Life* (New York, Ungar, 1956).

Hadley Cantril, *The Invasion from Mars: A Study in the Psychology of Panic* (Princeton, Princeton University, 1940). The sociological and psychological repercussions resulting from Orson Welles' broadcast of an imaginary invasion from Mars.

Fred W. Friendly, *Due to Circumstances Beyond Our Control* (New York, Random, 1967). An "inside" story by the former President of CBS News.

Roland Gelatt, *The Fabulous Phonograph: From Tin Foil to High Fidelity* (Philadelphia, Lippincott, 1955).

Paul Felix Lazarfeld, *The People Look at Radio: Report on a Survey Conducted by the National Opinion Research Center. . . .* (Chapel Hill, University of North Carolina, 1946).

William F. Lynch, S.J., *The Image Industries* (New York, Sheed & Ward, 1959).

Robert Lewis Shayon, *Television and Our Children* (New York, Longmans, 1951).

Harry J. Skornia, *Television and Society: An Inquest and Agenda for Improvement* (New York, McGraw-Hill, 1965).

David Manning White and Richard Averson, *Sight, Sound, and Society* (Boston, Beacon Press, 1968).

Max Wylie, *Clear Channels: Television and the American People* (New York, Funk & Wagnalls, 1955).

3 · Cartoons and Comic Strips

Stephen Becker, *Comic Art in America: A Social History of the Funnies, the Political Cartoons, Magazine Humor, Sporting Cartoons, and Animated Cartoons* (New York, Simon & Schuster, 1959).

The Best of Art Young, with an introduction by Heywood Broun (New York, Vanguard Press, 1936).

Herbert Block, *Herblock's Here and Now* (New York, Simon & Schuster, 1955). One of America's best political cartoonists, Block followed this collection with *Herblock's Special for Today* (New York, Simon & Schuster, 1958) and *Straight Herblock* (New York, Simon & Schuster, 1964).

Jules Feiffer, *Feiffer's Album* (New York, Random, 1963). Social satire.

Jules Feiffer, *The Great Comic Book Heroes* (New York, Dial, 1965).

George Harriman, *Krazy Kat* (New York, Holt, 1946).

Walt Kelly, *Ten Ever-Lovin' Blue-Eyed Years with Pogo* (New York, Simon & Schuster, 1959). Social satire.

Bill Mauldin, *Up Front* (New York, Holt, 1945). Mauldin made his reputation in *Stars and Stripes* during World War II. *Back Home* (New York, William Sloane Associates, 1947) was followed by *A Sort of a Saga* (New York, William Sloane Associates, 1949). He now draws political and social satire, collected in *What's Got Your Back Up?* (New York, Harper, 1961).

William Murrell, *A History of American Graphic Humor*, 2 vols. (New York, Whitney Museum of American Art, 1933–1938).

Charles M. Schulz, *The Peanuts Treasury* (New York, Holt, 1968). See also the numerous *Charlie Brown* volumes.

Martin Sheridan, *Comics and Their Creators: Life Stories of*

SPECIAL ASPECTS

American Cartoonists (Boston, Hale, Cushman & Flint, 1942).

Coulton Waugh, *The Comics* (New York, Macmillan, 1947).

Frederic Wertham, *Seduction of the Innocent* (New York, Rinehart, 1954).

David Manning White and Robert H. Abel, eds., *The Funnies: An American Idiom* (Glencoe, Free Press, 1963).

Gluyas Williams, *The Gluyas Williams Gallery* (New York, Harper, 1957).

V · LITERARY HISTORY

William Rose Benét, ed., *The Reader's Encyclopedia*, 2nd edition (New York, Crowell, 1965).

Marcus Cunliffe, *The Literature of the United States* (Baltimore, Penguin, 1954). A survey by an English historian.

Alice Payne Hackett, *70 Years of Best Sellers, 1895–1965* (New York, Bowker, 1967).

James David Hart, *The Oxford Companion to American Literature*, 4th edition, revised and enlarged (New York, Oxford, 1965).

James David Hart, *The Popular Book: A History of America's Literary Taste* (New York, Oxford, 1950).

Max John Herzberg, ed., *The Reader's Encyclopedia of American Literature* (New York, Crowell, 1962).

Granville Hicks, *The Great Tradition: An Interpretation of American Literature Since the Civil War*, revised edition (New York, Macmillan, 1935). A Marxist approach.

Clarence Hugh Holman, *A Handbook to Literature*, 3rd edition (Indianapolis, Odyssey Press, 1972). Based on the original edition by William Flint Thrall and Addison Hibbard, first published in New York in 1936 by Odyssey Press.

Rod William Horton and Herbert W. Edwards, *Backgrounds of American Literary Thought*, 2nd edition (New York, Appleton, 1967). First published in 1952 as *Backgrounds of American Literature*.

Leon Howard, *Literature and the American Tradition* (Garden City, Doubleday, 1960).

Stanley Jasspon Kunitz and Howard Haycraft, *American Authors, 1600–1900: A Biographical Dictionary of American Literature* (New York, Wilson, 1938).

Stanley Jasspon Kunitz and Howard Haycraft, *Twentieth Century Authors: A Biographical Dictionary of Modern Literature* (New York, Wilson, 1942). Supersedes *Living Authors*

(1931) and *Authors Today and Yesterday* (1933). In 1955, *Twentieth Century Authors: First Supplement* was issued under the editorial direction of Stanley Kunitz and Vineta Colby.

Richard Gordon Lillard, *American Life in Autobiography: A Descriptive Guide* (Stanford, Stanford University, 1956).

Frank Luther Mott, *Golden Multitudes* (New York, Macmillan, 1947). A survey of best sellers in American history.

Fred Lewis Pattee, *A History of American Literature since 1870* (New York, Century, 1915). A pioneer volume, it concludes with 1910.

Fred Lewis Pattee, *The New American Literature, 1890–1930* (New York, Century, 1930). Overlaps and continues its predecessor.

Arthur Hobson Quinn, with Kenneth B. Murdock, Clarence Gohdes, and George F. Whicher, *The Literature of the American People: An Historical and Critical Survey* (New York, Appleton, 1951).

Robert Ernest Spiller, Willard Thorp, Thomas H. Johnson, Henry Seidel Canby, Richard M. Ludwig, eds., *Literary History of the United States*, 3rd edition revised, 2 vols. (New York, Macmillan, 1963). This composite work was originally published in three volumes in 1948, followed by a bibliographical supplement in 1959. The four volumes were gathered into two in 1963. A second bibliographical supplement appeared in 1972.

Heinrich Straumann, *American Literature in the Twentieth Century*, 3rd revised edition (New York, Harper, 1965). This work by a Swiss scholar is an excellent one-volume survey of American literature in the first half of the twentieth century.

Willard Thorp, *American Writing in the Twentieth Century* (Cambridge, Harvard, 1960). In the Library of Congress Series in American Civilization.

William Peterfield Trent, John Erskine, Stuart Pratt Sherman, and Carl Van Doren, eds., *The Cambridge History of American Literature*, 3 vols. in 4 (New York, Putnam, 1917–

1921). Though superseded by *Literary History of the United States* (see Robert Ernest Spiller, above), the work has value, especially for its orderly bibliographies. A *Short History of American Literature* in one volume, based on the larger work, was published in 1922.

B · GENERAL REFERENCE WORKS

1 · *Closed Bibliographies*

Janet Margaret Agnew, "A Southern Bibliography: Fiction, Historical Fiction, Poetry, Biography," *University Bulletin of the Louisiana State University*, n.s., Vol. 31, no. 7; Vol. 32, nos. 8 and 11; Vol. 34, no. 7 (1939–1942).

American Literary Manuscripts: A Checklist of Holdings in Academic, Historical, and Public Libraries in the United States, comp. American Literature Group of the Modern Language Association of America (Austin, University of Texas, 1960).

Jacob Nathaniel Blanck, *Bibliography of American Literature*, 5 vols. (New Haven, Yale, 1955–). Vol. I. *Henry Adams to Donn Byrne* (1955); Vol. II. *George W. Cable to Timothy Dwight* (1957); Vol. III. *Edward Eggleston to Bret Harte* (1959); Vol. IV. *Nathaniel Hawthorne to Joseph Holt Ingraham* (1963); Vol. V. *Washington Irving to Henry Wadsworth Longfellow* (1969).

Jackson Robert Bryer, ed., *Fifteen Modern American Authors: A Survey of Research and Criticism* (Durham, Duke, 1969). A companion volume to the Stovall survey, noted below.

Catalog of Books Represented by Library of Congress Printed Cards Issued to July 31, 1942, 167 vols. (Ann Arbor, Edwards Brothers, 1942). Followed by *Supplement: Cards Issued August 1, 1942–December 31, 1947* (Ann Arbor, J. W. Edwards, 1948), 42 vols.; *Library of Congress Author Catalog . . . 1948–1952* (Ann Arbor, J. W. Edwards, 1953), 24 vols.; and *National Union Catalog: A Cumulative Author List . . . 1953–1957* (Ann Arbor, J. W. Edwards, 1958), 28 vols. All four gatherings will be replaced by *National Union*

Catalog: *Pre-1957 Imprints*, now in progress. See below under Open Guides.

Harry Hayden Clark, *American Literature: Poe Through Garland* (New York, Appleton, 1970).

Otis W. Coan and Richard G. Lillard, *America in Fiction: An Annotated List of Novels That Interpret Aspects of Life in the U.S., Canada, and Mexico*, 5th edition (Palo Alto, Pacific Books Publishers, 1967).

Arthur T. Dickinson, Jr., *American Historical Fiction*, 2nd edition (New York, Scarecrow Press, 1963). Almost 2,000 titles classified into periods of American history from Colonial times to 1962.

Clarence Gohdes, *Bibliographical Guide to the Study of the Literature of the U.S.A.*, 3rd edition (Durham, Duke, 1970). Provides "lists of books which will aid the professional student of the literature of the United States in the acquiring of information and in the techniques of research."

Otis L. Guernsey, Jr., ed., *Directory of the American Theater, 1894–1971* (New York, Dodd, Mead, 1971). A cumulative index to the *Best Plays* series (see below under Drama), but also a valuable guide in itself.

Philip May Hamer, ed., *A Guide to Archives and Manuscripts in the United States* (New Haven, Yale, 1961).

Clarence Hugh Holman, *The American Novel Through Henry James* (New York, Appleton, 1966).

Lewis Leary, *Articles on American Literature, 1900–1950* (Durham, Duke, 1954). Replaces an earlier edition (1947) covering the years 1920–1945. Supplemented by *Articles on American Literature, 1950–1967* (Durham, Duke, 1970).

Eugene Hudson Long, *American Drama from Its Beginnings to the Present* (New York, Appleton, 1970).

Blake Nevius, *The American Novel: Sinclair Lewis to the Present* (New York, Appleton, 1970).

Charles H. Nilon, *Bibliography of Bibliographies in American Literature* (New York, Bowker, 1970). Some 6,500 entries in four sections: Bibliography, Authors, Genre, and Auxiliary, the last one having 30 subheads.

Robert A. Rees and Earl N. Harbert, eds., *Fifteen American Authors Before 1900: Bibliographic Essays on Research and Criticism* (Madison, University of Wisconsin, 1971).

Louis Decimus Rubin, Jr., ed., *A Bibliographical Guide to the Study of Southern Literature* (Baton Rouge, Louisiana State, 1969).

Floyd Stovall, ed., *Eight American Authors: A Review of Research and Criticism* (New York, Modern Language Association, 1956). A paperbound edition with a bibliographical supplement covering 1955–1962, compiled by J. Chesley Matthews, was published by Norton in 1963.

George Thomas Tanselle, *Guide to the Study of United States Imprints* (Cambridge, Harvard, 1971). Principally concerned with printing and publishing, but it also contains "sections devoted to author lists, to genre lists, and to library catalogues."

Allen Tate, *Sixty American Poets, 1896–1944* (Washington, Library of Congress, 1945). A revised edition of this bibliography was prepared by Kenton Kilmer in 1954.

Darwin Theodore Turner, *Afro-American Writers* (New York, Appleton, 1970).

Union List of Little Magazines (Chicago, Midwest Inter-Library Center, 1956). An index of holdings in certain Midwestern libraries only.

James Leslie Woodress, *Dissertations in American Literature, 1891–1966* (Durham, Duke, 1968).

The following titles, originally open or continuing bibliographies, have become closed through cessation of publication.

The American Catalogue (New York, Bowker, 1881–1911). May be found in various forms of binding and volume. In general, it runs to 21 volumes, bound as 15, and is the "national trade bibliography" of books for the years covered. In 1941 it was reissued.

The American Year Book (New York, Appleton, 1911–1919, 1925–1951). Includes among other matters an annual survey of American literature.

The Annual Literary Index (New York, Publishers' Weekly, 1893–1905). Covers the years 1892–1904.

The Annual Library Index (New York, Publishers' Weekly, 1906–1911). Covers the years 1905–1910.

Appleton's Annual Cyclopaedia and Register of Important Events (New York, Appleton, 1876–1903). Vols. 1–15 cover the years 1861–1875; Vols. 16–35 (also known as n.s. Vols. 1–20) cover the years 1876–1895; Vols. 36–42 (also known as 3rd.s. Vols. 1–7) cover the years 1896–1902. There are various indexes; e.g., the index for 1876–1893 is in the 1893 volume.

The United States Catalog: Books in Print (Minneapolis and New York, Wilson, 1899–1928). Variously bound. This series should be distinguished from *Books in Print*, listed below under Open Guides, which is compounded from publishers' catalogues. Beginning in 1933, the supplement to the *United States Catalog* (covering the years 1928–1932) was published under the title *Cumulative Book Index*. For succeeding issues of this title, see below under Open Guides.

2 · *Open or Continuing Guides*

American Literary Scholarship, 1963: An Annual (Durham, Duke, 1965). Compiled annually since 1965. The first five volumes were edited by James Leslie Woodress. Beginning with the survey for 1968 (Durham, Duke, 1970), John Albert Robbins became editor.

The Americana Annual: An Encyclopedia of Current Events (New York, Americana Corp., 1923–). Useful for its annual survey of American literature.

The Book Review Digest (Minneapolis, Wilson, 1905–). Now published by Wilson in New York. Called the *Cumulative Book Review Digest* during the first year of publication.

Books in Print (New York, Bowker, 1948–). Issued annually, it is now in two volumes, one indexed by author, the other by title. Compounded from publishers' catalogues. Bowker also publishes annually, in two volumes, *Subject Guide to*

Books in Print: An Index to the Publishers' Trade List Annual.

Britannica Book of the Year (Chicago, Encyclopedia Britannica, 1948–). Includes among other matter an annual survey of American literature.

Catalogue of Copyright Entries (Washington, U.S. Government Printing Office, July 1, 1891–). Issued monthly or quarterly. Generally listed in library card catalogues under U.S. Copyright Office.

Cumulative Book Index (New York, Wilson, 1933–). Lists all books by American publishers. It appears monthly and is cumulated quarterly, semiannually, and annually.

Literary Market Place (New York, Bowker, 1940–). An annual business directory of American book publishing.

MLA International Bibliography. See *PMLA, Supplement,* below.

National Union Catalog (Washington, Library of Congress, 1956–). A cumulative author list representing Library of Congress printed cards and titles reported by other American libraries. It appears in nine monthly issues and is cumulated quarterly and annually by the Library of Congress, quinquennially by J. W. Edwards, Ann Arbor, Michigan.

National Union Catalog: Pre-1956 Imprints (Chicago and London, Mansell Information/Publishing Ltd., 1968–). A "repertory of the cataloged holdings of selected portions of the cataloged collections of the major research libraries of the United States and Canada plus the more rarely held items in the collections of selected smaller and specialized libraries." Begun in 1968, it will be completed in approximately ten years in about 610 volumes of about 700 pages each.

National Union Catalog of Manuscript Collections (Washington, Library of Congress, 1962–). The first issue, printing reproductions of cards issued for nearly 7,300 manuscript collections by the Library of Congress during the years 1959–1961, is the first of a series of what are now annual and cumulative volumes.

New International Yearbook (New York, Dodd, Mead, 1908–).

This is a successor to *International Yearbook 1899–1903*, published by Dodd, Mead in New York and covering the years 1898–1902. Each number contains a survey of American literature for the year. This annual should not be confused with the *International Year Book and Statesmen's Who's Who*, published in London by Burke's Peerage Limited beginning in 1955.

Paperbound Books in Print (New York, Bowker, 1955–). Began as a monthly. Since 1963, it has been cumulated three times a year (March, July, and November) under the title *Paperbound Books in Print: A Title, Author, Subject Index*. The monthly issues, published under the title *The Month Ahead*, offer previews of forthcoming books.

PMLA, Supplement (New York, Modern Language Association, 1923–). Contains an annual bibliography of scholarly investigation in American literature, beginning with 1922. In 1964, the title was changed to *MLA International Bibliography*. In 1970 it began to appear in a new multi-volume format, separate from, but published by, its parent journal *PMLA*. The bibliography for American literature is included in Vol. I of the four-volume set. For other annual bibliographies, see *American Quarterly* and *American Literature* under Critical List of Magazines, below.

Publishers' Weekly (New York, 1872–). Weekly. Each issue lists books just published, and the last issue in January gives the statistics of book production for the previous year. There are also quarterly "Announcement Numbers."

Readers' Guide to Periodical Literature (New York, Wilson, 1900–). Continues and supplements *Poole's Index to Periodical Literature* (New York) founded in 1848, which with various supplements and revisions lasted until 1908.

Union List of Serials in Libraries of the United States and Canada, 3rd edition, 5 vols. (New York, Wilson, 1965). Covers periodicals through December 31, 1949. Its successor is *New Serial Titles: A Union List of Serials Commencing Publication after December 31, 1949*, a monthly, quarterly, and annual publication issued by the Library of Congress. A two-volume gathering covering the years 1950–1960 was published in 1961 (Washington, Library of Congress), followed by *New Serial Titles, 1961–1965*, 2 vols. (New York, Bowker, 1966) and *New Serial Titles, 1966–1968*, 2 vols. (Washington, Library of Congress, 1969).

C · LITERARY HISTORIES OF SPECIALIZED SCOPE

John Watson Aldridge, *After the Lost Generation: A Critical Study of the Writers of Two Wars* (New York, McGraw-Hill, 1951).

John Watson Aldridge, *In Search of Heresy: American Literature in an Age of Conformity* (New York, McGraw-Hill, 1956).

Warner Berthoff, *The Ferment of Realism: American Literature, 1894–1919* (New York, Free Press, 1965).

John Mason Bradbury, *Renaissance in the South: A Critical History of the Literature, 1920–1960* (Chapel Hill, University of North Carolina, 1963).

Van Wyck Brooks, *America's Coming of Age* (New York, B. W. Huebsch, 1915). A study of the movement of revolt leading into the 1920s.

Van Wyck Brooks, *The Confident Years, 1885–1915* (New York, Dutton, 1952). The fifth volume in his survey of American literature.

Irene and Allen Cleaton, *Books and Battles: American Literature, 1920–1930* (Boston, Houghton Mifflin, 1937).

Malcolm Cowley, ed., *After the Genteel Tradition: American Writers since 1910* (New York, Norton, 1937). A group of interpretative essays.

James Frank Dobie, *Guide to Life and Literature of the Southwest*, revised edition (Dallas, Southern Methodist, 1952).

Bernard Ingersoll Duffey, *The Chicago Renaissance in American Letters: A Critical History* (East Lansing, Michigan State, 1954).

Wilbur Merrill Frohock, *Strangers to This Ground: Cultural Diversity in Contemporary American Writing* (Dallas, Southern Methodist, 1961).

Frederick John Hoffman, *The Twenties: American Writing in the Post-War Decade* (New York, Viking, 1955).

Jay Broadus Hubbell, *The South in American Literature, 1607–1900* (Durham, Duke, 1954).

Howard Mumford Jones, *The Bright Medusa* (Urbana, University of Illinois, 1952). A study of the movements leading into the 1920s.

Howard Mumford Jones, *The Theory of American Literature,* revised and enlarged edition (Ithaca, Cornell, 1965).

Dale Kramer, *Chicago Renaissance: The Literary Life in the Midwest, 1900–1930* (New York, Appleton, 1966).

Halford Edward Luccock, *American Mirror: Social, Ethical, and Religious Aspects of American Literature, 1930–1940* (New York, Macmillan, 1940).

John Albert Macy, *The Spirit of American Literature* (New York, Boni & Liveright, 1918). This pioneer work was for a time available in The Modern Library.

Jay Martin, *Harvests of Change: American Literature, 1865–1914* (Englewood Cliffs, Prentice-Hall, 1967).

Louis Decimus Rubin, Jr., and Robert D. Jacobs, eds., *South: Modern Southern Literature in Its Cultural Settings* (Garden City, Doubleday, 1961).

Louis Decimus Rubin, Jr., and Robert D. Jacobs, eds., *Southern Renascence: The Literature of the Modern South* (Baltimore, Johns Hopkins, 1953).

Edmund Wilson, *Classics and Commercials: A Literary Chronicle of the Forties* (New York, Farrar, 1950).

Edmund Wilson, *The Shores of Light: A Literary Chronicle of the Twenties and Thirties* (New York, Farrar, 1952). This interpretative work considers more than the decades enumerated.

Larzer Ziff, *The American 1890s: Life and Times of a Lost Generation* (New York, Viking, 1966).

D · SPECIAL THEMES

Daniel Aaron, *Writers on the Left: Episodes in American Lit-*

erary Communism (New York, Harcourt, 1961). Covers the period from 1912 to the early 1940s.

Jesse Bier, *The Rise and Fall of American Humor* (New York, Holt, 1968).

Walter Blair, *Horse Sense in American Humor, from Benjamin Franklin to Ogden Nash* (Chicago, University of Chicago, 1942).

John Mason Bradbury, *The Fugitives: A Critical Account* (Chapel Hill, University of North Carolina, 1958).

Benjamin Griffith Brawley, *The Negro in Literature and Art in the United States* (New York, Duffield & Co., 1929).

Edwin Harrison Cady, *The Gentleman in America: A Literary Study in American Culture* (Syracuse, Syracuse University, 1949).

Frederic Ives Carpenter, *American Literature and the Dream* (New York, Philosophical Library, 1955).

Bruce Cook, *The Beat Generation* (New York, Scribner, 1971).

Richard Allen Foster, *The School in American Literature* (Baltimore, Warwick & York, 1930).

Allen Guttmann, *The Conservative Tradition in America* (New York, Oxford, 1967). From Washington Irving to T. S. Eliot.

Allen Guttmann, *The Jewish Writer in America: Assimilation and the Crisis of Identity* (New York, Oxford, 1971).

Ima Honaker Herron, *The Small Town in American Literature* (Durham, Duke, 1939).

Anthony Channell Hilfer, *The Revolt from the Village, 1915–1930* (Chapel Hill, University of North Carolina, 1969).

Howard William Hintz, *The Quaker Influence in American Literature* (New York, Fleming H. Revell Co., 1940).

Frederick John Hoffman, *Freudianism and the Literary Mind*, 2nd edition (Baton Rouge, Louisiana State, 1957).

Irving Howe, *A World More Attractive: A View of Modern Literature and Politics* (New York, Horizon Press, 1963).

Nathan Irvin Huggins, *The Harlem Renaissance* (New York, Oxford, 1971). A survey of the artistic movement that in a sense preceded the social movement of "Black Liberation."

Sol Liptzin, *The Jew in American Literature* (New York, Bloch Publishing Co., 1966).

Halford Edward Luccock, *Contemporary American Literature and Religion* (Chicago, Willett, Clark & Co., 1934).

Edward Margolies, *Native Sons: A Critical Study of Twentieth-Century Negro American Authors* (Philadelphia, Lippincott, 1968).

Leo Marx, *The Machine in the Garden: Technology and the Pastoral Ideal in America* (New York, Oxford, 1964).

Albert Parry, *Garrets and Pretenders: A History of Bohemianism in America*, revised edition (New York, Dover, 1960). Two new chapters added. First published in 1933.

Donald Pizer, *Realism and Naturalism in Nineteenth-Century American Literature* (Carbondale, Southern Illinois, 1966).

William Schechter, *The History of Negro Humor in America* (New York, Fleet Press, 1970).

Franklin Dickerson Walker, *A Literary History of Southern California* (Berkeley, University of California, 1950).

Norris Wilson Yates, *The American Humorist: Conscience of the Twentieth Century* (Ames, Iowa State, 1964).

E · THE ENGLISH LANGUAGE IN AMERICA

Theodore Menline Bernstein, *Watch Your Language: A Lively, Informal Guide to Better Writing Emanating from the News Room of the New York Times* (New York, Atheneum, 1965). Originally published in 1958. See also his *The Careful Writer* (New York, Atheneum, 1965).

Lester V. Berrey and Melvin Van den Bark, *The American Thesaurus of Slang: With Supplement* (New York, Crowell, 1947).

Richard Bridgman, *The Colloquial Style in America* (New York, Oxford, 1966).

Sir William Alexander Craigie and James Root Hulbert, eds., *A Dictionary of American English on Historical Principles*, 4 vols. (Chicago, University of Chicago, 1938–1944). See also Joseph Abraham Weingarten, *Supplementary Notes to the Dictionary of American English* (New York, privately printed, 1948).

Bergen Evans and Cornelia Evans, *A Dictionary of Contemporary American Usage* (New York, Random, 1957).

Wilson Follett, *Modern American Usage: A Guide*, edited and completed by Jacques Barzun and others (New York, Hill & Wang, 1966).

George Philip Krapp, *The English Language in America*, 2 vols. (New York, Ungar, 1960). First published in 1925.

George Philip Krapp, *Modern English: Its Growth and Present Use*, revised by Albert H. Marckwardt (New York, Scribner, 1969). First published in 1909.

Charlton Laird, *Language in America* (New York, World, 1970).

Mitford McLeod Mathews, ed., *A Dictionary of Americanisms on Historical Principles*, 2 vols. (Chicago, University of Chicago, 1951). A shorter version is titled *Americanisms: A Dictionary of Selected Americanisms on Historical Principles* (Chicago, 1966).

Henry Louis Mencken, *The American Language*, 4th edition, corrected, enlarged, rewritten (New York, Knopf, 1936). Originally published in 1919. There were supplements in 1945 and 1948. A one-volume edition, abridged by Raven I. McDavid, Jr., and David W. Maurer, appeared in 1963.

Louise M. Myers, *Guide to American English*, 4th edition (Englewood Cliffs, PrenticeHall, 1966).

Margaret Nicholson, *A Dictionary of American-English Usage, Based on Fowler's Modern English Usage* (New York, Oxford, 1957).

William Richard Poirier, *A World Elsewhere: The Place of Style in American Literature* (New York, Oxford, 1966).

Carroll E. Reed, *Dialects of American English* (Cleveland, World, 1967).

George Rippey Stewart, *American Place-Names: A Concise and Selective Dictionary for the Continental United States of America* (New York, Oxford, 1970).

Harold Wentworth and Stuart Berg Flexner, *Dictionary of*

American Slang (New York, Crowell, 1960). A supplement by Flexner was added to the 1967 edition.

F · FICTION

1 · *The Novel*

a · *General Books*

John Watson Aldridge, ed., *Critiques and Essays on Modern Fiction, 1920–1951* (New York, Ronald, 1952).

Jonathan Baumbach, *The Landscape of Nightmare: Studies in the Contemporary Novel* (New York, New York University, 1965).

Joseph Warren Beach, *American Fiction, 1920–1940* (New York, Macmillan, 1941).

Nelson Manfred Blake, *Novelists' America: Fiction as History, 1910–1940* (Syracuse, Syracuse University, 1969).

Richard Volney Chase, *The American Novel and Its Tradition* (Garden City, Doubleday, 1957).

Alexander Cowie, *The Rise of the American Novel* (New York, American Book Co., 1948). Ends with Henry James.

Chester Emanuel Eisinger, *Fiction of the Forties* (Chicago, University of Chicago, 1963).

Harold Charles Gardiner, S.J., ed., *Fifty Years of the American Novel: A Christian Appraisal* (New York, Scribner, 1951). An anthology of essays.

Maxwell David Geismar, *Rebels and Ancestors: The American Novel, 1890–1915* (Boston, Houghton Mifflin, 1953).

Maxwell David Geismar, *The Last of the Provincials: The American Novel, 1915–1925* (Boston, Houghton Mifflin, 1947).

Maxwell David Geismar, *Writers in Crisis: The American Novel Between Two Wars* (Boston, Houghton Mifflin, 1942). Covers the years 1925–1940.

Maxwell David Geismar, *American Moderns: From Rebellion to Conformity* (New York, Hill & Wang, 1958). A midcentury view of the American novel.

Ihab Hassan, *Radical Innocence: Studies in the Contemporary American Novel* (Princeton, Princeton University, 1961).

81

Frederick John Hoffman, *The Modern Novel in America, 1900–1950* (Chicago, Regnery, 1951). A brief survey.

Marcus Klein, *After Alienation: American Novels in Mid-Century* (Cleveland, World, 1964).

Desmond Ernest Stewart Maxwell, *American Fiction: The Intellectual Background* (New York, Columbia, 1963).

Hermann Mohrmann, *Kultur- und Gesellschaftsprobleme des amerikanischen Romanes der Nachkriegszeit, 1920–1927* (Giessen, Nolte, 1934).

Sean O'Faolain, *The Vanishing Hero: Studies in Novelists of the Twenties* (Boston, Little, Brown, 1957).

Louis Decimus Rubin, Jr., and John Rees Moore, eds., *The Idea of an American Novel* (New York, Crowell, 1961). Selected documents "that bear on our intense and long-standing self-consciousness about the American novel."

Jean Simon, *Le roman américain au XXe siècle* (Paris, Boivin, 1950).

Tony Tanner, *City of Words: American Fiction, 1950–1970* (New York, Harper, 1971).

Edward Charles Wagenknecht, *Cavalcade of the American Novel, from the Birth of the Nation to the Middle of the Twentieth Century* (New York, Holt, 1952). Contains an excellent bibliography.

Helen Weinberg, *The New Novel in America: The Kafkan Mode in Contemporary Fiction* (Ithaca, Cornell, 1969).

b · *Special Topics*

Lars Åhnebrink (Aahnebrink), *The Beginnings of Naturalism in American Fiction: A Study of the Works of Hamlin Garland, Stephen Crane, and Frank Norris with Special Reference to Some European Influences, 1891–1903. Essays and Studies on American Language and Literature*, IX (Upsala, Sweden, The American Institute in the University of Upsala, 1950). Also published in America (Cambridge, Harvard, 1950).

James Osler Bailey, *Pilgrims Through Space and Time: Trends and Patterns in Scientific and Utopian Fiction* (New York, Argus Books, 1947). A reliable study.

Harry Bernard, *Le roman régionaliste aux Etats-Unis, 1913–1940* (Montreal, Editions Fides, 1949).

Joseph Leo Blotner, *The Modern American Political Novel, 1900–1960* (Austin, University of Texas, 1966).

George Bluestone, *Novels into Film* (Baltimore, Johns Hopkins, 1957).

Robert A. Bone, *The Negro Novel in America* (New Haven, Yale, 1958).

Stanley Cooperman, *World War I and the American Novel* (Baltimore, Johns Hopkins, 1967).

Dorothy Yost Deegan, *The Stereotype of the Single Woman in American Novels. A Social Study with Implications for the Education of Women* (New York, Columbia, 1951).

Leon Edel, *The Psychological Novel, 1900–1950* (New York, Lippincott, 1955).

Leslie Aaron Fiedler, *Love and Death in the American Novel,* revised edition (New York, Criterion Books, 1966).

James King Folsom, *The American Western Novel* (New Haven, College & University Press, 1966).

Warren French, *The Social Novel at the End of an Era* (Carbondale, Southern Illinois, 1966). Does not discuss Farrell, Dos Passos, O'Hara, or the proletarian school. Concentrates on *For Whom the Bell Tolls, The Grapes of Wrath, Night Rider, The Hamlet, Johnny Got His Gun,* and *Ararat.*

Wilbur Merrill Frohock, *The Novel of Violence in America,* revised and enlarged edition (Dallas, Southern Methodist, 1957).

Blanche Housman Gelfant, *The American City Novel* (Norman, University of Oklahoma, 1954).

Hugh Morris Gloster, *Negro Voices in American Fiction* (Chapel Hill, University of North Carolina, 1948).

Richard Boyd Hauck, *A Cheerful Nihilism: Confidence and "the Absurd" in American Humorous Fiction* (Bloomington, Indiana University, 1971).

Robert Humphrey, *Stream of Consciousness in the Modern Novel* (Berkeley, University of California, 1954).

Josephine Lurie Jessup, *The Faith of Our Feminists: A Study in the Novels of Edith Wharton, Ellen Glasgow, Willa Cather* (New York, Richard R. Smith, Publisher, 1950).

Ernest Erwin Leisy, *The American Historical Novel* (Norman, University of Oklahoma, 1950).

Robert Alexander Lively, *Fiction Fights the Civil War: An Unfinished Chapter in the Literary History of the American People* (Chapel Hill, University of North Carolina, 1957).

Kenneth Schuyler Lynn, *The Dream of Success: A Study of the Modern American Imagination* (Boston, Little, Brown, 1955). Treats Dreiser, London, Norris, Herrick, and Phillips.

John Ormsby Lyons, *The College Novel in America* (Carbondale, Southern Illinois, 1962).

Michael Millgate, *American Social Fiction: James to Cozzens* (New York, Barnes & Noble, 1964).

Wright Morris, *The Territory Ahead* (New York, Harcourt, 1958).

Walter Bates Rideout, *The Radical Novel in the United States, 1900–1954: Some Interrelations of Literature and Society* (Cambridge, Harvard, 1956).

Mark Schorer, ed., *Society and Self in the Novels* (New York, Columbia, 1956). English Institute Essays of 1955. Includes Schorer's own essay on Sinclair Lewis.

Walter Fuller Taylor, *The Economic Novel in America* (Chapel Hill, University of North Carolina, 1942).

Nancy M. Tischler, *Black Masks: Negro Character in Modern Southern Fiction* (University Park, Pennsylvania State University Press, 1969).

Charles Child Walcutt, *American Literary Naturalism: A Divided Stream* (Minneapolis, University of Minnesota, 1956).

W. Tasker Witham, *The Adolescent in the American Novel, 1920–1960* (New York, Ungar, 1964).

2 · *The Short Story*

There are innumerable collections of American short stories of various types, the purpose, scope, or kind of the anthology usually being indicated in the titles. The best place to find such volumes is in a large, or even a medium-size, library, public or academic. There are also innumerable books on how to write short stories.

a · *Continuing Collections*

The Best American Short Stories (Boston, Small, Maynard & Co., 1915–1925; New York, Dodd, Mead, 1926–1932; Boston, Houghton Mifflin, 1933–). This annual compilation was begun by Edward J. O'Brien, partly in protest against the "mechanical" or "commercial" magazine story, and is currently edited by Martha Foley and David Burnett. The introductory matter in each volume provides a valuable appraisal of tendencies in this literary form for the year covered. In 1965, Martha Foley edited *Fifty Best American Short Stories, 1915–1965* (Boston, Houghton Mifflin).

O. Henry Memorial Award Prize Stories (New York, Doubleday, 1921–). Originally founded under the editorship of Blanche Colton Williams as a counter-collection to the series listed above. Over the years the title has varied, the 1963 volume being *Prize Stories 1963: The O. Henry Awards*. Recent volumes have been edited by Paul Engle (1954–1959), Mary Stegner (1960), Richard Poirier (1961–1966), and William Abrahams (since 1966).

b · *General Books*

Edward Joseph Harrington O'Brien, *The Advance of the American Short Story*, revised edition (New York, Dodd, Mead, 1931).

Fred Lewis Pattee, *The Development of the American Short Story: An Historical Survey* (New York, Harper, 1923). Reprinted in 1966 (New York, Biblo & Tannen).

William Peden, *The American Short Story: Front Line in the National Defense of Literature* (Boston, Houghton Mifflin, 1964).

Ray Benedict West, Jr., *The Short Story in America* (Chicago, Regnery, 1956). Originally *The Short Story in America, 1900–1950*, published by Regnery in 1952.

Blanche Colton Williams, *Our Short Story Writers* (New York, Moffat, Yard & Co., 1920).

Despite the large number of titles having to do with modern poetry, it is difficult to assemble a select list of books principally concerned with the history and development of the art in the United States since 1890. Possibly as good a way as any to trace the history of the poetic movement since 1912 is to consult the files of the magazine expressly founded by Harriet Monroe to champion the new movement, *Poetry: A Magazine of Verse* (Chicago, 1912–). It is now edited by Daryl Hine.

Gay Wilson Allen, *American Prosody* (New York, American Book Co., 1935). Reprinted in 1966 (New York, Octagon Books).

Alfred Alvarez, *The Shaping Spirit: Studies in Modern English and American Poets* (London, Chatto & Windus, 1958). Published in New York by Scribner in 1958 under the title *Stewards of Excellence*.

Joseph Warren Beach, *Obsessive Images: Symbolism in Poetry of the 1930's and 1940's*, edited by William Van O'Connor (Minneapolis, University of Minnesota, 1960).

Richard Palmer Blackmur, *Language As Gesture: Essays in Poetry* (New York, Harcourt, 1952). Treats Pound, Eliot, Stevens, Cummings, and Moore, among others.

Louise Bogan, *Achievement in American Poetry, 1900–1950* (Chicago, Regnery, 1951).

John Mason Bradbury, *The Fugitives: A Critical Account* (Chapel Hill, University of North Carolina, 1958).

William Stanley Braithwaite, ed., *Anthology of Magazine Verse . . . and Yearbook of American Poetry* (New York, G. Sully & Co., 1913–1929).

Cleanth Brooks and Robert Penn Warren, *Understanding Poetry*, 3rd edition (New York, Holt, 1960). Although a textbook and anthology with commentary, it is included here because it has been, since it was first published in 1938, the most widely used introductory book explicating the reading and study of poetry.

Stanley Burnshaw, *The Seamless Web: Language-Thinking, Creative-Knowledge, Art-Experience* (New York, Braziller, 1970).

Glauco Cambon, *The Inclusive Flame: Studies in Modern American Poetry* (Bloomington, Indiana University, 1963). Focuses on Stevens, Williams, and Hart Crane.

John Ciardi, *How Does a Poem Mean?* (Boston, Houghton Mifflin, 1959).

Stanley Knight Coffman, *Imagism: A Chapter for the History of Modern Poetry* (Norman, University of Oklahoma, 1951).

Frederick William Conner, *Cosmic Optimism: A Study of the Interpretation of Evolution by American Poets from Emerson to Robinson* (Gainesville, University of Florida, 1949).

Babette Deutsch, *Poetry in Our Time*, revised edition (Garden City, Doubleday, 1963). Originally published in New York by Holt in 1952 and by Columbia in 1956.

Denis Donoghue, *Connoisseurs of Chaos: Ideas of Order in Modern American Poetry* (New York, Macmillan, 1965).

Elizabeth A. Drew, in collaboration with John L. Sweeney, *Directions in Modern Poetry* (New York, Norton, 1940).

Horace Gregory and Marya Zaturenska, *A History of American Poetry, 1900–1940* (New York, Harcourt, 1946). Covers the 1890s in part. Reprinted in 1969.

Richard Howard, *Alone with America: Essays on the Art of Poetry in the United States since 1950* (New York, Atheneum, 1969).

Edward Buell Hungerford, ed., *Poets in Progress: Critical Prefaces to Ten Contemporary Americans* (Evanston, Northwestern, 1962).

Randall Jarrell, *Poetry and the Age* (New York, Knopf, 1953).

Randall Jarrell, *The Third Book of Criticism* (New York, Farrar, 1969).

Carlin T. Kindilien, *American Poetry in the Eighteen Nineties*

. . . (Providence, Brown University Press, 1956). Based on the rich collections in the Brown University libraries, this is Vol. XX in the Brown University Studies.

Joseph Marshall Kuntz, ed., *Poetry Explication*, revised edition (Denver, Swallow, 1962). A checklist of interpretations since 1925 of British and American poems past and present.

Archibald MacLeish, *Poetry and Experience* (Boston, Houghton Mifflin, 1961).

Josephine Miles, *The Primary Language of Poetry in the 1940's* (Berkeley, University of California, 1951).

Joseph Hillis Miller, *Poets of Reality: Six Twentieth-Century Writers* (Cambridge, Harvard, 1965). Groups Eliot, Stevens, and Williams with Conrad, Yeats, and Dylan Thomas.

Ralph Joseph Mills, Jr., *Contemporary American Poetry* (New York, Random, 1965). Twelve essays on twelve poets.

Roy Harvey Pearce, *The Continuity of American Poetry* (Princeton, Princeton University, 1961). An introduction to both the theory and the history of American poetry.

Sister Mary Bernetta Quinn, *The Metamorphic Tradition in Modern Poetry* (New Brunswick, Rutgers, 1955). Discusses Pound, Eliot, Williams, Hart Crane, Stevens, and Jeffers.

Macha Louis Rosenthal, *The Modern Poets: A Critical Introduction* (New York, Oxford, 1960).

Macha Louis Rosenthal, *The New Poets: American and British Poetry since World War II* (New York, Oxford, 1967).

Karl Jay Shapiro, *In Defense of Ignorance* (New York, Random, 1960). Attacks Pound and Eliot.

Monroe Kirk Spears, *Dionysus and the City: Modernism in Twentieth-Century Poetry* (New York, Oxford, 1970). Ranges from Yeats and Pound to Robert Lowell and James Dickey.

Leonard Unger, *The Man in the Name: Essays on the Experience of Poetry* (Minneapolis, University of Minnesota, 1956).

Albert Douglass Van Nostrand, *Everyman His Own Poet: Romantic Gospels in American Literature* (New York, McGraw-Hill, 1968).

Hyatt Howe Waggoner, *American Poets from the Puritans to the Present* (Boston, Houghton Mifflin, 1968).

Hyatt Howe Waggoner, *The Heel of Elohim: Science and Values in Modern American Poetry* (Norman, University of Oklahoma, 1950).

Michael Yatron, *America's Literary Revolt* (New York, Philosophical Library, 1959). Devoted exclusively to Masters, Lindsay, Sandburg, and Populism.

H · DRAMA

Justin Brooks Atkinson, *Broadway: Nineteen Hundred to Nineteen Seventy* (New York, Macmillan, 1970).

Eric Russell Bentley, *The Dramatic Event: An American Chronicle* (New York, Horizon Press, 1954). Deals with the Broadway theater in 1952–1954.

Archie Binns and Olive Kooken, *Mrs. Fiske and the American Theatre* (New York, Crown, 1955). Not only a biography of Mrs. Fiske but also the chronicle of a struggle against the so-called "theatrical trust."

Robert Brustein, *The Theatre of Revolt: An Approach to the Modern Drama* (Boston, Little, Brown, 1964).

Harold Clurman, *The Fervent Years: The Story of the Group Theatre and the Thirties* (New York, Hill & Wang, 1957). Originally published by Knopf in 1945.

Harold Clurman, *The Naked Image: Observations in the Modern Theatre* (New York, Macmillan, 1966).

Lehman Engel, *The American Musical Theater: A Consideration* (New York, Macmillan, 1967).

John Gassner, *Form and Idea in Modern Theatre* (New York, Dryden, 1956).

Richard Gilman, *Common and Uncommon Masks: Writings on Theatre, 1961–1970* (New York, Random, 1971).

Martin Gottfried, *A Theater Divided: The Postwar American Stage* (Boston, Little, Brown, 1967).

Philip Graham, *Showboats: The History of an American Institution* (Austin, University of Texas, 1951).

Abel Green and Joe Laurie, Jr., *Show Biz from Vaude to Video* (New York, Holt, 1951).

Barnard Wolcott Hewitt, *Theatre, U.S.A., 1668–1957* (New York, McGraw-Hill, 1959). A general survey.

Morgan Yale Himelstein, *Drama Was a Weapon: The Left-Wing Theatre in New York, 1929–1941* (New Brunswick, Rutgers, 1962).

Glenn Hughes, *A History of the American Theatre, 1700–1950* (New York, Samuel French, 1951).

Wisner Payne Kinne, *George Pierce Baker and the American Theatre* (Cambridge, Harvard, 1954). Concerns the famous "47 Workshop" at Harvard University.

Joseph Wood Krutch, *The American Drama since 1918: An Informal History*, revised edition (New York, Braziller, 1957).

Mary Therese McCarthy, *Sights and Spectacles, 1937–1962* (New York, Farrar, 1963). A highly personal view of the drama during these years.

Richard Moody, *America Takes the Stage: Romanticism in American Drama and Theatre, 1750–1900* (Bloomington, Indiana University, 1955).

Lloyd R. Morris, *Curtain Time: The Story of the American Theatre* (New York, Random, 1953).

Montrose Jonas Moses and John Mason Brown, *The American Theatre As Seen by Its Critics, 1752–1934* (New York, Norton, 1934). Chiefly concerned with the later theater.

George Jean Nathan, *The Magic Mirror: Selected Writings on the Theatre*, edited by Thomas Quinn Curtiss (New York, Knopf, 1960).

George Jean Nathan, *The World of George Jean Nathan*, edited by Charles Angoff (New York, Knopf, 1952). A cross-section of his critical opinions over four decades.

Julia S. Price, *The Off-Broadway Theater* (New York, Scarecrow Press, 1962).

Arthur Hobson Quinn, *A History of the American Drama from the Civil War to the Present Day*, revised edition (New York, F. S. Crofts & Co., 1936).

LITERARY HISTORY

Richard Schechner, *Public Domain: Essays on the Theatre* (Indianapolis, Bobbs-Merrill, 1969).

Wieder David Sievers, *Freud on Broadway: A History of Psychoanalysis and the American Drama* (New York, Hermitage House, 1955).

A. Nicholas Vardac, *Stage to Screen* (Cambridge, Harvard, 1949). A study of pictorial staging from Garrick to Griffith, particularly in American theaters.

Gerald Weales, *American Drama since World War II* (New York, Harcourt, 1962).

Gerald Weales, *The Jumping-Off Place: American Drama in the 1960's* (New York, Macmillan, 1969).

The history of the Broadway theater during the period can be followed by consulting the *Best Plays* series, published in New York by Dodd, Mead. The bibliography is mildly complicated. *The Best Plays of 1894–1899*, a retrospective collection, was published in 1955; *The Best Plays of 1899–1909*, again retrospective, was published in 1944; and *The Best Plays of 1909–1919*, also retrospective, appeared in 1933. The annual volume, edited by Burns Mantle, first appeared in 1920 (Boston, Small, Maynard & Co.), for the season of 1919–1920. Since then, the *Best Plays* has appeared each year. Beginning in 1926, Dodd, Mead became the publisher. Mantle died in 1948. John Chapman continued the annual series through 1952, Louis Kronenberger through 1961, Henry Hewes through 1964, and Otis L. Guernsey, Jr., since 1965.

I · GENERAL PROSE AND CRITICISM

For a brief survey of American critical movements, 1915–1945, with bibliography, see *Literary History of the United States*, Robert E. Spiller and others, eds., 3rd edition (New York, Macmillan, 1963), pp. 1,358–1,373.

Conrad Aiken, *Collected Criticism from 1916 to the Present: A Reviewer's ABC*, edited by Rufus A. Blanchard (New York, Meridian Books, 1958).

Joseph Warren Beach, *The Outlook for American Prose* (Chicago, University of Chicago, 1926).

Clarence Arthur Brown, comp., *The Achievement of American Criticism: Representative Selections from Three Hundred Years of American Criticism*, with a foreword by Harry Hayden Clark (New York, Ronald, 1954).

Donald Davidson, *Southern Writers in the Modern World* (Athens, University of Georgia, 1958).

Bernard De Voto, *The Easy Chair* (Boston, Houghton Mifflin, 1955). Essays reprinted from *Harper's Magazine*.

Max Eastman, *The Literary Mind: Its Place in an Age of Science* (New York, Scribner, 1931).

William Elton, *A Guide to the New Criticism*, revised edition (Chicago, Modern Poetry Association, 1953). First published in 1949 under the title *A Glossary of the New Criticism* (Chicago, Modern Poetry Association).

James Thomas Farrell, *Literature and Morality* (New York, Vanguard Press, 1947).

Richard Jackson Foster, *The New Romantics: A Reappraisal of the New Criticism* (Bloomington, Indiana University, 1962).

Charles Irving Glicksberg, *American Literary Criticism, 1900–1950* (New York, Hendricks House, 1952).

William Dean Howells, *Criticism and Fiction* (New York, Harper, 1891).

William Dean Howells, *My Literary Passions* (New York, Harper, 1895).

Stanley Edgar Hyman, *The Armed Vision: A Study in the Methods of Modern Literary Criticism* (New York, Knopf, 1948). Revised and abridged in 1955 (New York, Vintage).

Henry James, *The American Essays*, edited with an introduction by Leon Edel (New York, Vintage, 1956).

Henry James, *The House of Fiction: Essays on the Novel*, edited with an introduction by Leon Edel (London, Rupert Hart-Davis, 1957).

Henry James, *Literary Reviews and Essays on American, English,* and *French Literature,* edited by Albert Mordell (New York, Twayne Publishers, 1959).

Alfred Kazin, *On Native Grounds: An Interpretation of Modern American Prose Literature* (New York, Reynal, 1942).

Lawrence Irwin Lipking and A. Walton Litz, eds., *Modern Literary Criticism, 1900–1970* (New York, Oxford, 1971). Concentrates on Pound, Eliot, Richards, and Frye.

Francis Otto Matthiessen, *The Responsibilities of the Critic: Essays and Reviews,* selected by John Rackliffe (New York, Oxford, 1952).

John Paul Pritchard, *Criticism in America: An Account of the Development of Critical Techniques from the Early Period of the Republic to the Middle Years of the Twentieth Century* (Norman, University of Oklahoma, 1956).

Richard Ruland, *The Rediscovery of American Literature* (Cambridge, Harvard, 1967). Discusses "the premises of critical taste, 1900–1940," with emphasis on Stuart Pratt Sherman, the New Humanists, H. L. Mencken, and F. O. Matthiessen.

Robert Ernest Spiller, *The Cycle of American Literature: An Essay in Historical Criticism* (New York, Macmillan, 1955).

Robert Wooster Stallman, ed., *Critiques and Essays in Criticism, 1920–1948, Representing the Achievement of Modern British and American Critics* (New York, Ronald, 1949).

Floyd Stovall, ed., *The Development of American Criticism* (Chapel Hill, University of North Carolina, 1955). Essays by Harry Hayden Clark and others.

Walter E. Sutton, *Modern American Criticism* (Englewood Cliffs, Prentice-Hall, 1963).

Lionel Trilling, *The Liberal Imagination: Essays on Literature and Society* (New York, Viking, 1950).

Lionel Trilling, *The Opposing Self: Nine Essays in Criticism* (New York, Viking, 1955).

Morton Dauwen Zabel, ed., *Literary Opinions in America: Essays Illustrating the Status, Methods, and Problems of Criticism in the United States in the Twentieth Century,* 3rd edition, revised, 2 vols. (New York, Harper, 1962).

BACKGROUNDS

J · BIOGRAPHY

Biography Index (New York, Wilson, 1946–). Covers biographical material in current books and magazines. Published quarterly; cumulated annually and triennially.

Current Biography (New York, Wilson, 1940–). Publishes "articles on people who are prominent in the news." Appears monthly; cumulated annually in *Current Biography Yearbook*.

Marion Dargan, *Guide to American Biography* (Albuquerque, University of New Mexico, 1949, 1952). In two parts. Part II covers the years 1815–1933.

John Mark Lonaker, *Contemporary Biography* (Philadelphia, University of Pennsylvania, 1934).

Dana Kinsman Merrill, *American Biography: Its Theory and Practice* (Portland, Bowker Press, 1957).

Edward Hayes O'Neill, *Biography by Americans, 1658–1936: A Subject Bibliography* (Philadelphia, University of Pennsylvania, 1939).

Edward Hayes O'Neill, *A History of American Biography, 1800–1935* (Philadelphia, University of Pennsylvania, 1939).

K · MAGAZINES

Frederick John Hoffman, Charles Allen, and Carolyn Farquhar Ulrich, *The Little Magazines: A History and a Bibliography*, 2nd edition (Princeton, Princeton University, 1966).

Index to Little Magazines (Denver, Swallow, 1949–). Now published by Swallow in Chicago. Originally issued each year, but 1953–1955 appeared as one volume in 1956; 1956–1957 as one volume in 1958; and so on. There have been various compilers, the latest issue being put together by Evelyn G. Lauer. Stephen H. Goode compiled two volumes that supplement retrospectively this continuing index: *Index to Little Magazines, 1943–1947* (Denver, Swallow, 1965) and *Index to Little Magazines, 1940–1942* (New York, Johnson Reprint Corp., 1967). Other volumes indexing pre-1940 publications are in preparation.

Frank Luther Mott, *American Journalism: A History, 1690–1960*, 3rd edition (New York, Macmillan, 1962).

Frank Luther Mott, *A History of American Magazines*, 5 vols. (Cambridge, Harvard, 1938–1968). The first volume was originally issued in 1930 in New York by Appleton. Vol. IV (1957) covers the years 1885–1905. Vol. V (1968), a posthumous volume titled *Sketches of 21 Magazines, 1905–1930*, includes a cumulative index to the five volumes.

Theodore Bernard Peterson, *Magazines in the Twentieth Century*, 2nd edition (Urbana, University of Illinois, 1964).

Carolyn Farquhar Ulrich and Eugenia Patterson, *Little Magazines: A List* (New York, New York Public Library, 1947).

James Playsted Wood, *Magazines in the United States: Their Social and Economic Influence*, 2nd edition (New York, Ronald, 1956).

L · AMERICAN PUBLISHING

1 · General Books

Herbert Smith Bailey, Jr., *The Art and Science of Book Publishing* (New York, Harper, 1970).

Bowker Lectures on Book Publishing (New York, Bowker, 1957). Contains the first 17 Bowker Memorial Lectures, 1935–1956, delivered at the New York Public Library.

Pierce Butler, ed., *Librarians, Scholars, and Booksellers at Mid-Century: Papers Presented before the Sixteenth Annual Conference of the Graduate Library School of the University of Chicago* (Chicago, University of Chicago, 1953).

Orion Howard Cheney, *Economic Survey of the Book Industry, 1930–1931* (New York, National Association of Book Publishers, 1931). Reprinted in New York by Bowker in 1949 and 1960. A *Supplementary Report* by the Employing Bookbinders of America and a *Review* by the National Association of Book Publishers were issued in New York in 1932.

Chandler B. Grannis, ed., *What Happens in Book Publishing*, 2nd edition (New York, Columbia, 1967).

Harold K. Guinzburg, Robert William Frase, and Theodore

Waller, *Books and the Mass Market* (Urbana, University of Illinois, 1953). The fourth annual Windsor Lectures.

Gene R. Hawes, *To Advance Knowledge: A Handbook on American University Press Publishing* (New York, American University Press Services, 1967).

Henry Charles Link and Harry Arthur Hopf, *People and Books: A Study of Reading and Book-Buying Habits* (New York, Book Industry Committee of the Book Manufacturers' Institute, 1946).

Charles Allan Madison, *Book Publishing in America* (New York, McGraw-Hill, 1966).

Jesse William Markham and others, *An Economic-Media Study of Book Publishing* (New York, American Textbook Publishers, 1966).

William Miller, *The Book Industry* (New York, Columbia, 1949). Part of the investigation known as the Public Library Inquiry.

Raymond Howard Shove, *Cheap Book Production in the United States, 1870–1891* (Urbana, University of Illinois, 1937).

Madeleine Bettina Stern, *Imprints on History: Book Publishers and American Frontiers* (Bloomington, Indiana University, 1956).

Albert Douglass Van Nostrand, *The Denatured Novel* (Indianapolis, Bobbs-Merrill, 1960). A study of the relation between commercial pressures and artistic purposes in marketing books.

2 · *Particular Publishers*

Alfred A. Knopf: Quarter Century (New York, privately printed, 1940). Articles by Willa Cather, H. L. Mencken, and eight others.

Ellen B. Ballou, *The Building of the House: Houghton Mifflin's Formative Years* (Boston, Houghton Mifflin, 1970).

Edward William Bok, *The Americanization of Edward Bok* (New York, Scribner, 1920). Often reprinted. The "success story" of the editor of the *Ladies' Home Journal*.

George Britt, *Forty Years—Forty Millions: The Career of Frank A. Munsey* (New York, Farrar, 1935).

Roger Burlingame, *Endless Frontiers: The Story of McGraw-Hill* (New York, McGraw-Hill, 1959).

Cass Canfield, *The Publishing Experience* (Philadelphia, Lippincott, 1969).

Cass Canfield, *Up and Down and Around* (New York, Harper's Magazine Press, 1971).

Edward Howard Dodd, *The First Hundred Years: A History of the House of Dodd, Mead, 1839–1939* (New York, Dodd, Mead, 1939).

George Henry Doran, *Chronicles of Barabbas, 1884–1934* (New York, Harcourt, 1935). Chiefly concerns George H. Doran Co.

William Webster Ellsworth, *A Golden Age of Authors: A Publisher's Recollection* (Boston, Houghton Mifflin, 1919). Chiefly concerns the Century Co.

Eugene Exman, *The House of Harper: 150 Years of Publishing* (New York, Harper, 1967).

E. McClung Fleming, *R. R. Bowker: Militant Liberal* (Norman, University of Oklahoma, 1952).

James Lauren Ford, *Forty-Odd Years in the Literary Shop* (New York, Dutton, 1921). General reminiscences chiefly of New York literary life.

Walker Gilmer, *Horace Liveright: Publisher of the Twenties* (New York, David Lewis, 1970).

Ferris Greenslet, *Under the Bridge: An Autobiography* (Boston, Houghton Mifflin, 1943). Chiefly concerns Houghton Mifflin Co.

Henry Holt, *Garrulities of an Octogenarian Editor* (Boston, Houghton Mifflin, 1923). Chiefly concerns Henry Holt & Co.

Robert Underwood Johnson, *Remembered Yesterdays* (Boston, Little, Brown, 1923). By an editor of the *Century Magazine*.

Raymond Lincoln Kilgour, *Estes and Lauriat: A History, 1872–1898, with a Brief Account of Dana Estes and Company, 1898–1914* (Ann Arbor, University of Michigan, 1957).

Sidney Kramer, *A History of Stone & Kimball and Herbert S. Stone & Co., with a Bibliography of Their Publications, 1893–1905* (Chicago, Norman W. Forgue, 1940).

Grant Martin Overton, *Portrait of a Publisher, and the First Hundred Years of the House of Appleton, 1825–1925* (New York, Appleton, 1925).

Walter Hines Page, *A Publisher's Confession,* new edition (Garden City, Doubleday, 1923). The publishing house is of course the house of Doubleday.

George Haven Putnam, *George Palmer Putnam: A Memoir, Together with a Record of the Earlier Years of the Publishing House Founded by Him* (New York, Putnam, 1912). This George Palmer Putnam should not be confused with George Palmer Putnam, the younger, named below.

George Haven Putnam, *Memories of a Publisher, 1865–1915,* second edition (New York, Putnam, 1923).

George Palmer Putnam, *Wide Margins: A Publisher's Autobiography* (New York, Harcourt, 1942).

Quentin Reynolds, *The Fiction Factory, or, From Pulp Row to Quality Street: The Story of 100 Years of Publishing at Street & Smith* (New York, Random, 1955).

Frank Leopold Schick, *The Paperbound Book in America: The History of Paperbacks and Their European Background* (New York, Bowker, 1958).

Ellery Sedgwick, *The Happy Profession* (Boston, Little, Brown, 1946). By an editor of the *Atlantic Monthly.*

Frederick Abbot Stokes, *A Publisher's Random Notes, 1800–1935* (New York, New York Public Library, 1935). One of the Bowker Lectures.

John William Tebbel, *George Horace Lorimer and The Saturday Evening Post* (Garden City, Doubleday, 1948).

Lewis Frank Tooker, *The Joys and Tribulations of an Editor* (New York, Century, 1924). Concerns the *Century Magazine.*

John Hall Wheelock, *Editor to Author: The Letters of Maxwell E. Perkins* (New York, Scribner, 1950). Wheelock not only selected and edited the letters of the famous editor at Scribner's but also supplied a running commentary.

VI · CRITICAL LIST OF MAGAZINES

The following selective list includes magazines of general character or of specifically literary, critical, ideational, or scholarly interest, of concern to the student of American literature; and magazines of opinion likely to illumine thought and writing since 1890.

ACCENT: A QUARTERLY OF NEW LITERATURE (1940–1960), Urbana. Published by the English Department of the University of Illinois.

AMERICAN HERITAGE: THE MAGAZINE OF HISTORY (1949–), New York. Quarterly; bimonthly. Sponsored by the American Association for State and Local History and the Society of American Historians, Inc., it treats American history, from all angles, for the general intelligent reader.

AMERICAN LITERATURE (1929–), Durham, North Carolina. Quarterly. The official scholarly publication of the American Literature Group of the Modern Language Association, it is useful for its critical articles as well as for current bibliographies of scholarly investigation. See Thomas Frederic Marshall, *An Analytical Index to American Literature, Vols. I–XXX, March 1929–January 1959* (Durham, Duke University, 1963).

The AMERICAN MAGAZINE (1905–1955), New York. Monthly. Originally the organ of the "Muckrakers," this magazine after a few years changed character and became simply another household periodical.

The AMERICAN MERCURY (1924–), New York. Monthly. Founded by Alfred A. Knopf as a vehicle for H. L. Mencken and George Jean Nathan, this periodical was characteristic of the twenties, but by 1934, following the withdrawal of both men, it had changed character. Three members were titled *The New American Mercury* (December 1950–February 1951), then the old title was restored. The present *American Mercury*, published in South Gate, California, is more political than literary. Since June 1966 it has incorporated *Western Destiny, Folk,* and *Northern World.*

AMERICAN QUARTERLY (1949–), Minneapolis; Philadelphia. Quarterly. Created at the University of Minnesota by the Program in American Studies. In 1951 it moved to the University of Pennsylvania. Annual "annotated interdisciplinary bibliographies of current articles in American Studies" are published in the Summer Supplement.

The AMERICAN REVIEW. See The [American] BOOKMAN.

The AMERICAN SCHOLAR (1932–), formerly New York, now Washington. Quarterly. Supported by Phi Beta Kappa, this magazine contains articles appraising the American scene and debates current political, economic, and cultural questions.

The AMERICAN SPECTATOR (1932–1937), New York. Monthly. Originally an organ for George Jean Nathan, Ernest Boyd, Van Wyck Brooks, this periodical changed character in 1935.

The ANTIOCH REVIEW (1941–), Yellow Springs, Ohio. Quarterly. Opinion and criticism.

The ARENA (1889–1909), Boston. Monthly. Founded by Benjamin O. Flower and mostly edited by him, this periodical fought for economic and social reform and for realism in the arts.

The ATLANTIC MONTHLY (1857–), Boston. Monthly. Still a leading general literary periodical, heretofore conservative in taste and outlook, *The Atlantic* has been an institution. Recent editors include Horace E. Scudder, 1890–1898; Walter Hines Page, 1898–1899; Bliss Perry, 1899–1909; Ellery Sedgwick, 1909–1938; Edward Weeks, 1938–1966; and Robert Manning, 1966–.

The BILLBOARD (1894–), Cincinnati. Weekly. Since 1960 the title varies. A theatrical trade paper with special emphasis on the worlds of burlesque, carnivals, fairs, the circus, popular music, night club entertainment, vaudeville, radio, and television. See also *Variety,* below.

The [American] BOOKMAN (1895–1933), New York. Monthly.

In its earlier years supposedly an organ of genteel criticism, this magazine changed character under Burton Rascoe (1928–1929), who made it a periodical of controversy. Seward Collins (1930–1933) turned it into the organ of the Neohumanists. It was superseded by *The American Review* (1933–1937), New York. A monthly except for July and August. Not to be confused with the English *Bookman* (1891–1934) nor with *The American Bookman* (founded 1943), New York, a quarterly, which in 1945 merged with *Philosophic Abstracts* (1939–1954).

BOOKS ABROAD (1927–), Norman, Oklahoma. Quarterly. A gallant attempt to keep abreast of and interpret foreign literature in terms relevant to American readers.

BROOM: AN INTERNATIONAL MAGAZINE OF THE ARTS (1921–1924). Monthly. Published successively in Rome, Berlin, and New York, it was an avant-garde magazine of the twenties.

The CENTURY ILLUSTRATED MAGAZINE (1881–1930), New York. Monthly. This magazine was preceded by *Scribner's Monthly* (1870–1881), not to be confused with the contemporary of *The Century*, *Scribner's Magazine* (q.v.). One of the great magazines of its time, *The Century* published a notable series of Civil War memoirs by generals and others; it did much to awaken Northern sympathy for the South after Reconstruction as well as to arouse interest in national issues, and was one of the leading periodicals in the encouragement of art, particularly through its own illustrations. Richard Watson Gilder edited it from 1881 to 1909. The title varies. In 1930 it merged with *The Forum* (q.v.).

The CHAP BOOK (1894–1898), Chicago. Semimonthly. This magazine contained material by Stephen Crane, Eugene Field, Henry James, William Vaughn Moody, Hamlin Garland, and others. In 1898 it merged with *The* [Chicago] *Dial* (q.v.).

COLLEGE ENGLISH (1939–), Champaign, Illinois. Eight times a year (October–May). The official organ of the National Council of Teachers of English, it frequently carries interesting articles on current writers. It was preceded by *The English Journal* (q.v.).

COMMENTARY: A JOURNAL OF SIGNIFICANT THOUGHT AND OPINION ON CONTEMPORARY ISSUES (1945–), New York. Monthly. Edited by Norman Podhoretz. This magazine, published under the auspices of the American Jewish Committee, absorbed *The Contemporary Jewish Record*. It expresses the Jewish point of view on national and international issues but is not hidebound and includes some fiction as well as thoughtful reviews of books, films, and theater.

The COMMONWEAL (1924–), New York. Weekly. Offers opinion and reviews of literature, art, and public affairs from the Catholic point of view.

The COSMOPOLITAN MAGAZINE (1866–), New York. Monthly. This magazine has undergone various changes of title, the most important occurring in 1925 when it became for a time *Hearst's International Cosmopolitan*. A vehicle for fiction in earlier years, it is now mostly a household magazine.

The CRITIC (1881–1906), New York. Monthly. An organ for the Genteel Tradition, it merged into *Putnam's Magazine* in 1906. *Putnam's* ceased publication in 1910.

CRITICISM: A QUARTERLY FOR LITERATURE AND THE ARTS (1959–), Detroit. Published by the Department of English of Wayne State University. Although it examines "the art and literature of all periods and nations," a large portion of the journal, in recent issues, has been devoted to American authors.

CRITIQUE: STUDIES IN MODERN FICTION (1956–), Minneapolis. Three times a year. Supersedes *Faulkner Studies* (1952–1954, Denver). It is devoted chiefly to criticism of American fiction.

The [Chicago] DIAL (1880–1929), Chicago; New York. Monthly; semimonthly; biweekly; monthly. Not to be confused with the transcendentalist *Dial* (1840–1844), this magazine was conservative in taste until 1916, when it removed to New

York, where it was in the vanguard of the new writing, under the editorship of Conrad Aiken, Randolph Bourne, and Van Wyck Brooks. In 1919, Scofield Thayer became the editor; in 1925, Marianne Moore.

The DOUBLE-DEALER (1921–1926), New Orleans. Monthly. An avant-garde magazine for the South, including, however, Northern writers temporarily resident in New Orleans.

DRAMA MAGAZINE (1911–1931), Chicago. Quarterly; monthly; irregular. The organ of the Drama League of America, expressing the vague idealism of the theater "movement" of the period.

DRAMA SURVEY: A REVIEW OF DRAMATIC LITERATURE AND THE THEATRICAL ARTS (1961–), Minneapolis. Three times a year. Concerned chiefly with European and classic drama, it also prints articles and book reviews on the American theater.

The ENGLISH JOURNAL (COLLEGE EDITION) (1928–1939), Chicago. Nine times a year. Founded in 1912, *The English Journal* was published by the National Council of Teachers of English for high schools. It was superseded in 1939 by *College English* (q.v.).

ESQUIRE (1933–), Chicago. Monthly. This "magazine for men" is distinguished by cartoons and drawings supposed to have a special masculine appeal. Its articles are rather obviously "sophisticated," but it occasionally publishes literary work of importance, such as F. Scott Fitzgerald's "The Crack-Up." Lately it has become more sober, even political, in tone, and its articles have improved in literary quality.

ETC: A REVIEW OF GENERAL SEMANTICS (1943–), Chicago; San Francisco since 1955. Quarterly. From its inception it has been under the editorship of S. I. Hayakawa.

The FORUM (1886–1950), New York. Monthly; quarterly. Chiefly a magazine of debate on contemporary problems, it occasionally published fiction. Henry Goddard Leach was editor from 1923 to 1940. In 1930 it absorbed *The Century* (q.v.); in 1940 it merged with *Current History* to become *Current History and Forum*; and from 1940 to 1950 it was again published as an independent magazine.

The FREEMAN (1920–1924), New York. Weekly. A brilliant, liberal magazine founded by Van Wyck Brooks, Albert Jay Nock, Francis Nielson, and others. It contained excellent literary criticism. *The Freeman Book* (New York, B. W. Huebsch, 1924) is an anthology of gleanings from its pages.

The FRONTIER AND MIDLAND (1920–1939), Missoula, Montana. Three issues a year. Founded by H. G. Merriam at the University of Montana as a medium for regionalism, *The Frontier* in 1933 took over *The Midland* (q.v.). It began life as *The Montanan* (1920) and acquired its *Frontier* title after a few issues.

The FUGITIVE (1922–1925), Nashville, Tennessee. Quarterly; bimonthly; quarterly. Devoted to poetry, principally that of Donald Davidson, Merrill Moore, John Crowe Ransom, Allen Tate, and Robert Penn Warren. A *Fugitive Anthology* (New York, Harcourt, 1928) was made from its pages.

HARPER'S MAGAZINE (1850–), New York. Monthly. Originally *Harper's Monthly Magazine* (to 1925), this magazine began chiefly as a reprint periodical containing British literature. Henry Mills Alden was editor from 1869 to 1919, probably the longest term of service of its kind in American history. Howells occupied the famous Editor's Easy Chair from 1901 to 1921, as did Bernard De Voto from 1935 until his death in 1955. Crucial changes of policy occurred in 1900 and in 1925. Recently the magazine has become less a literary vehicle than one of social and political discussion and is mainly staff-written.

HOUND AND HORN (1927–1934), Cambridge; New York. Quarterly. Founded at Harvard University by Lincoln Kirstein as an avant-garde publication, it included work by R. P. Blackmur, Kenneth Burke, T. S. Eliot, Katherine Anne Porter, Gertrude Stein, and Allen Tate. The editorial office was moved to New York in 1930.

The HUDSON REVIEW (1948–), New York. Quarterly. A literary periodical expressive of, though not dominated by, the "New Criticism."

JOURNAL OF AMERICAN STUDIES (1967–), Manchester,

England. Twice a year. Publishes "work by specialists of any nationality on American history, literature, politics, geography and related subjects," as well as book reviews, review articles, and notes on work in progress.

JOURNAL OF MODERN LITERATURE (1970–), Philadelphia. Five issues a year. Concentrates on "research-based studies of literature published during the past century."

JUDGE (1881–1939), New York. Weekly. One of the three great comic magazines of the period, regularly publishing cartoons, light verse, quips, short stories, and informal essays. See also *Puck* and *Life*, below.

The KENYON REVIEW (1939–1968), Gambier, Ohio. Quarterly. Largely the creation of John Crowe Ransom, this magazine was one of the more prominent periodicals of the "New Criticism."

LADIES' HOME JOURNAL (1883–), Philadelphia. Monthly. Under the editorship of Edward J. Bok, this characteristically American magazine rose to a circulation of over two million, whereupon after thirty years of editing Bok turned to other fields, having persuaded the American housewife to want what he wanted her to want.

The LARK (1895–1897), San Francisco. Monthly. One of the famous "little magazines" of the nineties, its announced policy was "gaiety."

LIFE (before it became a picture magazine) (1883–1936), New York. Weekly. Disputed leadership with *Puck* and *Judge* in the field of humorous writing and drawing. Less political than either. It became a Henry Luce publication in 1936.

The LITTLE REVIEW (1914–1929), Chicago; New York; Paris. Irregular. This famous and unbusinesslike periodical was the work of Margaret Anderson. See her *My Thirty Years' War* (New York, Covici, Friede, 1930).

The MASSES (1911–1917), New York. Monthly. Originally edited by Max Eastman, this magazine included among its contributors Floyd Dell and John Reed. It was the Marxist organ of its time, suppressed in World War I and revived as *The Liberator* (1918–1924). It contained some of the finest black-and-white art work of the period. Unfortunately files are rare. See *New Masses*, below.

McCLURE'S MAGAZINE (1893–1929), New York. Monthly. Famous as a muckraking magazine, this periodical was also notable for its low price. It was the product of S. S. McClure and was edited from 1902 to 1906 by Lincoln Steffens, with Ida M. Tarbell and Ray S. Baker among the contributors. The title varies.

The MIDLAND (1915–1933), Iowa City; Chicago. Monthly. Established by John T. Frederick as a regional magazine, this periodical suffered a variety of changes and in 1933 was merged with *The Frontier* (q.v.).

M'LLE NEW YORK (1895–1899), New York. Fortnightly. Vance Thompson edited this magazine, supposed to be "Bohemian" and "French." James G. Huneker was an important contributor.

MODERN DRAMA (1958–), Lawrence, Kansas. Quarterly. Short articles and book reviews.

MODERN FICTION STUDIES (1955–   ), Lafayette, Indiana. Quarterly. Published by the Department of English of Purdue University and devoted to "criticism, scholarship, and bibliography of American, English, and European fiction since about 1800." Special numbers (usually spring or autumn) deal entirely with an individual author. Maurice Beebe has been assembling the invaluable checklists since the first issue.

The MODERN QUARTERLY (1923–1940), Baltimore. Quarterly; monthly. Retitled in 1933 *The Modern Monthly*, this magazine "of the newer spirit" was edited by V. F. Calverton and was leftist in viewpoint.

The NATION (1865–), New York. Weekly. Founded by E. L. Godkin, editor from 1865 to 1881, *The Nation* did much for science, the acceptance of Darwinism, civil service reform, and literary criticism. Under Paul E. More, editor from 1909 to 1914, it became a conservative critical journal, but Oswald Garrison Villard (1918–1933) turned it into a leading liberal weekly. The current editor is Carey McWilliams.

MAGAZINES

NEW MASSES (1926–1948), New York. Monthly; weekly. Successor to *The Masses* (q.v.) and *The Liberator*, this magazine was edited by Joseph Freeman, Michael Gold, and other proletarian critics. It became the fighting organ of Marxism. In 1948 it merged with another Marxist journal under the name *Masses and Mainstream*.

The NEW REPUBLIC (1914–), New York; Washington. Weekly. Founded by Herbert Croly, this liberal weekly had a brilliant staff during World War I, including Robert Morss Lovett, Malcolm Cowley, and Walter Lippmann. Its later years were less distinguished, but lately it has undergone a renaissance.

The NEW YORK REVIEW OF BOOKS (1963–), New York. Biweekly, except when it appears once every three weeks in July, August, September, and January. A lively literary newspaper, noted for lengthy and articulate reviews.

The NEW YORKER (1925–), New York. Weekly. The chief organ of "sophisticated" urban wit, with such contributors as James Thurber, Ogden Nash, and others, this magazine is also a crusader against intolerance and obscurantism. Harold Ross edited the magazine from 1925 to 1951. Do not confuse with *New York* magazine.

NEWSWEEK (1933–), New York. Weekly. The chief rival of *Time* (q.v.), this magazine has departments devoted to books, movies, radio, theater, music, and so on.

NOVEL: A FORUM ON FICTION (1967–), Providence, Rhode Island. Three times a year. It seeks "to report on the novel's newness, to define its protean nature, and to accommodate its richness and variety through comparative, historical and comprehensive approaches."

The OUTLOOK (1870–1935), New York. Weekly; monthly. This magazine was the organ of the liberal Protestant point of view, including the social gospel, and had for contributors Hamilton Wright Mabie, Lyman Abbott, and Theodore Roosevelt, among others. The title varies.

The PACIFIC SPECTATOR (1947–1956), Stanford, California. Quarterly. Devoted to the humanities and edited by a group at Stanford University headed by John W. Dodds.

The PARIS REVIEW (1953–), Paris. Erratic in publication and frequently undated. Publishes chiefly poetry, fiction, and art, but the long interviews with writers are valuable for the student of literature as well as of creative writing.

The PARTISAN REVIEW (1934–), New York. Monthly; quarterly. Originally showing Marxist tendencies, this magazine is now a periodical of literary theory and criticism.

POET LORE (1889–1953), Philadelphia: Boston. Quarterly. Originally edited by Charlotte Porter and Helen A. Clarke, this magazine has been a medium for genteel discussion of the art of literature, but even more importantly a vehicle for translating Continental drama into English.

POETRY (1912–), Chicago. Monthly. Founded by Harriet Monroe, this is the oldest and most important of existing poetry magazines. It championed the "Poetic Renaissance."

PUBLISHERS' WEEKLY (1872–), New York. Weekly. The most neglected source material in the field of American literary history can be found in the files of this magazine.

PUCK (1877–1918), New York. Weekly. This comic magazine had a brilliant line of editors, including Henry C. Bunner (1878–1896), Harry Leon Wilson (1896–1902), and John Kendrick Bangs (1904–1905). Joseph Keppler's political cartoons were influential social commentary.

The READER'S DIGEST (1922–), Pleasantville, New York. Monthly. This magazine, theoretically a parasite on other magazines, is the creation of De Witt Wallace. In its various forms (there are American, British, Canadian, Spanish, Portuguese, Swedish, Arabic, Chinese, Finnish, Danish, and other editions, besides one in Braille and a "talking record" edition for the blind) it has the largest circulation in the world. For a somewhat unsympathetic account, see John Bainbridge, *Little Wonder; or, The Reader's Digest and How It Grew* (New York, Reynal, 1946).

REEDY'S MIRROR (1891–1920), St. Louis. Weekly. The creation of William Marion Reedy (1862–1920), this wandering periodical (St. Louis being one of its homes) first published *The Spoon River Anthology* and work by John Gould Fletcher, Julia Peterkin, and others. The title varies.

MAGAZINES

The REPORTER (1949–1968), New York. Biweekly. Founded by Max Ascoli, who was both editor and publisher, this magazine aimed at disseminating facts and ideas chiefly political, but it also published critical reviews, literary essays, and occasionally fiction.

THE SATURDAY EVENING POST (1821–1969), Philadelphia. Weekly; biweekly. A general magazine *not* founded by Benjamin Franklin. Its special articles were well, if sometimes mechanically, written; its fiction, though frequently tending to type, was sometimes excellent; its poetry was negligible; and its politics were conservative. Recently (1971) there has been an attempt to revive it as a quarterly.

The SATURDAY REVIEW (1924–), New York. Weekly. Founded as *The Saturday Review of Literature* by Henry Seidel Canby, Amy Loveman, and others (seceders from the old New York *Post*), it has been in recent years under the leadership of Norman Cousins and Harrison Smith. A critical weekly that took a middle-of-the-road position in literary theory, it expanded to include departments concerned with travel, education, drama, movies, and recorded music; and under Cousins it also insisted on the desirability of better world organization. Late in 1971 it was bought by a group headed by John J. Veronis and Nicolas H. Charney, who propose to develop it into four monthly magazines on a rotating scheme so that readers receive a separate monthly each week: *The Saturday Review of the Arts, The Saturday Review of Education, The Saturday Review of Science,* and *The Saturday Review of the Society.* Norman Cousins, the last of the original editors, resigned.

SCIENCE AND SOCIETY: AN INDEPENDENT JOURNAL OF MARXISM (1936–), New York. Quarterly. For the intellectual Marxists.

The SCIENTIFIC AMERICAN (1845–), New York. Monthly. Currently the most intelligent magazine edited for the lay reader in the world of science, it is intended to fill the gap between the technical journal and the merely popular science magazine. The original editor was Orson D. Munn, and it was once a magazine of invention as well as of scientific research. The mode of publication varied over the years; and a *Scientific American Supplement* ran from 1876 to 1919. The title varies.

SCRIBNER'S MAGAZINE (1887–1939), New York. Monthly. This famous literary magazine was one of the chief cultural periodicals in the Genteel Tradition, with many famous names appearing among its contributors. It came to a sad end as *Scribner's Commentator* (1939-1942).

SECESSION (1922–1924), various places. Irregular. A characteristic expatriate periodical, it was edited by Gorham B. Munson and others. It published Hart Crane.

The SEVEN ARTS (1916–1917), New York. Monthly. Short-lived but influential, this magazine had among its contributors Theodore Dreiser, Vachel Lindsay, Amy Lowell, H. L. Mencken, Sherwood Anderson, and Randolph Bourne. In 1917 it merged with *The Dial* (q.v.).

SEWANEE REVIEW (1892–), Sewanee, Tennessee. Quarterly. Founded at the University of the South and edited first by William P. Trent, then by William S. Knickerbocker, this magazine devoted itself mainly to cultural material of interest to the South. Later it was captured by the "New Criticism." In recent years, under the editorship of Monroe K. Spears and, since 1961, of Andrew Lytle, it has published distinguished fiction and poetry as well as critical articles on international literature and lengthy book reviews.

The SMART SET (1890–1930), New York. Monthly. Founded as a scandal sheet, it was sold in 1900 to John Adams Thayer. This influential magazine, neglected by librarians, was edited in its best days by H. L. Mencken and George Jean Nathan. No periodical did more for "sophistication" and realism. The title varies. Carl R. Dolmetsch edited *The Smart Set: A History and Anthology* (New York, Dial, 1966).

SOUTH ATLANTIC QUARTERLY (1902–), Durham, North Carolina. Quarterly. Highly academic, this magazine is chiefly devoted to scholarly general articles. It was founded by John Spencer Bassett.

The SOUTHERN REVIEW (1935–1942; 1965–), Baton Rouge.

Quarterly. Merged into *The Kenyon Review* (q.v.) in 1942; revived in 1965. It publishes fiction, poetry, and reviews as well as critical articles, many of them lengthy.

SOUTHWEST REVIEW (1915–), Dallas, Texas. Quarterly. Founded as *The Texas Review* at Austin and originally edited by Stark Young, this regional periodical moved to Southern Methodist University and changed its name in 1924.

STUDIES IN SHORT FICTION (1963–), Newberry, North Carolina. Quarterly. Devoted exclusively to "serious commentary on short fiction," reviews, and notes.

SURVEY and SURVEY GRAPHIC (1897–1932; 1933–1949; 1949–1953), New York. Monthly. This magazine, ostensibly for the social worker, carried from time to time able and dispassionate reports on all sorts of social, economic, and educational problems. Mostly it was issued as a monthly. In 1933 it was superseded by two separate periodicals, which again combined in January 1949.

TEXAS QUARTERLY (1958–), Austin, Texas. A magazine of general cultural comment, publishing fiction and poetry as well as essays on literature, art, philosophy, science, and politics. Illustrations have been of high quality.

TDR: TULANE DRAMA REVIEW (1955–), New Orleans; since 1967, New York. Quarterly. Superseded *The Carleton Drama Bulletin* (1949–1954) and *The Carleton Drama Review* (1955–1956). In 1967 it was renamed *TDR: The Drama Review*. It includes long articles on drama, theater, and acting, playscripts, interviews, book reviews, and bibliographies.

THEATRE SURVEY: THE AMERICAN JOURNAL OF THEATRE HISTORY (1960–), Pittsburgh. Semiannually.

THIS QUARTER (1925–1932), Paris. Irregular. An expatriate magazine.

TIME (1932–), New York. Weekly. This famous magazine, published by the Luce interests, prides itself on a special style and accuracy. Both have been severely attacked. It has departments concerned with books, art, music, theater, movies, etc., and occasionally publishes lengthy articles on prominent literary figures.

TLS: TIMES LITERARY SUPPLEMENT (1902–), London. Weekly. This major English book review has wide coverage, including America and the Continent.

transition (1927–1938), Paris; The Hague; New York; Paris. Irregular. Originally edited by Eugene Jolas and Elliot Paul, this avant-garde magazine published fiction, poetry, criticism, drawings, photographs, and plates of contemporary art.

TRI-QUARTERLY (1958–1965, n.s. 1965–), Evanston, Illinois. Three times a year. Until 1965, titled *Northwestern University Tri-Quarterly*. It publishes poetry and fiction as well as criticism of literature, art, and films.

VARIETY (1905–), New York. Weekly. A theatrical trade paper covering the legitimate theater, vaudeville, films, popular music, nightclub entertainment, radio, and television. See also *The Billboard*, above.

VIRGINIA QUARTERLY REVIEW (1925–), Charlottesville, Virginia. Quarterly. A conservative magazine especially associated with the Upper South, though it is national and even international in its interests.

The YALE REVIEW (1892–), New Haven. Quarterly. Long edited by Wilbur L. Cross, this quarterly attained national prominence about 1910 as a relatively conservative journal of literature, politics, and opinion. It continues to publish distinguished critical prose on a wide variety of subjects.

It should be noted that during the last twenty-five or thirty years most leading universities and colleges have founded magazines of criticism, opinion, and general literature, commonly quarterlies. Other representative titles could be included in the above list, but limitations of space have prevented mention of every such periodical.

VII · CHIEF HISTORICAL
EVENTS, 1890–1971

1889–1893 BENJAMIN HARRISON (R), PRESIDENT

1889–91 Invention of motion pictures.

1890 Ending of the American frontier. Sherman Anti-Trust Act. Sherman Silver Purchase Act. The McKinley Tariff. Pan-American Congress (James G. Blaine, Secretary of State). First electrocution for murder, Auburn, New York, prison. Ellis Island opened as immigration depot.

1892 Homestead steel strike. Dr. Rudolf Diesel patented an internal combustion engine operating on pulverized fuel.

1893–1897 GROVER CLEVELAND (D), PRESIDENT

1893 Panic of 1893. Repeal of Sherman Silver Purchase Act. World's Columbian Exposition, Chicago. Opening of the University of Chicago.

1894 First public showing of Edison's Kinetoscope in New York. March of "Coxey's Army" on Washington. Pullman Car Company strike. The Wilson-Gorman Tariff Act.

1895 Roentgen announced discovery of X-rays. Invention of the Vitascope. The Selden patent marked practical beginning of the automobile industry in the United States. Marconi sent first wireless message. Venezuelan boundary dispute.

1896 Completion of the Vitascope and first showing of motion pictures at Koster and Bials Music Hall, New York City. In Paris, Becquerel announced the radioactivity of uranium. Creation of Greater New York (union of five boroughs). Bryan-McKinley campaign ("Sixteen to one").

1897–1901 WILLIAM MCKINLEY (R), PRESIDENT

1897 The Dingley Tariff.

1898 In Paris the Curies and associates announced the discovery of radium. Sending of the first radiogram. Spanish-American War (Battle of Manila Bay, San Juan Hill, destruction of the Spanish fleet in Cuban waters). Annexation of the Hawaiian Islands. Annexation of Puerto Rico and the Philippine Islands.

1899 Philippine Insurrection under Aquinaldo (to 1901). Tension with Germany over the Samoan Islands. Universal Peace Conference at The Hague. Beginning of the Boer War (to 1902).

1899–1901 The Boxer Rebellion in China; intervention by the Great Powers; beginning of agitation for an "Open Door" policy (John Hay, Secretary of State).

1900 Opening of the Paris Exposition. The Gold Standard Act. Beginning of the campaign by Dr. Walter Reed and associates to wipe out yellow fever.

1901 WILLIAM MCKINLEY (R), PRESIDENT

1901–1905 THEODORE ROOSEVELT (R), PRESIDENT

1901 President McKinley was shot at the Buffalo Exposition and died on September 14, 1901. He was succeeded by Vice-President Theodore Roosevelt. First radio signal sent across the Atlantic Ocean by Marconi.

1902 First radio message sent. Blockade of Venezuela by European powers. American occupation of Cuba ended and the Republic of Cuba proclaimed. First International Court of Arbitration opened at The Hague. Pennsylvania anthracite coal strike. Creation of the Reclamation Service.

1903 The Wright brothers announced the first successful flight of a heavier-than-air machine. *The Great Train Robbery*, first successful American commercial motion picture. First transcontinental automobile trip, New York to San Francisco. Massacre of Jews at Kichinev, Russia. Republic of Panama recognized by the United States.

1904 New York subway opened. Northern Securities Case. Panama Canal brought under American auspices (completed 1914). Russo-Japanese War began (ended by the Treaty of Portsmouth, 1905).

1905–1909 THEODORE ROOSEVELT (R), PRESIDENT

1905 First motion picture theater ("nickelodeon") opened in Pittsburgh. Beginning of political battle between Speaker Joseph G. Cannon and conservative senators, on the one hand, and a "progressive" group, on the other, for control of the Republican party. First Russian parliament (Duma) opened.

1906 Trial of Harry K. Thaw for killing Stanford White. San Francisco fire and earthquake. Hepburn (Railway Rate) Act. Pure Food Act (amended 1912).

1907 Panic of 1907 checked by J. P. Morgan and Co. and by U.S. government. *Ben Hur*, first multiple-reel motion picture, exhibited. Oklahoma became a state. Immigration Act checked entrance of Japanese into the United States. Second Hague Conference.

1908 American fleet sent around the world (1907–1909). Danbury Hatters' case (1902–1914). Root-Takahira agreement admitted Japan's special interest in Asia. Austro-Hungary annexed Bosnia and Herzegovina.

1909–1913 WILLIAM HOWARD TAFT (R), PRESIDENT

1909 Admiral Robert E. Perry reached the North Pole. Louis Blériot flew across the English Channel. Payne-Aldrich Tariff Act. Agitation for "conservation."

1910 Mann-Elkins Act increased the powers of the Interstate Commerce Commission. Hague Tribunal settled Newfoundland fisheries dispute between United States and Great Britain. Controversy between Gifford Pinchot, foremost advocate of conservation under Roosevelt, and Richard A. Ballinger, Secretary of the Interior, seemed to many liberals to threaten the maintenance of Roosevelt's public land policy. "Insurgent" Republicans reduced powers of the Speaker of the House. Return of Theodore Roosevelt from abroad and his proclamation of the "New Nationalism." Boy Scouts of America founded.

1911 First transcontinental airplane flight, by O. P. Rogers. Roald Amundsen reached the South Pole. Supreme Court ordered dissolution of the Standard Oil "trust" and of the American Tobacco Company as monopolies. Commercial treaty with Japan. Mexican Revolution started.

1912 Captain R. F. Scott reached the South Pole. Creation of the Progessive (Bull Moose) Party. Eight-hour day for federal employees. New Mexico and Arizona became states. Taft-Roosevelt-Wilson election. Creation of the Republic of

China. Sinking of the S.S. *Titanic*. First Balkan War (against Turkey). Founding of Camp Fire Girls. Renewal of the Triple Alliance.

1913–1917 WOODROW WILSON (D), PRESIDENT

1913 Ratification of the Sixteenth Amendment (income tax) and the Seventeenth Amendment (popular election of U.S. senators). Underwood Tariff Act. Creation of the Federal Reserve system. Second Balkan War.

1914 Showing of D. W. Griffith's film *The Birth of a Nation*. First ship passed through the Panama Canal. Meeting of the Second International at Brussels. U.S. Marines landed at Vera Cruz. Murder of the Austrian Archduke Francis Ferdinand at Sarajevo precipitated the First World War. Invasion of Belgium. First Battle of the Marne. Battle of Ypres. Stalemate on the Western front. American declaration of neutrality.

1915 Reorganization of the Ku Klux Klan. American recognition of the Carranza government in Mexico. Japan forced the "Twenty-one Demands" on China. Turkey entered the war on the German side. Italy entered the war on the side of the Entente. Failure of the Dardanelles expedition. Russian defeat on the Eastern front. Defeat and occupation of Serbia. Increasing importance of the Mesopotamian front. German submarine sank S.S. *Lusitania*. Preparedness movement in the United States.

1916 Federal statute closed interstate commerce to products of child labor. Mooney and Billings convicted of bomb outrage in San Francisco (pardoned 1939). Germans attacked Verdun. Russian successes against Austria. Romania conquered by the Central Powers. British advance in Palestine. Indecisive naval battle of Jutland.

1917–1921 WOODROW WILSON (D), PRESIDENT

1917 Copper strike at Bisbee, Arizona, settled by vigilance committee. Puerto Ricans became American citizens. Lansing's note to Japan recognized Japan's "special interest in China." United States entered the war on the side of the Entente, April 6. Second battle of Ypres. Italian disaster at Caporetto.

Capture of Jerusalem by the British. Russian breakdown and revolution. Proclamation of Russian Republic and eventual capture of power by the Bolsheviki. Emergence of Lenin and Trotsky.

1918 Woodrow Wilson enunciated the Fourteen Points. Russian-German peace signed at Brest-Litovsk. Second Battle of the Marne. Collapse of Bulgaria and Turkey. American attack at St. Mihiel. Collapse of Austria. Abdication of the German Kaiser and proclamation of the German Republic. Armistice declared, November 11.

1919 First "artificial disintegration of the nucleus" announced by Rutherford. First crossing of the Atlantic by air (Alcock and Brown). Boston police strike. Eighteenth Amendment (prohibition) adopted (effective 1920). Versailles Peace Conference, ending the war and creating the League of Nations. Civil war spread in Russia. U.S. Senate rejected the Versailles Treaty. Russian-Polish war (to October 1920).

1920 First commercial radio broadcasting station, KDKA, opened in Pittsburgh. Beginning of the Sacco-Vanzetti case (April 15; trial, May 21, 1921; execution, August 22, 1927). Nineteenth Amendment (woman suffrage) went into effect. League of Nations founded at Geneva.

1921–1923 WARREN GAMALIEL HARDING (R), PRESIDENT
1923–1925 CALVIN COOLIDGE (R), PRESIDENT

1921 Successful extraction of insulin by Banting, Best, and MacLeod (made public in 1922). Joint resolution by Congress declared peace with Germany and Austria. Washington Conference on limitation of armaments (to 1922). Founding of Fascist party in Italy. Beginning of famine in Russia. Announcement of New Economic Policy by Lenin.

1922 Fordney–McCumber Tariff Act. Transfer of oil reserves (Teapot Dome) by presidential order from Navy Department to Department of Interior. Bonus bill vetoed by Harding. Fascists march on Rome. Mussolini became dictator. Creation of the U.S.S.R. (proclaimed July 6, 1923).

1923 First (partial) talking movies shown at Rivoli Theatre, New York. Hitler's abortive "Beerhall Putsch" at Munich. French and Belgian troops occupied the Ruhr. President Harding died on August 2, and was succeeded by Vice-President Calvin Coolidge. Dictatorship established in Spain (Primo de Rivera).

1924 Soviet constitution adopted. First round-the-world air flight. First performance of Gershwin's *Rhapsody in Blue*. Investigation, by the Walsh Committee of the U.S. Senate, of scandals in the Harding regime. Inauguration of the Dawes plan for Germany. Evacuation of the Ruhr by the French and Belgians. Death of Nikolai Lenin. British Labor Government recognized the Soviets. Accord between Soviet Russia and China (Sun Yat-sen).

1925–1929 CALVIN COOLIDGE (R), PRESIDENT

1925 Scopes trial in Dayton, Tennessee. Congress authorized contracts with airlines for carrying mail. Nine-Power Treaty for limitation of armaments.

1926 New York-London telephone service established. Admiral Byrd circled the North Pole by plane. Pilsudski became dictator of Poland. U.S. Senate refused to adhere to World Court without reservations. Germany admitted to the League of Nations.

1927 Charles A. Lindbergh made nonstop solo flight, New York to Paris. First successful sound film, *The Jazz Singer*, shown in New York. First television transmission, New York to Washington, Battle in Nicaragua between U.S. Marines and rebels under Sandino. Disarmament conference at Geneva. Severance of diplomatic relations between Great Britain and Russia.

1928 All-talking motion picture, *The Lights of New York*, shown at Strand Theatre, New York. Fifteen powers signed the Briand-Kellogg Pact in Paris, renouncing war as an instrument of national policy (ratified by U.S. Senate, January 15, 1929). Chiang Kai-shek became President of China. Trotsky and his followers exiled from Russia. Rise of Joseph Stalin.

1929–1933 HERBERT HOOVER (R), PRESIDENT

1929 Admiral Byrd flew to the South Pole. Conviction of Albert B. Fall, former Secretary of the Interior, for accepting a bribe from E. L. Doheny. Stock market crash October 29 marked beginning of the Great Depression. The Papal State revived as Vatican City. The Five-Year Plan begun in Russia.

1930 Drought in Far Western states. Hawley-Smoot Tariff Act passed. Hoover plan for unemployment relief. London Naval Conference. Sinclair Lewis awarded Nobel Prize in Literature. The French evacuated Baden and the Rhineland. Liquidation of the kulaks in Russia.

1931 Report of the Wickersham Commission on law enforcement. Japan invaded Manchuria. Proclamation of the Spanish Republic. Banking crisis in Austria. Great Britain abandoned the gold standard.

1932 March of the "Bonus Army" on Washington. The Lindbergh kidnapping case. Reconstruction Finance Corporation authorized. The Scottsboro case before the Supreme Court. Manchuria became Japanese puppet state (Manchukuo). The Japanese attacked Shanghai. Salazar became dictator of Portugal. End of the first Five-Year Plan in Russia.

1933–1937 FRANKLIN D. ROOSEVELT (D), PRESIDENT

1933 Adoption of the Twentieth Amendment (abolishing the "Lame Duck" Congress) and of the Twenty-First Amendment (repeal of prohibition). Closing of American banks and stock exchanges. The "Hundred Days" of the New Deal (AAA, NRA, PWA, WPA, CCC, etc.) Creation of the Tennessee Valley Authority. Federal insurance of bank deposits. United States recognized the Soviet Union. Adolf Hitler became Chancellor of Germany. Beginning of large-scale persecution of the Jews in Germany. Failure of the London economic conference through refusal of the United States to join in an international agreement for stabilizing currency. The Reichstag fire.

1934 The Johnson Act forbade American loans to countries defaulting on debt payments. The Catholic Legion of Decency formed. Philippine Independence Act passed. Nazi storm troopers killed numerous party leaders in a "blood purge." On the death of Hindenberg, Hitler became President as well as Chancellor of Germany. Russia joined the League of Nations. Signing of the Polish-German nonaggression pact. Outbreak of the Italian-Ethiopian war (to 1935).

1935 Beginnings of the CIO. Passage of the Federal Social Security Act. Creation of the Resettlement Administration and the National Labor Relations Board. The NRA declared unconstitutional. The Saar returned to Germany by plebiscite. Hitler repudiated the Treaty of Versailles. Jews lost citizenship in Germany. Economic sanctions against Italy. End of the Bolivia-Paraguay struggle for the Chaco.

1936 Vogue of Father Coughlin's "Union for Social Justice." Passage of the Bonus Act. The AAA declared unconstitutional. Nye investigation into the munitions industry. Outbreak of the Spanish Civil War (to 1939). Death in England of George V; abdication of Edward VIII; proclamation of George VI. Eugene O'Neill awarded Nobel Prize in Literature. Japan and Germany signed the anti-Comintern pact. Proclamation of the "Rome-Berlin Axis." Buenos Aires conference agreed to Latin-American neutrality in case of war between any two American nations.

1937–1941 FRANKLIN D. ROOSEVELT (D), PRESIDENT

1937 Economic "recession." Proposed reform of the Supreme Court precipitated controversy. Wagner Act declared constitutional. Roosevelt's "quarantine" speech at Chicago. U.S. Neutrality Act. The "China" incident provoked by Japanese. Japanese bombed the U.S.S. *Panay*. Interference by European powers in the Spanish Civil War. Emergence of the Franco dictatorship in Spain.

1938 Formation of the Dies Committee. Pearl Buck awarded Nobel Prize in Literature. Hitler invaded Austria. Hitler demanded the Sudeten area from Czechoslovakia. Munich Conference.

1939 Fission of the uranium nucleus announced by Hahn and Strassman. Invasion of Czechoslovakia by Hitler. Italy annexed Albania. Border war on Manchurian frontier between Japan and Russia. Russian-German nonaggression pact. Finno-Russian War (to 1940), leading to annexation by Russia of parts of Finland. Pius XI succeeded by Pius XII. Germany invaded Poland September 1 and thus began

World War II. Declaration of national emergency in the United States.

1940 Selective Service Act passed (by one vote in the House). End of the "phoney" war as Germany successively invaded Denmark, Norway, the Low Countries, and France. Churchill became Prime Minister. British army rescued from Dunkirk. Formation of the Vichy government in France. Battle of Britain. Italy attacked Greece. The "destroyer deal" with Great Britain. Death of Trotsky in Mexico after an assassin's attack.

1941–1945 FRANKLIN D. ROOSEVELT (D), PRESIDENT

1941 Announcement of the "Four Freedoms" by Roosevelt and of the Atlantic Charter by Roosevelt and Churchill. Creation of Lend-Lease. U.S. Marines occupied Iceland. United States occupied Greenland. Roosevelt appealed to Japanese Emperor for peace. Germany invaded Russia. Overrunning of the Balkan countries, including Greece. Sneak attack on Pearl Harbor by the Japanese, December 7. Declaration of war by the United States.

1942 Fall of Singapore. Loss of the Philippines. Struggle for control of the Pacific. American-British invasion of North Africa. Twenty-six nations declared the desirability of creating the United Nations.

1943 Race riots in Detroit and Harlem. Repeal of the Chinese Exclusion Act. Establishment of UNRRA. German retreat from Stalingrad. German surrender in North Africa. Fall of Mussolini and occupation of much of Italy by the Germans.

1944 Supreme Court upheld constitutional right of Negroes to vote in primary elections. Allied invasion of Normandy under direction of General Dwight D. Eisenhower. Reconquest of the Philippines by General Douglas MacArthur.

1945 FRANKLIN D. ROOSEVELT (D), PRESIDENT
1945–1949 HARRY S. TRUMAN (D), PRESIDENT

1945 President Roosevelt died, April 12, and was succeeded by Vice-President Harry S. Truman. Russians reached Berlin. German collapse and surrender, May 7. Dropping of first atomic bomb on Hiroshima, August 6. Surrender of Japan,

August 14. United Nations conference held at San Francisco, creating that body and also UNESCO (United Nations Educational, Scientific and Cultural Organization). Discovery in Germany of the horrors of the concentration camps, followed by arrest of chief criminals. General MacArthur took over the government of Japan.

1946 Establishment of the U.S. Atomic Energy Commission. Further tests of atomic bombs at Bikini. Radar beam reached the moon. First meeting of the United Nations and of UNESCO. Abdication of Victor Emanuel III and proclamation of Italian republic. Ending of hostilities, December 31. Philippines became independent Republic.

1947 Announcement of the Marshall Plan. Selective Service Act expired. Creation of the (unified) Department of Defense. Taft-Hartley Act passed. Pakistan and India became autonomous commonwealths. U.N. partition of Palestine.

1948 First peacetime selective service bill passed. Economic Cooperation Administration established to administer U.S. contributions to the Marshall Plan. Appearance in national politics of the "Dixiecrat" party in the South and the "Progressive" party (Henry A. Wallace) nationally. Beginning of the Alger Hiss case (conviction 1950). Mohandas K. Gandhi assassinated. Communists took over Czechoslovakia. Proclamation of the State of Israel. The Berlin blockade and airlift. T. S. Eliot awarded the Nobel Prize in Literature.

1949–1953 HARRY S. TRUMAN (D), PRESIDENT

1949 President Truman announced evidence of an atomic explosion in Russia. American Communist leaders convicted of conspiracy (Judge Medina); conviction upheld by the Supreme Court (1950). End of the Nuremberg trials and conviction of chief war criminals. War between Israel and other (Arab) nations. Chiang Kai-shek resigned as President of China. Western Powers ended military government of Western Germany. Beginning of Tito deviation from Russia. North Atlantic Treaty Organization agreement signed by ten nations.

HISTORICAL EVENTS

1950 The Atomic Energy Commission directed to work toward creating a hydrogen bomb. Attempt to assassinate Truman. Peace Treaty with Japan. Soviet boycott of the Security Council of the United Nations. United States recalled all consular officers from Communist China. India proclaimed a Republic. Vietnam declared a sovereign nation within the French Union. Invasion of South Korea by forces from the North and subsequently by Chinese "volunteers." William Faulkner awarded Nobel Prize in Literature. Proclamation of national emergency in the United States.

1951 Creation of the U.S. Commission on Internal Security. Passage of a bill setting up machinery for Universal Military Service. Adoption of the Twenty-Second Amendment (limiting the President to two terms). General MacArthur recalled from Korea. Opening of NATO headquarters in Europe. Treaty of peace with Japan signed by forty-nine nations, but not by Soviets. Nationalization of the oil industry in Iran. Occupation of Tibet by the Chinese. Communist China branded as an aggressor by the U.N. Armistice negotiations opened in Korea.

1952 King George VI died; Elizabeth II proclaimed Queen. Increasing racial tensions in Africa (Union of South Africa, Tunisia, Egypt, and the Sudan). Japanese Peace Treaty put in force. Formal establishment of the European Defense Community. Keel of the first atomic submarine laid. Puerto Rico made a commonwealth. Dwight D. Eisenhower and Richard M. Nixon elected over Adlai E. Stevenson and John J. Sparkman, the first Republicans elected to the presidency and the vice-presidency since the administration of Hoover. U.S. Atomic Energy Commission announced hydrogen bomb test at Eniwetok.

1953–1957 DWIGHT D. EISENHOWER (R), PRESIDENT

1953 Stalin died. United States agreed to assist West Germany in rearmament when the European Defense Community became effective. Creation of the Department of Health, Education, and Welfare in the Cabinet. United Nations passed resolution calling for peace in Korea. Top of Mt. Everest reached by Hillary and Tenzing. Egypt proclaimed

1 2 3

a republic. Korean armistice signed at Panmunjom. Russia announced possession of the hydrogen bomb. Earl Warren made Chief Justice of the Supreme Court. In an address at the United Nations, President Eisenhower called for an international pool of fissionable materials for peaceful purposes.

1954 The *Nautilus*, first nuclear-powered submarine in the U.S. Navy, launched at Groton. Nasser became Premier of Egypt. U.S. Senate defeated the "Bricker amendment" limiting the treaty-making power of the President. The most powerful U.S. thermonuclear device to date exploded at Bikini. Army-McCarthy dispute resulted in official hearings in Washington. Supreme Court unanimously ruled that racial segregation in the public schools is unconstitutional. Security clearance denied to J. Robert Oppenheimer by the Atomic Energy Commission. President Eisenhower signed bill outlawing the Communist party; also bill opening the way for the private development of nuclear power. Ernest Hemingway awarded Nobel Prize in Literature. Censure of Senator Joseph McCarthy voted in the Senate.

1955 Winston Churchill retired as Prime Minister of Great Britain. The Federal Republic of Germany (West Germany) attained full sovereignty. U.S. Supreme Court ruled that the states must end racial segregation in public schools within a "reasonable time." U.S. Air Force Academy dedicated in Colorado. The first international conference on the peaceful uses of atomic energy held in Geneva. Ford Foundation announced grant of $500,000,000 to 4,157 colleges, hospitals, and universities. Start of Negro boycott of buses in Montgomery, Ala., led by the Reverend Martin Luther King, Jr.

1956 In Russia, Khrushchev attacked the Stalin legend and the cult of individualism. Pakistan formally became an Islamic republic. Molotov resigned as Russian Foreign Minister. British evacuated the Suez Canal Zone. Nasser elected President of Egypt. United States and Great Britain withdrew offer to assist financially in the Aswan Dam project. Nasser proclaimed nationalization of the Suez Canal. Soviet-Japanese peace treaty signed. Anti-Soviet riots in Hungary. Israel invaded the Sinai Peninsula; British and French forces bombarded Egyptian oil fields. U.N. General Assembly called for withdrawal of Israeli-British-French forces. Soviet troops crushed the Hungarian rebellion. End of bus segregation in Montgomery, Alabama. British and French forces evacuated from Egypt.

1957–1961 DWIGHT D. EISENHOWER (R), PRESIDENT

1957 European Common Market formed. U.S. Congress passed civil rights legislation giving federal courts power to hold offenders on criminal contempt charges and creating a Civil Rights Division in the Department of Justice. In Little Rock, Arkansas, Governor Faubus ordered the Arkansas National Guard to prevent integration at Central High School; President Eisenhower ordered federal troops to enforce the court order requiring integration. U.S.S.R. launched first artificial satellite and first intercontinental ballistic missile. U.S. submarine *Nautilus* made successful trip under Arctic ice. Atomic power station opened in Shippingport, Pennsylvania. United States launched "Atlas," first American intercontinental ballistic missile.

1958 U.S.-U.S.S.R. cultural exchange pact signed. Van Cliburn winner of Tchaikovsky International Piano Contest in Russia. Suez Canal settlement. Khrushchev became Premier of U.S.S.R. De Gaulle in full political control of France. U.S. submarine *Skate* remained underwater for more than thirty-one days. U.S. Marines landed in Lebanon. Sherman Adams, assistant to President Eisenhower, forced to resign. John XXIII became Pope. United States launched first "talking satellite."

1959 Alaska and Hawaii became 49th and 50th states. Federal courts proclaimed legal failure of Virginia's "massive resistance" to integration. First U.S. weather station in space. John Foster Dulles resigned as Secretary of State; succeeded by Christian Herter. St. Lawrence Seaway opened for traffic, April 25. *Lady Chatterley's Lover* freed from charge of pornography by federal court in New York. Khrushchev visited United States. Antarctica became a "scientific preserve" by treaty signed by several nations. Strife-torn Cyprus became a republic.

1960 Construction of Aswan Dam begun in Egypt by Nasser with aid from U.S.S.R. U.S.S.R.-Cuba Economic Pact. France became fourth nuclear power. First important Negro "sit-down" in Greensboro, North Carolina, to desegregate restaurants. New racial outburst in Union of South Africa; South Africa condemned by U.N. Security Council. U.S. "spy" plane shot down by U.S.S.R. Israelis captured Adolf Eichmann; Eichmann sentenced to death. Belgian Congo became independent. Castro seized oil refineries in Cuba; signed pact with Communist China. Television debates between Richard Nixon and John Kennedy. Kennedy, first Roman Catholic to become President, elected by narrow margin.

1961–1963 JOHN F. KENNEDY (D), PRESIDENT
1963–1965 LYNDON B. JOHNSON (D), PRESIDENT

1961 United States broke diplomatic relations with Cuba. Formation of U.S. Peace Corps. Union of South Africa withdrew from British Commonwealth of Nations. Bay of Pigs invasion of Cuba failed. Soviet astronaut Gagarin, first human space traveler, safely orbited the globe. Freedom Rider movements to force desegregation in interstate travel began in May; U.S. marshals forced to intervene because of riots in Montgomery, Alabama. U.S. astronaut Alan Shepard made successful trip 115 miles into space in suborbital rocket flight. Kennedy-Khrushchev conference in Vienna. Rift between U.S.S.R. and Communist China increasingly evident. U.S.S.R. exploded biggest nuclear bomb. U Thant chosen as U.N. Secretary General to succeed Dag Hammarskjöld, who died in a plane crash. Castro announced Communist aims.

1962 Organization of American States ostracized Cuba. John H. Glenn became first U.S. astronaut to orbit the earth. U.S. rocket hit the moon. U.S. troops sent to Thailand because of explosive situation in nearby countries. U.S. Supreme Court outlawed official prayer in New York schools. James Meredith's admission into University of Mississippi enforced, despite rioting. Pope John XXIII opened Ecumenical Council. Crisis over Soviet bases in Cuba. John Steinbeck awarded Nobel Prize in Literature. Richard Nixon defeated for governorship of California.

1963 De Gaulle rejected Great Britain's membership in the European Common Market. United States resumed underground nuclear testing. Pope John XXIII issued his encyclical *Pacem in Terris* outlining a plan for safeguarding peace in the atomic age. Antisegregation drive in Birmingham, Alabama, led to arrest of the Reverend Martin Luther King, Jr., and sixty others. Major Gordon Cooper completed a successful 22-orbit space flight. Governor Wallace of Alabama, confronted by National Guard troops, stepped aside to allow two Negroes to enroll in the University of Alabama. President Kennedy asked Congress to enact the most far-reaching civil rights legislation to date. The United States, Great Britain, and the Soviet Union initiated a test ban agreement prohibiting nuclear testing on land, in space, and under water. James Meredith received a degree from the University of Mississippi, becoming its first Negro alumnus. About 200,000 persons, white and Negro, marched peacefully on Washington to dramatize the fight for civil rights legislation. President Kennedy assassinated in Dallas; Vice-President Lyndon B. Johnson sworn in as the 36th President, November 22. Lee Harvey Oswald, the alleged assassin, shot and killed by Jack Ruby, November 24.

1964 U.S. Supreme Court ruled that districts for both houses in state legislatures must be "substantially equal" in population. Racial violence erupted in Harlem section of New York City and continued through August in New Jersey, Pennsylvania, and Illinois. Three young civil rights workers found murdered in Mississippi. Warren Commission declared Lee Harvey Oswald solely responsible for the assassination of President Kennedy. U.S.S.R. orbited three men in a single space capsule. Nikita Khrushchev replaced as leader of the Soviet Union by Leonid Brezhnev and Aleksei Kosygin. Communist China announced its first test explosion of a nuclear bomb. President Johnson re-elected in a landslide, defeating Senator Barry Goldwater.

BACKGROUNDS

1965 Federal indictments returned against 18 men in connection with 1964 slaying of three civil rights workers in Mississippi. Sir Winston Churchill died. Racial strife over Nego voter registration continued in Alabama. Malcolm X, Black Muslim leader, assassinated. U.S. District Judge dismissed felony indictments against 17 of the 18 men in Mississippi. The Early Bird, world's first communication satellite, was launched. Air Vice-Marshal Mguyen Cao Ky appointed Premier of South Vietnam. Majors James McDivitt and Edward White completed four-day, 62-orbit space flight, including first space walk by an American. Adlai Stevenson died in London. A six-day race riot in the Watts section of Los Angeles. Lt. Col. Gordon Cooper and Lt. Comdr. Charles Conrad in eight-day space flight. Vietnam War accelerated. United States achieved first manned space flight rendezvous.

1966 President Johnson and South Vietnamese Premier Ky met in Honolulu to discuss war problems. France announced its withdrawal from NATO and ordered all NATO bases removed from French soil by April 1967. President Sukarno of Indonesia gave over virtual control of his country to Lt. Gen. Suharto. United States began B–52 bombing raids of North Vietnam. Surveyor 1 made the first U.S. soft landing on the moon. Gemini 9 in 3-day space flight. U.S. bombed Hanoi. Race riots in seven major cities. Gemini 10 in brief flight. Gemini 11 made a first-orbit docking with another vehicle. Gemini 12 completed the last of the Gemini program flights.

1967 Three U.S. astronauts killed in a flash fire during an Apollo spacecraft launching. Twenty-one Latin-American states banned nuclear weapons by treaty from South America, Central America, and the Caribbean. First U.S.A.-U.S.S.R. consular treaty. Military junta seized control in Greece. President Nasser of Egypt forced evacuation of U.N. peace force along Egyptian-Israeli boundaries and closed Gulf of Aqaba to Israeli shipping. In a six-day war, Israel defeated all enemy Arab states and seized control of the Sinai Peninsula, the Gaza strip, Golan Heights, and much Jordanian territory west of the Jordan River, including Old Jerusalem (in 1969 Israel announced determination to retain much of these areas). Thurgood Arnold became the first Negro appointee to the U.S. Supreme Court. Racial violence in Newark, Detroit, and other cities. Thousands of protestors against Vietnam War barred by force from the Pentagon. Beginning of British withdrawal from southern Arabia territories.

1968 North Korean patrol boats seized U.S.S. *Pueblo*. Seven Vietcong attacks on South Vietnam cities; U.S. embassy in Saigon temporarily seized by Vietcong; reconquest of Hue from North Vietnamese after 25-day battle and loss of 11,000 dead. North Vietnam and United States agree to begin peace talks in Paris. U.S. astronauts Borman, Anders, and Lovell return from orbiting the moon ten times. Report of President's committee on civil disorders: fear of racial warfare. Pollution of air, earth, and water a growing issue. Assassination of the Reverend Martin Luther King, Jr. Assassination of Senator Robert F. Kennedy. Pierre Trudeau became Prime Minister of Canada. President Johnson announced decision to retire from the presidency and a partial cessation of bombing in North Vietnam. About 1,000 New York police ended a week-long student occupation of Columbia University buildings. Sixty-two nations signed a nuclear nonproliferation treaty. Richard M. Nixon and Spiro T. Agnew nominated at Republican convention in Miami; Hubert H. Humphrey and Edmund C. Muskie nominated at Democratic Convention in Chicago amid violent street riots. Nixon won by a wide margin in the Electoral College, but Democrats retained control of Congress.

1969– RICHARD M. NIXON (R), PRESIDENT

1969 Serious rioting in Northern Ireland. An oil slick closed the harbor of Santa Barbara, California; accidents to seagoing tankers raised question of ocean pollution elsewhere. Highjacking of airplanes became an international problem. Chinese and Soviet military clashes along eastern Siberian border. Pope Paul VI denounced dissent in Roman Catholic Church. Over 400 police removed protesting Harvard students from occupied buildings. De Gaulle resigned as President of France; succeeded by Georges Pompidou. Justice Abe Fortas resigned from the Supreme Court; Walter E. Burger became 15th Chief Justice, succeeding Earl Warren. U.S. astronauts Neil A. Armstrong and Edwin E. Aldrin, Jr. were first men to walk on the moon. The S.S. *Manhattan* was first commercial vessel through the Northwest Passage. Vice-President Agnew assailed television stations for their bias in news coverage. The United States agreed to return Okinawa to Japan. First U.S. draft lottery since World War II was instituted.

1970 Increase in plane highjacking and kidnapping of consular, ministerial, and ambassadorial personnel throughout the world. U.S. combat troops moved into Cambodia, but increasing numbers of troops were withdrawn from Southeast Asia. Army inquiry into responsibility for alleged massacres of Vietnamese civilians at My Lai involved former head of West Point and Lt. William Calley, Jr., among others. Acquittal of "Chicago Seven" of conspiracy charges, but conviction of five on charge of inciting to riot during the Democratic Convention of 1968. Campus riots reached climax in the burning of a bank in Santa Barbara, California; the killing of four students at Kent State University and wounding of others; and the destruction of a million-dollar research building at the University of Wisconsin and death of a research worker. Reportedly 448 U.S. universities and colleges went "on strike" or closed during the year. Destruction of townhouse in Greenwich Village by bomb, supposedly the work of Weathermen, a revolutionary group. Tensions between Israel and Arab states gave way to a 90-day ceasefire between Israel and Egypt; various Arab states, notably Jordan, put down guerrillas by force. Chinese Communist leader Mao Tse-tung demanded world revolution against U.S. imperalism. Attempt to assassinate Pope Paul VI in Philippines. Soviet spacecraft landed on Venus. Senate rejected G. Harrold Carswell for Supreme Court but accepted Harry A. Blackmun. Congress passed Omnibus Crime Control Act. U.S. railroad strike ended by injunction. Growing uneasiness about the state of the American economy. Death of President Nasser of Egypt. First complete synthesis of a gene.

1971 South Vietnam's "incursion" into Laos ended in retreat. Lt. William Calley, Jr., found guilty of premeditated murder at My Lai in 1968. Unemployment rate rose markedly. Red China invited U.S. table tennis players to compete in Peking. Supreme Court ordered busing of students to achieve racial desegregation. Antiwar militants disrupted Washington and the Capitol. Egypt and U.S.S.R. sign 15-year pact. Three Soviet astronauts died on return from three-week space journey. The Pentagon Papers, leaked to the press by Daniel Ellsberg, published by major newspapers; injunction issued by District Court to stop publication overruled by Supreme Court; Ellsberg indicted. U.S. Senate rejected a plan calling for total troop withdrawal from Vietnam by December 31, 1971. Adoption of the Twenty-Sixth Amendment (reduces voting age in all elections to 18). President Nixon announced a visit to Red China. Apollo 15 landed on the moon; astronauts spent three days in exploration. Freeze on wages and prices in attempt to combat inflation. Gun battle at San Quentin prison; Soledad Brother George Jackson killed. Attica, New York, prison riot ended; 32 inmates and nine hostages dead. United States and Russia agreed on a system to avert accidental nuclear warfare. Rioting in Northern Ireland increased. U.N. Assembly seated Mao Tse-tung's Chinese Communists and ousted Chiang Kai-shek's Nationalists.

Reading Lists of
American Literature
since 1890

I · AMERICAN LITERATURE
1890–1919

A · THE GENTEEL TRADITION

1 · The Genteel Tradition: "Culture"

In 1890 the cultural life of the United States was largely dominated by a complex of inherited values now ironically called the Genteel Tradition, after George Santayana's use of the phrase in *The Genteel Tradition at Bay* (1931). This complex of values was in general satisfactory to the inheritors of the tradition of (1) Anglo-Saxon (2) Protestant (3) middle-class America. It involved, among other matters:

a. A strong belief in metaphysical and moral idealism, in origin partly Platonic and partly Christian.

b. An equally strong belief that the highest cultural sanction is ethical, both in education ("liberal" education) and in the arts.

c. The general assumption that culture was self-culture; i.e., that the individual has within him capacities for self-directed growth and maturation in the light of such examples as Goethe, Arnold, and James Russell Lowell. The ideal was to become a well-rounded individual of noble purpose and refined intelligence.

The doctrine of culture in the Genteel Tradition may be studied in such representative works as these:

James Thompson Bixby (1843–1921), *The Crisis in Morals*, 1891 (reissued in 1900 as *The Ethics of Evolution*)
George William Curtis (1824–1892), *From the Easy Chair*, 1892 (There are two subsequent volumes: *Other Essays from the Easy Chair*, 1893, and *From the Easy Chair, Third Series*, 1894, which also illustrate genteel values.)
Charles W. Eliot (1834–1926), *American Contributions to Civilization and Other Essays and Addresses*, 1897

Charles W. Eliot, *Educational Reform: Essays and Addresses*, 1898

Robert Grant (1852–1940), *Reflections of a Married Man*, 1892

Robert Grant, *The Art of Living*, 1899

Robert Grant, *Search-Light Letters*, 1899

Life and Letters of Edward Everett Hale, 2 vols., 1917 (Hale lived from 1822 to 1909.)

Thomas Wentworth Higginson (1823–1911), *Cheerful Yesterdays*, 1898

Hamilton Wright Mabie (1845–1916), *My Study Fire*, 1890

Hamilton Wright Mabie, *Books and Culture*, 1896

Barrett Wendell (1855–1921), *Liberty, Union and Democracy*, 1906 (The discussion of democracy is especially revelatory.)

Barrett Wendell, *The Privileged Classes*, 1908 (Note the implications of the title essay.)

Woodrow Wilson (1856–1924), *Mere Literature and Other Essays*, 1896

George Edward Woodberry (1855–1930), *Studies in Letters and Life*, 1890

2 · *The Genteel Tradition: The Theory of the Arts*

In all the arts, but especially in painting and literature (and notably in poetry), upholders of the tradition clung to a set of canons. Four elements were especially important:

a. Art is the expression of the highest idealism, whether that idealism be interpreted to mean purposefulness in the cosmos, purposefulness in the life of the soul, or purposefulness in the life of the state.

b. Although good work in both the classic and the romantic schools was acceptable to the Genteel Tradition, art was acceptable principally as an expression of the highest morality (nobility).

c. Since, however, the weakness of the romantic tradition was likely to be "excess" or else formlessness, art as discipline was central (restraint, workmanship, craftsmanship).

d. The business of criticism was steadily to hold before artist and audience ideal standards not so much dogmatically conceived as garnered from traditional practice in Western Europe, New England, and (in lesser degree) other parts of the United States.

The theory of art (and of criticism) can be gleaned from careful reading of such critics as these:

William C. Brownell (1851–1928), *French Art*, 1892 (especially Chs. 1 and 3)

William C. Brownell, *American Prose Masters*, 1909 (Note especially the fresh interpretation of James Fenimore Cooper.)

Edmund C. Stedman (1833–1908), *The Nature and Elements of Poetry*, 1892 (especially Chs. 2 and 8)

William Wetmore Story (1819–1895), *Conversations in a Studio*, 2 vols., 1890

William Wetmore Story, *Excursions in Art and Letters*, 1891

Charles Dudley Warner (1829–1900), *The Relation of Literature to Life*, 1896

George Edward Woodberry (1855–1930), *The Heart of Man*, 1899 (Note the Platonic overtones of "A New Defence of Poetry.")

The practice of poetry in the Genteel Tradition may be studied in a great number of volumes. One anthology, however, summed up the period: Edmund C. Stedman, ed., *An American Anthology*, 1900. Characteristic poetry within the tradition may be read, *inter alia*, in such pieces as these:

Richard Watson Gilder, "Ode" (474–475), "The Celestial Passion" (475), "The Heroic Age" (478)
Louise Imogen Guiney, selections (664–667)
Lloyd Mifflin, sonnets (496–498)
Lizette Woodworth Reese, selections (609–612)

Characteristic books of poetry in the tradition are:
Thomas Bailey Aldrich (1836–1907), *Unguarded Gates and Other Poems*, 1895 (*Writings*, 8 vols., 1897; 9 vols., 1907)
Richard Hovey (1869–1900), *Along the Trail: A Book of Lyrics*, 1898. (Hovey also wrote an ambitious cycle of verse dramas, never completed, on the Arthurian Legends:
The Quest of Merlin, 1891
The Marriage of Guenevere, 1891
The Birth of Galahad, 1898
Taliesin, 1899
The Holy Grail, 1902—fragmentary.
George Cabot Lodge (1837–1909), *The Song of the Wave and Other Poems*, 1898
Louise Chandler Moulton (1835–1908), *Poems*, 1889
Lizette Woodworth Reese (1856–1935), *A Handful of Lavender*, 1891
George Santayana (1863–1952), *Sonnets and Other Verses*, 1894–1896, 1906
George Santayana, *A Hermit of Carmel and Other Poems*, 1901
Trumbull Stickney (1874–1904), *Dramatic Verses*, 1902
Trumbull Stickney, *Poems*, 1905
Trumbull Stickney, *The Poems of Trumbull Stickney*, ed. Amberys R. Whittle, 1972
George Edward Woodberry, *The North Shore Watch and Other Poems*, 1890
George Edward Woodberry, *Selected Poems*, 1933

1890–1919

3 · *The Regional and the Local*

Regionalism, cultural pluralism, or the doctrine that the United States is composed of culturally autonomous regions (New England, the South, the Far West) offered writers in the Genteel Tradition both a challenge and an opportunity. On the one hand localism, through its insistence on recording actual speech and custom, seemed to deny the validity of universal or idealized art; on the other hand, if properly managed, localism revealed the ideal in the actual, the universal in the present, the general in the particular. (A title like "A Village Lear" by Mary E. Wilkins Freeman illustrates this attempt.)

Techniques were developed in local color by which the flavorsomeness of provinciality was fused with a general philosophy of ideal conduct, typicality of human nature, and the dominance of universal moral standards, usually Christian. Favorite forms were the short story and the tale; the novel and poetry were less successful.

Earlier, simpler, and more sentimentalized versions of local color may be illustrated from:

Rose Terry Cooke (1827–1892), *Huckleberries Gathered from New England Hills*, 1891

Characteristic volumes in the period, arranged by regions, are these:

NEW ENGLAND

Alice Brown (1857–1948), *Meadow-Grass*, 1895
Alice Brown, *Tiverton Tales*, 1899
Mary E. Wilkins Freeman (1862–1930), *A New England Nun and Other Stories*, 1891
Mary E. Wilkins Freeman, *Jane Field*, 1893
Sarah Orne Jewett (1849–1909), *A Native of Wimby and Other Tales*, 1893
Sarah Orne Jewett, *The Country of the Pointed Firs*, 1896

Sarah Orne Jewett, *The Queen's Twin and Other Stories*, 1899
Edith Wharton (1862–1937), *Ethan Frome*, 1911

NEW YORK AND PENNSYLVANIA

Margaret Deland (1857–1944), *Old Chester Tales*, 1898
Margaret Deland, *Dr. Lavendar's People*, 1903
Margaret Deland, *The Awakening of Helena Ritchie*, 1906
Edward N. Wescott (1846–1898), *David Harum*, 1898

THE MIDWEST

James Whitcomb Riley (1849–1916), *Poems Here at Home*, 1893
James Whitcomb Riley, *Neighborly Poems*, 1897
Booth Tarkington (1869–1946), *The Gentleman from Indiana*, 1899
"Octave Thanet" (Alice French, 1850–1934), *Stories of a Western Town*, 1893

THE SOUTH

George Washington Cable (1844–1925), *Old Creole Days*, 1879
George Washington Cable, *The Grandissimes*, 1880
Charles W. Chesnutt (1858–1932), *The Conjure Woman*, 1899
Kate Chopin (1851–1904), *Bayou Folk*, 1894
Kate Chopin, *A Night in Acadie*, 1897
Paul Laurence Dunbar (1872–1906), *Lyrics of Lowly Life*, 1896
Mary Hallock Foote (1847–1938), *The Led-Horse Claim*, 1883
Grace King (1852–1932), *Balcony Stories*, 1893
F. Hopkinson Smith (1838–1915), *Colonel Carter of Cartersville*, 1891

THE FAR WEST

Mary Austin (1868–1934), *The Land of Little Rain*, 1903

4 · *Historical Romance*

The vogue of historical romance, especially after 1898, owed much to British success in the field (Robert Louis Stevenson, Conan Doyle, Rider Haggard, Stanley J. Weyman etc.), and much to the nationalism ebullient after the Spanish-American War. It posed certain problems to the Genteel Tradition analogous to those presented by local color. How reconcile the locus of an historical event with universal idealism? A solution was to create a usable past for the tradition by equating the hero and heroine of the historical novel with a philosophy of ideal conduct, and then fusing ideal conduct with an interpretation of history, providential in fact, known as "American idealism." The following novels are representative of the vogue:

Mary H. Catherwood (1847–1902), *The Romance of Dollard*, 1889 (French settlement and exploration in the Old Northwest)

Winston Churchill (1871–1947), *Richard Carvel*, 1899 (American Revolution)

Winston Churchill, *The Crisis*, 1901 (Civil War)

Winston Churchill, *The Crossing*, 1904 (the George Rogers Clark expedition)

"Charles E. Craddock" (Mary Noailles Murfree, 1850–1922), *The Story of Old Fort Loudon*, 1899 (Colonial Tennessee)

Paul Leicester Ford (1865–1902), *Janice Meredith*, 1899 (the Revolutionary period in the Middle Colonies)

Thomas A. Janvier (1849–1913), *The Aztec Treasure House: A Romance of Contemporaneous Antiquity*, 1890 (Mexico)

Mary Johnston (1870–1936), *Prisoners of Hope*, 1898 (Colonial Virginia)

Mary Johnston, *To Have and To Hold*, 1900 (Colonial Virginia)

Mary Johnston, *Audrey*, 1902 (Colonial Virginia)

S. Weir Mitchell (1829–1914), *Hugh Wynne, Free Quaker*, 1897 (Revolutionary Philadelphia)

S. Weir Mitchell, *The Red City*, 1907 (the presidency of Washington)

Thomas Nelson Page (1853–1922), *Red Rock,* 1898 (Civil War and Reconstruction in Virginia)

Maurice Thompson (1844–1901), *Alice of Old Vincennes,* 1900 (the Old Northwest)

5 · *Travel*

Although travel literature has been from the earliest period an important element in American letters, the Genteel Tradition put its special stamp on this branch of nonfictional prose. Not the scientific expedition, not the voyage of geographical exploration, not the pragmatical book of advice to emigrants, but the travel book as the record of a "broadening" experience, the result of being exposed to an older, richer, or alien culture, was the theme of volumes characteristic of the tradition. Such a book was an explication of an alien culture (a) in terms of life older, richer, or wiser than that in the United States; and (b) in terms of social controls usually seen from the point of view of a governing class—the "gentlemen and ladies" of the alien culture. But it might also explicate the exotic or the far away. Typical volumes of the period are these:

Charles A. Dana (1819–1897), *Eastern Journeys,* 1898
Richard Harding Davis (1864–1916), *About Paris,* 1895
Charles M. Flandrau (1871–1938), *Viva Mexico!* 1908
Lafcadio Hearn (1850–1904), *Two Years in the French West Indies,* 1890
Lafcadio Hearn, *Glimpses of Unfamiliar Japan,* 1894
William Dean Howells (1837–1920), *London Films,* 1905
William Dean Howells, *Certain Delightful English Towns,* 1906
William Dean Howells, *Roman Holidays,* 1908
William Dean Howells, *Seven English Cities,* 1909
Henry James (1843–1916), *A Little Tour in France,* 1885
Henry James, *Essays in London and Elsewhere,* 1893
Henry James, *English Hours,* 1905
Henry James, *The American Scene,* 1907
John La Farge (1835–1910), *An Artist's Letters from Japan,* 1897
Percival Lowell (1855–1916), *Occult Japan,* 1895
Edward Sylvester Morse (1838–1925), *Glimpses of China and Chinese Homes,* 1902
Edward Sylvester Morse, *Japan Day by Day,* 1917

F. Hopkinson Smith (1838–1915), *A White Umbrella in Mexico*, 1889

Charles Warren Stoddard (1843–1909), *A Cruise under the Crescent: From Suez to San Marco*, 1898

Edith Wharton (1862–1937), *Italian Villas and Their Gardens*, 1904

Edith Wharton, *Italian Backgrounds*, 1905

Edith Wharton, *A Motor-Flight Through France*, 1908

6 · *The Literature of Entertainment*

The phrase "literature of entertainment" is misleading. No attitude of condescension, however, is implied. In an era not yet affected by movies, radio, or television, writers faced problems resulting from the fact that the theater and the novel were two chief means of rational amusement. Both were dominated by the supposed requirements of women of the middle and upper classes, notably the young girl, whom H. H. Boyesen called "the iron madonna." Literature as purified entertainment for this purpose was both theorized and exemplified during the period.

The theory of literature as entertainment may be studied in these books:

Francis Marion Crawford (1854–1909), *The Novel: What It Is,* 1893
Brander Matthews (1852–1929), *Aspects of Fiction and Other Ventures in Criticism,* 1896 (Note the emphasis on technique as a mode of securing attention.)
Brander Matthews, *The Historical Novel and Other Essays,* 1901 (Note especially the implications of the title essay.)

Characteristic examples of fiction as entertainment are these:

Thomas Bailey Aldrich (1836–1907), *Two Bites at a Cherry,* 1894
Henry Cuyler Bunner (1855–1896), *Short Sixes,* 1890
Francis Marion Crawford, *Sant' Ilario,* 1889
Francis Marion Crawford, *A Cigarette Maker's Romance,* 1890
Francis Marion Crawford, *Don Orsino,* 1892 (The Saracinesca series, probably his most enduring claim to fame, consists of *Saracinesca,* 1887; *Sant' Ilario,* 1889; *Don Orsino,* 1892; and *Corleone,* 1896.)
Francis Marion Crawford, *Casa Braccio,* 2 vols., 1894
Francis Marion Crawford, *Via Crucis,* 1898
Francis Marion Crawford, *In the Palace of the King,* 1900 (a story of Philip II of Spain)
Paul Leicester Ford (1865–1902), *The Great K & A Train Robbery,* 1897

Henry Blake Fuller (1857–1929), *The Chevalier of Pensieri Vani*, 1890

George Barr McCutcheon (1866–1928), *Graustark*, 1901

George Barr McCutcheon, *Brewster's Millions*, 1903

Booth Tarkington (1869–1946), *Monsieur Beaucaire*, 1900

7 · *The Literature of Childhood*

Following upon the success of Louisa May Alcott (*Little Women*, 1868–69; *Little Men*, 1871) and Mark Twain (*Tom Sawyer*, 1876; *Huckleberry Finn*, 1885), the last third of the nineteenth century and the opening decades of the twentieth century produced a library of fiction that treated childhood gravely or sympathetically. Most such material was written within the Genteel Tradition in the sense that the ethical and religious prepossessions of the cultured group were made the canons by which childhood was judged. The following volumes, of varying degree of literary merit or complexity, are relevant:

L. Frank Baum (1865–1919), *The Wonderful Wizard of Oz*, 1900

John Bennett (1865–1956), *Master Skylark: A Story of Shakespeare's Time*, 1897

Gelett Burgess (1866–1951), *Goops and How To Be Them*, 1900

Stephen Crane (1871–1900), *Whilomville Stories*, 1900

Charles G. Finney (1905–), *Past the End of the Pavement*, 1939

Henry James (1843–1916), *What Maisie Knew*, 1897

Owen M. Johnson (1878–1952), *The Varmint*, 1910

Owen M. Johnson, *The Tennessee Shad*, 1911

James Whitcomb Riley (1849–1916), *Rhymes of Childhood*, 1891

Booth Tarkington (1869–1946), *Penrod*, 1914

Jean Webster (1876–1916), *Daddy Long Legs*, 1912

William Allen White (1868–1944), *The Court of Boyville*, 1899

Kate Douglas Wiggin (1856–1923), *Rebecca of Sunnybrook Farm*, 1903

8 · *Humor*

Two strains have dominated the development of humor in American literature: (a) urbane humor, represented by a succession of authors extending from Benjamin Franklin and Washington Irving to Dorothy Parker and E. B. White; and (b) folk humor, represented by folk tales about Paul Bunyan and Tony Beaver. Among "literary" humorists who have sought to exploit popular humor are Mark Twain, Artemus Ward, Josh Billings, and eventually Will Rogers. The problem for the Genteel Tradition was to refine folk humor while retaining its tang. Among the instruments working toward this end were the three great comic magazines of the late nineteenth and early twentieth century: *Puck*, 1877–1918, *Judge*, 1881–1939, and *Life*, 1883–1936. Humorists in the Genteel Tradition engaged in reconciling these two strains of humor (omitting Mark Twain) are represented by the following titles:

George Ade (1866–1944), *Fables in Slang*, 1900
George Ade, *More Fables*, 1900
John Kendrick Bangs (1862–1922), *A Houseboat on the Styx*, 1896
Guy Wetmore Carryl (1873–1904), *Fables for the Frivolous*, 1898
Guy Wetmore Carryl, *Grimm Tales Made Gay*, 1902
Finley Peter Dunne (1867–1936), *Mr. Dooley in Peace and War*, 1898
Finley Peter Dunne, *Mr. Dooley's Opinions*, 1901
John Ames Mitchell (1845–1918), *The Last American*, 1889
Frank R. Stockton (1834–1902), *The Casting Away of Mrs. Lecks and Mrs. Aleshine*, 1886
Frank R. Stockton, *The Great War Syndicate*, 1889
Frank R. Stockton, *The Great Stone of Sardis*, 1898
Edward W. Townsend (1855–1942), *Chimmie Fadden, Major Max, and Other Stories*, 1895
Harry Leon Wilson (1867–1939), *Ruggles of Red Gap*, 1915
Harry Leon Wilson, *Merton of the Movies*, 1922

9 · *The West*

Until the rise of Hollywood and the resultant easy connection between California and New York, the antinomy of East and West had been constant in American culture. The West was at once jealous of and subservient to the more experienced East; the East was both condescending and terrified before the lawless energy of the West—an area defined in the 1890s as the Great Plains, the Rocky Mountains, the intervening area, and the Pacific Coast. An image of the West was formed in which at least five elements can be ascertained:

a. Surprise
b. Plenitude
c. Vastness
d. Melancholy
e. Incongruity—especially the incongruity of the petty human element against the naked grandeur of God's handiwork, as exemplified in the Yosemite Valley, the Grand Canyon, and other characteristic Western natural phenomena.

On the whole, though not uniformly, the expression of Western life was kept uneasily in check by the imposition of genteel standards of achievement and control, which, though by no means unsympathetic to Western energy and Western democracy, nevertheless evaluated Western ebullience by its eventual acquiescence in Eastern standards. In varying degree these elements can be studied in the following books:

Andy Adams (1859–1935), *The Log of a Cowboy,* 1903
Andy Adams, *Reed Anthony, Cowman,* 1907
Thomas Hornsby Ferril (1896–), *New and Selected Poems,* 1952
Thomas Hornsby Ferril, *Words for Denver and Other Poems,* 1966
Zane Grey (1875–1939), *Riders of the Purple Sage,* 1912
Alfred Henry Lewis (c.1858–1914), *Wolfville,* 1897
Alfred Henry Lewis, *Wolfville Days,* 1902
John Muir (1838–1914), *The Mountains of California,* 1894
John Muir, *Our National Parks,* 1901
John Muir, *Travels in Alaska,* 1915

Eugene Manlove Rhodes (1869–1934), *Stepsons of Light,* 1921
Eugene Manlove Rhodes, *Copper Streak Trail,* 1922
Theodore Roosevelt (1858–1919), *The Wilderness Hunter,* 1893
Owen Wister (1860–1938), *The Virginian,* 1902

C · FORCES HOSTILE TO THE GENTEEL TRADITION

10 · *The Fin de Siècle Spirit*

The Genteel Tradition eventually lost its cultural dominance. The reasons for its decline were complex, but among them was the emergence of new values and forces in art and thought with which the tradition was unprepared to cope. Three outstanding elements of "revolt" were these:

a. The acceptance in the United States, at least in cities having some pretension to cosmopolitanism ("sophistication"), of the *fin de siècle* spirit.

b. The acceptance among educated Americans of the evolutionary hypothesis, an acceptance that, despite the emergence of the "Social Gospel" as a practical *via media* between Darwinism and Christianity, deepened the difficulties of the idealist position.

c. The enthusiastic proclamation of realistic and naturalistic theories of art, especially by the rising generation of novelists.

By the *fin de siècle* spirit one means, briefly, the emotional attitudes consequent on the pessimistic belief that civilization was inevitably declining. Sensitive souls could find existence bearable only by throwing themselves into a life of sensation and of art. The philosophic attitude of pessimism was encouraged by the discovery of Schopenhauer, von Hartmann, Omar Khayyám, Wagner, Nordau, and Nietzsche. The prestige of the Decadent and Art-for-Art's-Sake movements in London, coupled with des-ultory information about an analogous development in French, German, and Italian poetry, also helped to sustain an American aesthetic revolt.

One or another phase of American pessimism may be studied in the following books:

Ignatius Donnelly (1831–1901), *Caesar's Column*, 1891
Edgar Saltus (1855–1921), *The Philosophy of Disenchantment*, 1885
Edgar Saltus, *The Anatomy of Negation*, 1886
George Santayana (1863–1952), *Lucifer*, 1899
"Mark Twain" (Samuel L. Clemens, 1835–1910), *The Mysterious Stranger*, 1916

The aesthetic and impressionist movements can be studied in these titles:

Bliss Carman (1861–1929) and Richard Hovey (1864–1900), *Songs from Vagabondia*, 1894

Chap-Book Essays, 1896

H. C. Chatfield-Taylor (1865–1945), *Two Women and a Fool*, 1895

Lafcadio Hearn (1850–1904), *Chita: A Memory of Last Island*, 1889

Lafcadio Hearn, *Exotics and Retrospectives*, 1898

Lafcadio Hearn, *Shadowings*, 1900

Lafcadio Hearn, *Fantastics and Other Fancies*, 1914

James Gibbons Huneker (1860?–1921), *Melomaniacs*, 1902

James Gibbons Huneker, *Iconoclasts*, 1905

James Gibbons Huneker, *Promenades of an Impressionist*, 1910

James Gibbons Huneker, *Painted Veils*, 1920

Harry Thurston Peck (1856–1914), *The Personal Equation*, 1898

Percival Pollard (1869–1911), *Their Day in Court*, 1909

Edgar Saltus, *Imperial Purple*, 1892

Vance Thompson (1863–1925), *French Portraits*, 1900

11 · *The American Interpretation of Evolution*

Although the work of Lyell (*Principles of Geology*, 1830–1833, often re-edited and reprinted) was known to American geologists, and although Darwin's *Origin of Species* (1859) was immediately debated by American scientists and theologians, discussion did not grow heated over the problem of evolution until the publication of Huxley's *Man's Place in Nature* (1863) and Darwin's *The Descent of Man* (1871). The appearance of Huxley at the ceremonies opening The Johns Hopkins University (1876) and the virtual underwriting of Herbert Spencer (1820–1903) by American money so that he might complete the 10-volume *Synthetic Philosophy* (the last volume appeared in 1896–1897) were events of importance in the controversy. Spencer's sweeping generalizations appealed to the American love of broad statement; his distrust of state action pleased industrial leaders; and his vague generalization that progress was virtually assured to man by evolution pleased reformers and labor leaders, committed as they were to a principal of voluntarism.

The American parallel to Spencer is *Outlines of Cosmic Philosophy*, 2 vols. (1874), by John Fiske. Less formal but equally cogent treatments of the evolutionary hypothesis may be read in such works as the following:

John Fiske (1842–1901), *Excursions of an Evolutionist*, 1884 (especially the essays, "Our Aryan Forefathers" and "The Meaning of Infancy," the last being Fiske's original contribution to evolutionary theory)

John Fiske, *The Destiny of Man*, 1884 (Key chapters are 1–4, 10, 15–16.)

John Fiske, *The Idea of God as Affected by Modern Knowledge*, 1886 (Key chapters are 5–7, 11, 14.)

John Fiske, *A Century of Science*, 1899

John Fiske, *Through Nature to God*, 1899 (Note the evolutionary implications in "The Cosmic Roots of Love and Self-Sacrifice.")

William James (1842–1910), *The Principles of Psychology*, 2 vols., 1890 (Note especially the theory of the function of the brain and the theory of instincts.)

Henry F. Osborn (1857–1935), *From the Greeks to Darwin*, 1894

Josiah Royce (1855–1916), *Fugitive Essays*, 1920 (Note the essay on "The Nature of Voluntary Progress.")

Andrew D. White (1832–1918), *A History of the Warfare of Science with Theology in Christendom*, 2 vols., 1896

12 · *The Application of Evolutionary Theory*

The evolutionary hypothesis affected and still affects all departments of American culture. Those who struggled with the problem of the relation of the evolutionary hypothesis to the social
present and the probable future of American life may be divided
into two broad categories: one group interpreted evolution,
imaginatively or philosophically, as supporting a doctrine of
loyalty to idealism, social progress, and religious "modernism,"
usually taking shape as the "Social Gospel"; another, more disillusioned, group tended to the point of view that progress was
an illusion, state action for ameliorative purposes a piece of
sentimentality, and altruism a cloak for ruthless competition in
the struggle for existence.

The following writers interpreted evolution as a challenge to
a more heroic loyalty to the ideal:

> William Vaughn Moody (1869–1910), *Poems and Plays,* 2 vols.,
> 1912 (See especially *The Masque of Judgment,* 1900, *The
> Fire-Bringer,* 1904, and the unfinished *Death of Eve,* among
> the poetic dramas; and among the poems, "Gloucester
> Moors," "The Menagerie," "Ode on a Soldier Fallen in the
> Philippines," "Ode in Time of Hesitation," and "The
> Troubling of the Waters.")
> Josiah Royce (1855–1916), *The Philosophy of Loyalty,* 1908

The Catholic position on social amelioration is well expressed
in:

> John L. Spaulding (1840–1916), *Socialism and Labor,* 1902

The general doctrine of the Social Gospel may be studied in
the following:

> Lyman Abbott (1835–1922), *The Evolution of Christianity,*
> 1892 (especially Chs. 1, 8–9)
> Washington Gladden (1836–1918), *Ruling Ideas of the Present
> Age,* 1895
> Washington Gladden, *How Much Is Left of the Old Doctrines?*
> 1899

Walter Rauschenbusch (1861–1918), *Christianity and the Social Crisis*, 1907 (Note especially the chapters on "The Present Crisis" and "The Stake of the Church in the Social Movement.")

Walter Rauschenbusch, *Christianizing the Social Order*, 1912 (Key chapters are those on "The Case of Christianity Against Capitalism," "Economic Democracy," and "The Economic Basis for Fraternity.")

Among novels dramatizing the Social Gospel are the following:

Winston Churchill (1871–1947), *The Inside of the Cup*, 1913
Charles M. Sheldon (1857–1946), *In His Steps*, 1896
Albion W. Tourgée (1838–1905), *Murvale Eastman, Christian Socialist*, 1890

The view of progress under evolution is less roseate in such writers as these:

Oliver Wendell Holmes (1841–1935), *Collected Legal Papers*, 1920 (especially "The Path of the Law," "The Theory of Legal Interpretation," and "Law in Science and Science in Law")

William James (1842–1910), *Varieties of Religious Experience*, 1902 (especially Chs. 4, 10, 20)

Alfred Thayer Mahan (1840–1914), *The Influence of Sea Power upon History, 1600–1783*, 1890

Theodore Roosevelt (1858–1919), *The Winning of the West*, 4 vols., 1889–1896 (In the competition of races the "Anglo-Saxons" must conquer to live.)

Theodore Roosevelt, *The Rough Riders*, 1899

William Graham Sumner (1840–1910), *Essays*, ed. Albert Galloway Keller and Maurice R. Davie, 2 vols., 1934 (See especially "Religion and Mores," "War," "Earth Hunger," and "The Forgotten Man" in Vol. I; "What Makes the Rich Richer and the Poor Poorer?" and "The Conquest of the United States by Spain" in Vol. II.)

William Graham Sumner, *Folkways*, 1907 (on the relativity of morals)

Frederick Jackson Turner (1861–1932), *The Frontier in American History*, 1920 (an expansion of his famous paper of

1893, "The Significance of the Frontier in American History")

Thorstein Veblen (1857–1929), *The Theory of the Leisure Class*, 1899 (especially Chs. 3, 4, 14)

Thorstein Veblen, *The Theory of Business Enterprise*, 1904

13 · *The Forces of Realism: William Dean Howells*

If the phases of American literary history were denominated by
the names of their principal authors, the period covered by this
part of the outline would be called the Age of Howells. Chief
exponent of a theory of realism, cultured exponent during the
period of a mild but sincere form of gradualistic socialism, William Dean Howells (1837–1920) befriended younger and more
daring authors and himself exemplified a quality of fictional
realism devoted to the sympathetic presentation of average
middle-class American life. Representative works by him are
these:

LITERARY THEORY

Criticism and Fiction, 1891
Heroines of Fiction, 2 vols., 1901 (In the course of these ami-
    able comments on fictional heroines Howells also uttered a
    great deal of valuable technical advice on the writing of
    fiction.)
Literature and Life, 1902

FICTION

The Rise of Silas Lapham, 1885
Annie Kilburn, 1888
A Hazard of New Fortunes, 1890
The Shadow of a Dream, 1890
The Quality of Mercy, 1892
The World of Chance, 1893
The Landlord at Lion's Head, 1897
The Son of Royal Langbrith, 1904
The Vacation of the Kelwyns, 1920

SOCIALISTIC UTOPIANISM

A Traveler from Altruria, 1894
Through the Eye of a Needle, 1907

14 · *The Forces of Realism: The Contemporaries of Howells*

From 1890 to his death in 1916, Henry James, in the eyes of
present-day critics a greater writer than Howells, lived principally in England or on the Continent except for occasional visits
to his native land, which he observed almost with the eyes of an
alien. In 1915 he became a British subject. His influence was
greater after World War I than before, but insofar as it was felt
by writers in the period 1890–1920, it was a technical influence
on psychological fiction. Probably his most influential work of
literary theory was *Notes on Novelties* (1914). Titles of his novels
that contributed to American realism from 1890 on are these:

Henry James (1843–1916), *The Tragic Muse*, 1890
Henry James, *The Spoils of Poynton*, 1897
Henry James, *What Maisie Knew*, 1897
Henry James, *The Awkward Age*, 1899
Henry James, *The Wings of the Dove*, 1902
Henry James, *The Ambassadors*, 1903
Henry James, *The Golden Bowl*, 1904

Other lesser writers, more immediately in touch with American
life, advanced the cause of realism. Representative writers and
representative novels by them follow:

Gertrude Atherton (1857–1948), *Patience Sparhawk and Her
    Times*, 1897
Gertrude Atherton, *Senator North*, 1900
Gertrude Atherton, *Black Oxen*, 1923
Arlo Bates (1850–1918), *The Puritans*, 1898 (a novel of Boston,
    which should be read in conjunction with its predecessors,
    The Pagans, 1888, and *The Philistines*, 1889)
H. H. Boyesen (1848–1895), *The Mammon of Unrighteousness*,
    1891
Francis Marion Crawford (1854–1909), *Katharine Lauderdale*,
    1894 (followed the next year by a sequel, *The Ralstons*)
Francis Marion Crawford, *Adam Johnstone's Son*, 1896
Margaret Deland (1857–1944), *John Ward, Preacher*, 1888
Edward Eggleston (1837–1902), *The Faith Doctor*, 1891
Harold Frederic (1856–1898), *The Lawton Girl*, 1890

Harold Frederic, *The Copperhead*, 1893
Harold Frederic, *The Damnation of Theron Ware*, 1896
Robert Grant (1852–1940), *Unleavened Bread*, 1900
Robert Grant, *The Chippendales*, 1909 (followed in 1931 by
a sequel, *The Dark Horse*)
"Mark Twain" (Samuel L. Clemens, 1835–1910), *Pudd'nhead
Wilson*, 1894
"Mark Twain," *The Man That Corrupted Hadleyburg*, 1900
Charles Dudley Warner (1829–1900), *The Golden House*, 1894
Charles Dudley Warner, *That Fortune*, 1899

15 · *The Forces of Naturalism: The Meliorists*

Distinctions between realism and naturalism are hard to make. Naturalism, however, tends to concentrate on the concept of man as a superior animal rather than as an individual soul and on his more elemental motives, and therefore on the more disagreeable or physiologically unpleasant events of life. Naturalism often adopts a theory of physical determinism that strikes alike at the roots of idealism and of altruism. Many American novelists, though accepting naturalistic themes and even naturalistic concepts of character, felt that naturalism, by discarding supernatural or idealistic presuppositions, would open the road to necessary reforms in society, supposedly based on scientific truth. American naturalists, therefore, tend to fall into two divisions: the meliorists or "soft" naturalists, who are but imperfect exponents of rigorous naturalism; and the determinists, who follow with greater consistency the logic of nineteenth-century science, in which events in a closed universe are beyond the control of an individual. The following list gives representative works by "soft" naturalists (some critics deny they are naturalists at all); the next list (16) gives representative work by the "hard" naturalists.

An imperfect theory of fictional naturalism may be read in:

Hamlin Garland (1860–1940), *Crumbling Idols,* 1894 (Much light is thrown on both Garland and his contemporaries by his *Son of the Middle Border,* 1917, and *Roadside Meetings,* 1930.)
Frank Norris (1870–1902), *The Responsibilities of the Novelist,* 1903

Representative works of fiction which, naturalistic in part, nevertheless seek improvement in the social and political order are these:

Hamlin Garland, *Main-Travelled Roads,* 1891
Hamlin Garland, *A Spoil of Office,* 1892
Hamlin Garland, *Prairie Folks,* 1893
Hamlin Garland, *Rose of Dutcher's Coolly,* 1895

Hamlin Garland, *Jason Edwards*, 1897
Jack London (1876–1916), *The Call of the Wild*, 1903
Jack London, *The Sea-Wolf*, 1904
Jack London, *The Iron Heel*, 1907
Jack London, *Martin Eden*, 1909
Frank Norris, *McTeague*, 1899
Frank Norris, *The Octopus*, 1901
Frank Norris, *The Pit*, 1903

16 · *The Forces of Naturalism: The Determinists*

For comment, see the headnote to list 15 above.

Ambrose Bierce (1842–1914?), *In the Midst of Life,* 1898 (originally published in 1891 as *Tales of Soldiers and Civilians*)

Ambrose Bierce, *Can Such Things Be?* 1893

Stephen Crane (1871–1900), *Maggie: A Girl of the Streets,* 1893, 1896 (first published privately under the pseudonym "Johnston Smith," then revised for the 1896 printing under his own name)

Stephen Crane, *The Red Badge of Courage,* 1895

Stephen Crane, *George's Mother,* 1896

Stephen Crane, *The Monster and Other Stories,* 1899 (contains "The Blue Hotel")

Theodore Dreiser (1871–1945), *Sister Carrie,* 1900 (first printed in 1900 but withheld from circulation by the publisher; reissued in 1912)

Theodore Dreiser, *Jennie Gerhardt,* 1911

Theodore Dreiser, *The Financier,* 1912

Theodore Dreiser, *The Titan,* 1914

Theodore Dreiser, *The "Genius,"* 1915

Theodore Dreiser, *An American Tragedy,* 1925

Theodore Dreiser, *The Stoic,* 1947 (With *The Financier* and *The Titan* this book constitutes the "Trilogy of Desire." The main character, Frank Cowperwood, is a fictional treatment of the Philadelphia tycoon Charles T. Yerkes.)

D · MOVEMENTS OF RECONSTRUCTION

17 · *New Viewpoints in Social Interpretation*

From 1893 to 1897–1898 the country suffered from "The Panic of 1893." The American experiment seemed to be headed for disaster, industrial democracy looked impossible, and American society appeared to be "sick." By and large the middle classes were unaware of the nature of the sociological puzzle confronting the country. Consequently an important library of books appeared designed to describe sympathetically a variety of American "underdogs" and to indicate ways of improving the condition both of the misfits and of the American commonwealth. The "tramp" was discovered; the slums were dramatized; problems of the Negro and of the immigrant were posed. A selected list of such books follows:

Jane Addams (1860–1935), *Twenty Years at Hull-House*, 1910
Jane Addams, *The Second Twenty Years at Hull-House*, 1930
Mary Antin (1881–1949), *The Promised Land*, 1912
George Washington Cable (1844–1925), *The Negro Question*, 1888
Josiah Flynt (Willard) (1869–1907), *Tramping with the Tramps*, 1899
Josiah Flynt (Willard), *Notes of an Itinerant Policeman*, 1900
Laurence Gronlund (1846–1899), *Our Destiny*, 1891
Laurence Gronlund, *The New Economy*, 1898
Jack London (1876–1916), *The People of the Abyss*, 1903
Simon N. Patten (1852–1922), *The New Basis of Civilization*, 1907
Jacob A. Riis (1849–1914), *How the Other Half Lives*, 1890
Jacob A. Riis, *The Making of an American*, 1901
Lester Frank Ward (1841–1913), *The Psychic Factors of Civilization*, 1893 (Though a commentary on his *Dynamic Sociology*, 1883, it can be read independently.)
Booker T. Washington (1856–1915), *Up from Slavery*, 1901
Walter A. Wyckoff (1865–1908), *The Workers: The East*, 1897
Walter A. Wyckoff, *The Workers: The West*, 1898

18 · *Social Reform: Program and Experience*

The disturbing discovery that large classes of Americans and of persons resident in America were not enjoying the fruits of an ideal democratic society led to considering ways and means to achieve practical reform within the existing political order. The climax of this movement was the Progressive ("Bull Moose") Movement, which reached its height in the election of 1912 when Theodore Roosevelt battled successfully to defeat Taft and unsuccessfully to defeat the "New Freedom" of Woodrow Wilson. The characteristic literary expression corresponding to the political movement was the literature of muckraking, which except for the name was not new in the twentieth century. Much of the muckraking library was ephemeral, although some of it has lasting value. The most sagacious volume rising out of the progressivism of the early twentieth century and a key book for the interpretation of American life before World War I is:

Herbert D. Croly (1869–1930), *The Promise of American Life,* 1909

Other general books of more than ephemeral value include:

Herbert Demarest Lloyd (1847–1903), *Wealth Against Commonwealth,* 1894 (especially Chs. 5, 14, 24, 25)
Lincoln Steffens (1866–1936), *The Shame of the Cities,* 1904

Autobiographical writings by the progressives are at once documents of primary importance for understanding the doctrine of change within the American system and valuable revelations of character or personality. Among them are:

Tom L. Johnson (1854–1911), *My Story,* 1911
Robert M. La Follette (1855–1925), *Autobiography,* 1913
Lincoln Steffens, *Autobiography,* 1931

Insight into the general mood of progressivism may be gained from:

John Jay Chapman (1862–1933), *Causes and Consequences,* 1898

Theodore Roosevelt (1858–1919), *The Strenuous Life,* 1900
Woodrow Wilson (1856–1924), *The New Freedom,* 1913
The Public Papers of Woodrow Wilson, ed. Ray Stannard
   Baker and William E. Dodd, 6 vols., 1925–1927 (particularly
   the two volumes entitled *The New Democracy*)

19 · *Novels of Social and Political Reform*

Like *Pilgrim's Progress*, the novel of political exposure, designed to dramatize the conflict between political righteousness and moral idealism, on the one hand, and on the other the sinister forces of political corruption and amoral business enterprise, personified in the gangster, the grafter, the briber, the bribe-taker, and the boss, assured readers of the eventual victory of what is good and pure. Many of these books contain vivid and sympathetic studies of political personalities or record in fictional guise dramatic, political, and economic struggles. Representative works are here listed:

Winston Churchill (1871–1947), *Coniston*, 1906
Winston Churchill, *Mr. Crewe's Career*, 1908
Paul Leicester Ford (1865–1902), *The Honorable Peter Stirling*, 1894
Ellen Glasgow (1874–1945), *The Voice of the People*, 1900
Ellen Glasgow, *The Romance of a Plain Man*, 1909
Robert Herrick (1868–1938), *The Web of Life*, 1900
Robert Herrick, *Memoirs of an American Citizen*, 1905
Robert Herrick, *Clark's Field*, 1914
Alfred Henry Lewis (c.1858–1914), *The Boss*, 1903
David Graham Phillips (1867–1911), *The Cost*, 1904
David Graham Phillips, *The Deluge*, 1905
David Graham Phillips, *The Plum Tree*, 1905
David Graham Phillips, *Light-Fingered Gentry*, 1907
David Graham Phillips, *The Second Generation*, 1907
David Graham Phillips, *Susan Lenox: Her Fall and Rise*, 1917
Upton Sinclair (1878–1968), *The Jungle*, 1906
Brand Whitlock (1869–1934), *The Thirteenth District*, 1902
Brand Whitlock, *The Turn of the Balance*, 1907

20 · *The Interpretation of Fiction*

Other novelists dug deeper and saw further. They were gravely alarmed by the transition from an agrarian into an industrial society, from a social order having relatively fixed moral codes into a society living by the spending standard, and from an epoch still retaining the heroic flavor of the pioneer to an era dedicated in William James's phrase to the worship of the bitch goddess Success.

In New York City, the slow corruption of the "natural" aristocracy of Little Old New York by the intrusion of vulgar wealth was chronicled by Edith Wharton (1862–1937) in such novels as these:

The House of Mirth, 1905
The Reef, 1912
The Custom of the Country, 1913
The Age of Innocence, 1920
Hudson River Bracketed, 1929

What Mrs. Wharton did for a city, Ellen Glasgow (1874–1945) in some sense did for a whole commonwealth, her native state of Virginia, as in:

The Deliverance, 1904
The Miller of Old Church, 1911
Virginia, 1913
Life and Gabriella, 1916
Barren Ground, 1925
They Stooped to Folly, 1929
The Sheltered Life, 1932
Vein of Iron, 1935

In the Middle West, Booth Tarkington (1869–1946) broadened the lens to take in a whole region moving from a village republic to a megalopolitan culture in:

The Turmoil, 1915

The Magnificent Ambersons, 1918
Alice Adams, 1921
The Midlander, 1923

And for the Great Plains, Willa Cather (1876–1947) chronicled a similar transition, although hope arose (as in the case of the other novelists) through the appearance of characters of integrity, even amid vulgarity:

The Song of the Lark, 1915
My Ántonia, 1918
A Lost Lady, 1923
The Professor's House, 1925
Death Comes for the Archbishop, 1927

21 · *Governing Philosophies*

While novelists were penetrating deeper into American life, American philosophy, now fully mature, was digging deeper still, posing the problem of relativism against the absolute, and endeavoring to fuse the implications of nineteenth-century science, notably physics and biology, with some of the traditional postulates of the metaphysician. Not all the authors listed below were technical philosophers. Moreover, the kind of information necessary to grasp the relation between professional philosophical systems and the influence of a point of view on the intellectual life of the country does not require expertise in logic and metaphysics. The titles that follow seem to be more readable volumes by writers whose formal treatises, if they wrote any, may lie beyond the comprehension of readers untrained in epistemology and logic.

Thus, though the most important of Royce's philosophical works seems to be *The World and the Individual,* 2 vols. (1900–1901), the following titles give at least a working acquaintance with his thought.

Josiah Royce (1855–1916), *The Spirit of Modern Philosophy,* 1892 (especially the General Introduction and, *inter alia,* the discussions of Hegel and Schopenhauer)
Josiah Royce, *Studies of Good and Evil,* 1898
Josiah Royce, *The Hope of the Great Community,* 1916

Interesting in connection with Royce is a book by an opponent of his:

Francis Ellingwood Abbot (1836–1903), *The Way Out of Agnosticism,* 1890

A darker interpretation of the course of history appears in the following:

Brooks Adams (1848–1927), *The Law of Civilization and Decay,* 1895
Brooks Adams, *America's Economic Supremacy,* 1900
Brooks Adams, *The New Empire,* 1902

Henry Adams (1838–1918), *Mont St.-Michel and Chartres*, 1904
Henry Adams, *The Education of Henry Adams*, 1907 (published in 1918)
Brooks Adams and Henry Adams, *The Degradation of the Democratic Dogma*, 1919 (includes Henry Adams' *Letter to Teachers of American History*, 1910, and "The Tendency of History," 1909, with introductory matter by Brooks Adams)

A greater degree of affirmation, even of optimism, was expressed by two philosophers thought to be more characteristic of the twentieth century than any of the above:

John Dewey (1859–1952), *The School and Society*, 1899
John Dewey, *Democracy and Education*, 1916
Joseph Ratner, ed. (1901–), *Intelligence in the Modern World: John Dewey's Philosophy*, 1939 (an anthology of characteristic writings by Dewey, prefaced by an elaborate introduction, in which Sec. 11, "Science and Philosophy of Education," is especially informative)
William James (1842–1910), *The Will To Believe and Other Essays*, 1897
William James, *Pragmatism*, 1907

Influenced by evolution but standing aloof from the others is George Santayana. Representative volumes by him are:

George Santayana (1863–1952), *Interpretations of Poetry and Religion*, 1900
George Santayana, *The Life of Reason*, 5 vols., 1905–1906
George Santayana, *Scepticism and Animal Faith*, 1923
George Santayana, *The Last Puritan*, 1936 (fiction)
George Santayana, *The Realm of Being*, 4 vols., 1942 (includes the four "realms," concerning which volumes were earlier published as follows: *Essence*, 1927; *Matter*, 1930; *Truth*, 1937; *Spirit*, 1940)
Logan P. Smith, ed., *Little Essays Drawn from the Writings of George Santayana*, 1920

F · NEW DIRECTIONS

22 · The Drama

Before the advent of Eugene O'Neill (1888–1953), American theaters prospered on melodrama, sensationalism, "domestic" drama, the star system, and Shakespeare. Many plays were surreptitiously "borrowed" from Europe without acknowledgment. From 1895, theaters were controlled by the Theatrical Syndicate and later by the United Booking Office. New York City was the center for drama, and the rest of the nation was "the road." Realism was slow to be accepted on the stage in spite of the advances in American fiction, between 1890 and World War I, and the appearance abroad of Ibsen, Strindberg, Hauptmann, Wedekind, and other naturalists (who often turned into symbolists). Much of what entertained American audiences in these years was subliterary though good theater; but a few playwrights tried to break new ground with problem plays, witty satire, fantasy, political issues, and the inevitable psychological analyses. This list is chronological to indicate the trends:

James A. Herne (1838–1901), *Margaret Fleming*, 1890
Augustus Thomas (1857–1934), *Alabama*, 1891
Clyde Fitch (1865–1909), *Captain Jinks of the Horse Marines*, 1901
Clyde Fitch, *The Climbers*, 1901
Clyde Fitch, *The Girl with the Green Eyes*, 1902
Clyde Fitch, *The City*, 1909
Langdon Mitchell (1862–1935), *The New York Idea*, 1902
David Belasco (1859–1931), *The Girl of the Golden West*, 1905
William Vaughn Moody (1869–1910), *The Great Divide*, 1906
Winchell Smith (1872–1933) and Byron Ongley (? –1915), *Brewster's Millions*, 1906 (from the novel by George Barr McCutcheon)
Edward Sheldon (1886–1946), *The Nigger*, 1907

Eugene O'Neill's first productions were one-act plays of the sea, notably *The Long Voyage Home* (1917) and *The Moon of the Caribbees* (1918). When he moved from Provincetown to

Broadway, he began a career that firmly established him as America's most gifted playwright. His best early plays are:

The Emperor Jones, 1920
Anna Christie, 1921
"The Hairy Ape," 1921

The major works of the next decade include:

Desire under the Elms, 1924
All God's Chillun Got Wings, 1924
The Great God Brown, 1928
Strange Interlude, 1928
Mourning Becomes Electra, 1931
Ah, Wilderness! 1933

O'Neill broke a long silence with *The Iceman Cometh* in 1946. After his death in 1953, Broadway saw three more of his plays, the first of which, *Long Day's Journey into Night* (1956), sparked an O'Neill revival and is considered by many critics to be his masterpiece.

23 · *The Poetic Renaissance: Preliminary*

Just prior to World War I the most forward-looking movement in American letters, judged from the point of view of subsequent developments, was probably the Poetic Renaissance, which may be dated from the founding of *Poetry: A Magazine of Verse* by Harriet Monroe (1860–1936) in Chicago in 1912. This movement not only sought to end the whole nineteenth-century manner in verse, but also served as a bridge into the development of poetry in the twentieth century subsequent to World War I. Most of the poets were affected by both World Wars and by the world events of the thirties. As a whole, however, the names grouped here may be thought of as constituting a transition movement between the first half of the period under survey in this guide and the later portion.

The initial struggle concerned poetic language, figures of speech, and the subject matter of verse. This struggle swirled around the doctrine of "Imagism," which was for a time an international matter, part of the conflict occurring in London and part of it in the United States. The two leaders (and chief combatants) were Amy Lowell and Ezra Pound:

Amy Lowell (1874–1925), *Six French Poets*, 1915
Amy Lowell, *Tendencies in Modern American Poetry*, 1917
Amy Lowell, *Selected Poems*, ed. John Livingston Lowes, 1928
Ezra Pound (1885–   ), *Personae*, 1909
Ezra Pound, *The Spirit of Romance*, 1910
Ezra Pound, *Ripostes*, 1912
Ezra Pound, *Instigations*, 1920
Ezra Pound, *Hugh Selwyn Mauberley*, 1920
Ezra Pound, *Poems, 1918–21*, 1921
Ezra Pound, *Personae: The Collected Poems of Ezra Pound*, 1926
Ezra Pound, *Make It New*, 1934
Ezra Pound, *The Cantos: I–CXVII*, 1970
The Letters of Ezra Pound, 1907–1941, ed. D. D. Paige, 1950

Two Americans, in addition to Pound and Lowell, were major contributors:

1 7 4

"H. D." (Hilda Doolittle Aldington, 1886–1961), *Collected Poems*, 1925 (reprinted 1940)
John Gould Fletcher (1886–1950), *Preludes and Symphonies*, 1922 (reprinted 1930)
John Gould Fletcher, *Selected Poems*, 1938

The English poets of the group were Richard Aldington, T. E. Hulme, F. S. Flint, and, briefly, D. H. Lawrence.

The movement of Imagism in the United States can also be followed in:

Some Imagist Poets, 1915
Some Imagist Poets, 1916
Some Imagist Poets, 1917 (These three volumes were under the general supervision of Amy Lowell.)
An Imagist Anthology, 1930

24 · *The Poetic Renaissance: Fulfillment*

The lasting achievements of the Poetic Renaissance, so far as popular favor is concerned, must be distinguished from its lasting achievements among the passionate few devoted to "advanced" poetry. The four or five names most generally known achieved a general audience denied to the others. These poets fall into two groups: those from the Middle West and those associated with New England.

> Vachel Lindsay (1879–1931), *General William Booth Enters into Heaven and Other Poems*, 1913
> Vachel Lindsay, *The Congo and Other Poems*, 1914
> Vachel Lindsay, *Collected Poems*, 1925
> Vachel Lindsay, *Selected Poems*, 1931
> Edgar Lee Masters (1869–1950), *Spoon River Anthology*, 1915
> Carl Sandburg (1878–1967), *Chicago Poems*, 1916
> Carl Sandburg, *Cornhuskers*, 1918
> Carl Sandburg, *Smoke and Steel*, 1920
> Carl Sandburg, *Slabs of the Sunburnt West*, 1922
> Carl Sandburg, *The People, Yes*, 1936

The two poets associated with New England are:

> Robert Frost (1874–1963), *A Boy's Will*, 1913
> Robert Frost, *North of Boston*, 1914
> Robert Frost, *Mountain Interval*, 1916
> Robert Frost, *New Hampshire*, 1923
> Robert Frost, *The Poetry of Robert Frost*, ed. Edward Connery Lathem, 1969
> Edwin Arlington Robinson (1869–1935), *Collected Poems*, 1937 (replaces earlier volumes by the same title issued in 1921, 1927, 1929, and 1931; and includes, *inter alia*, *The Town Down the River*, 1910; *The Man Against the Sky*, 1916; *Merlin*, 1917; *Lancelot*, 1920; *Roman Bartholow*, 1923; *The Man Who Died Twice*, 1924; *Tristram*, 1927; *Cavender's House*, 1929; and *King Jasper*, 1935)
> Edwin Arlington Robinson, *Selected Poems*, ed. Morton Dauwen Zabel, 1965

25 · *The Impact of World War I*

Perhaps the most difficult job of the historical imagination among students of American literature too young to have lived through the period is to envision the profound shock that World War I gave to America. There had been other recent wars, often bloody and determined—one between Russia and Japan and two Balkan wars—but these were in remote places. Suddenly Western Europe burst into flame; and it is hard to say whether the Americans were more disturbed by the revelation of international perfidy on a grand scale or by reports of the vast, gray-green German army pouring through Belgium. The war shortly came to be interpreted in familiar fashion as a conflict between good and evil. In this melodrama, Germany was the villain, France was thought of in terms of Joan of Arc, and Great Britain appeared as the old bulldog full of pluck, losing campaigns but winning the last battle. The fact that the Archduke Francis Ferdinand of Austria had been murdered in Sarajevo was passed over, the "scrap of paper" having obliterated other moral considerations. The sinking of the *Lusitania* underlined the moral issues. That the war was far more complex, deadly, destructive, monotonous, and self-seeking than this simple pattern of right and wrong was only gradually understood, and the contrast between the theory of an age-old struggle between good and evil and the later revelation of military stupidities and diplomatic irresponsibility produced in the twenties a new spirit of cynicism.

This list of books by American writers reporting on the war or supporting the interpretation of the conflict as a simple moral issue is representative. It omits books by British and French writers that were equally influential in shaping American opinion.

Mildred Aldrich (1853–1928), *A Hilltop on the Marne*, 1915

Gertrude Atherton (1857–1948), *Life in the War Zone*, 1916

Richard Harding Davis (1864–1916), *With the Allies*, 1914 (This contains a great picture of the German armies marching endlessly through Brussels. See Chs. 1, 3, 6, 10.)

Arthur Guy Empey (1883–1963), *Over the Top*, 1917 (Vastly popular, this book narrates with sang-froid the experiences of an American volunteer in the British army. See the useful "Tommy's Dictionary of the Trenches," pp. 281 ff.)

Floyd Gibbons (1887–1939), *And "They Thought We Wouldn't Fight,"* 1918 (By an immensely influential war correspondent. For characteristic passages, see Chs. 1, 7, 8.)

Robert Herrick (1868–1938), *The World Decision*, 1916 (By an enthusiast for the cause of the Allies. See especially the section on France.)

Frederick Palmer (1873–1958), *My Year of the Great War*, 1915 (By a correspondent and military historian. Note especially Chs. 2, 9, 11.)

Edith Wharton (1862–1937), *Fighting France*, 1915

Brand Whitlock (1869–1934, *Belgium*, 1918–19 (by the American minister to Belgium)

Brand Whitlock, *Letters and Journal*, ed. Allan Nevins, 2 vols., 1936 (The material on the German march into Belgium illuminates the American attitude.)

Woodrow Wilson (1856–1924), *In Our First Year of War*, 1918 (See especially his speeches to Congress asking for a declaration of war, April 2, 1917, and giving terms of peace, January 9, 1918, as well as his interpretation of the war as a moral crusade.)

Owen Wister (1860–1938), *The Pentecost of Calamity*, 1915 (Virtually a classic, this book persuaded Americans that Germany was wrong.)

26 · *The New Spirit and the War Novels*

Even before disillusioned young Americans returned from Europe to write a library of war novels, a sense of stir, vaguely referred to as the "New Spirit" was felt by a younger generation in revolt against their elders. Partly this was directed against the still powerful Genteel Tradition; partly this was caused by the American discovery of Freud and his contemporary psychologists (A. A. Brill published a translation of Freud's *The Interpretation of Dreams* in 1913 and followed this by other works); partly the movement represented an awareness of new tendencies in painting (the Armory Show of 1913 was the discovery by America of such European developments as distortion, nonrepresentational art, and similar "radical" ideas), in poetry (the French symbolists enjoyed a new vogue), in Continental drama, and in new experiments in prose, particularly fiction (the stream-of-consciousness method). The war novels capitalized on the belief that the elder generation failed to understand the world and drove American fiction farther in the direction of naturalism. The books here listed are accordingly divided into two sections: (i) books expressing the feeling of the younger generation in revolt; and (ii) novels reporting on the conviction of participants in the war that life was not in the least like the orthodox American interpretation of battle, sex, idealism, or democracy.

I

New writers appeared to question conventional American postulates about literary values, idealism as a social force, and the traditional classics of American letters. They may be roughly divided into critics of society and critics of literature, though most writers were both.

EMPHASIS ON LITERARY CRITICISM

Max Eastman (1883–1969), *The Enjoyment of Poetry*, 1913 (Poetry must either disappear or change its nature in an age of science.)
Henry L. Mencken (1880–1956), *A Book of Prefaces*, 1917
Henry L. Mencken, *Selected Prejudices*, 1927 (chosen from suc-

cessive volumes of *Prejudices* for 1919, 1920, 1922, 1924, 1926, 1927)

Joel E. Spingarn (1875–1939), *The New Criticism*, 1911

Joel E. Spingarn, *Creative Criticism: Essays on the Unity of Genius and Taste*, 1917 (includes the preceding volume.)

EMPHASIS ON CULTURAL AND SOCIAL CRITICISM

Randolph Bourne (1886–1918), *Youth and Life*, 1913

Randolph Bourne, *Untimely Papers*, 1919

Randolph Bourne, *The History of a Literary Radical*, 1920

Waldo Frank (1889–1967), *Our America*, 1919

Waldo Frank, *The Rediscovery of America*, 1928

George Santayana (1863–1952), *The Genteel Tradition at Bay*, 1931

EXPERIMENTATION BASED ON EUROPEAN INFLUENCES

William E. Leonard (1876–1944), *Two Lives*, 1922 (published in 1925)

Gertrude Stein (1874–1946), *Selected Writings*, ed. Carl Van Vechten, 1946

FICTION REPRESENTING THE "NEW MANNER," THE "NEW PSYCHOLOGY"

Sherwood Anderson (1876–1941), *Winesburg, Ohio*, 1919

Sherwood Anderson, *Poor White*, 1920

Sherwood Anderson, *Dark Laughter*, 1925

Floyd Dell (1887–1969), *Mooncalf*, 1920

Floyd Dell, *The Briary Bush*, 1921

Floyd Dell, *Janet March*, 1923

Zona Gale (1874–1938), *Miss Lulu Bett*, 1920

Ernest Poole (1880–1950), *The Harbor*, 1915

II

THE WAR NOVELS

Thomas Boyd (1898–1935), *Through the Wheat*, 1923

E. E. Cummings (1894–1962), *The Enormous Room*, 1922

John Dos Passos (1896–1970), *One Man's Initiation*, 1920

John Dos Passos, *Three Soldiers*, 1921

William Faulkner (1897–1962), *Soldiers' Pay*, 1926
William Faulkner, *Sartoris*, 1929
F. Scott Fitzgerald (1896–1940), *This Side of Paradise*, 1920
(Although Fitzgerald saw no fighting, this book represents the disruption caused by such forces as the draft and enlistment.)
Ernest Hemingway (1899–1961), *The Sun Also Rises*, 1926
.Ernest Hemingway, *A Farewell to Arms*, 1929
"William March" (William Edward March Campbell, 1893–1954), *Company K*, 1933

27 · *The New Spirit in Fiction and Poetry*

The general stir in twentieth-century American letters cannot be closely defined, but in a broad sense the shift from the older basis of an art conceived as representation and as governed by ethical idealism to a new theory of art resulted from the fusion, during World War I and after, of (a) renewed awareness of contemporary or recent European experimentation in all the arts; (b) the long-run effects of American participation in the war and of such aftermaths as the Russian Revolution and worldwide anarchy; and (c) an increasing awareness that the psychology of the irrational (Freud, Jung, Adler) was only part of a universal revolt from the intellectual premises of rationalism into a movement that was to reach its climax in the philosophy of existentialism. The American response to the thought of Bergson ("creative evolution") is an unassessed element of some importance. Eventually interest in Bergson yielded to more dramatic philosophic outlooks of Europeans like Kierkegaard and Sartre. The shift conditioned all serious American writing, but may be especially traced in novelists less concerned with social commentary (than the writers in list 29, for instance) and, of course, in the poets.

THE "NEW FICTION"

Conrad Aiken (1889–   ), *Blue Voyage*, 1927
Conrad Aiken, *Great Circle*, 1933
Maxwell Bodenheim (1893–1954), *Replenishing Jessica*, 1925
William Faulkner (1897–1962), *The Sound and the Fury*, 1929
William Faulkner, *As I Lay Dying*, 1930
William Faulkner, *Sanctuary*, 1931
William Faulkner, *Light in August*, 1932
William Faulkner, *Absalom, Absalom!* 1936
William Faulkner, *The Hamlet*, 1940
F. Scott Fitzgerald (1896–1940), *The Beautiful and Damned*, 1922
F. Scott Fitzgerald, *Tender Is the Night*, 1934
Waldo Frank (1889–1967), *Rahab*, 1922
Ludwig Lewisohn (1882–1955), *The Case of Mr. Crump*, 1926

Thomas Wolfe (1900–1938), *Look Homeward, Angel,* 1929
Thomas Wolfe, *Of Time and the River,* 1935
Thomas Wolfe, *The Web and the Rock,* 1939
Thomas Wolfe, *You Can't Go Home Again,* 1940

POETRY IN THE "NEWER" MANNER

Leonie Adams (1899–   ), *Poems: A Selection,* 1954
Conrad Aiken, *The Jig of Forslin,* 1916
Conrad Aiken, *The Charnel Rose, Senlin (A Biography), and Other Poems,* 1918
Conrad Aiken, *John Deth, a Metaphysical Legend, and Other Poems,* 1930
Conrad Aiken, *Collected Poems,* 1953
Conrad Aiken, *The Morning Song of Lord Zero,* 1963
Louise Bogan (1897–   ), *Collected Poems, 1923–1953,* 1954
Hart Crane (1899–1932), *Collected Poems,* ed. Waldo Frank, 1933
E. E. Cummings (1894–1962), *Poems, 1923–1954,* 1954
E. E. Cummings, *95 Poems,* 1958
E. E. Cummings, *73 Poems,* 1963
T. S. Eliot (1888–1965), *Poems,* 1920
T. S. Eliot, *The Waste Land,* 1922
T. S. Eliot, *Ash-Wednesday,* 1930
T. S. Eliot, *Four Quartets,* 1943 (*Burnt Norton* began the series in 1936. The later parts, published separately, are *East Coker,* 1940; *The Dry Salvages,* 1941; *Little Gidding,* 1942.)
T. S. Eliot, *Collected Poems, 1909–1962,* 1963
Edna St. Vincent Millay (1892–1950), *Collected Poems,* comp. Norman Millay, 1956
Wallace Stevens (1879–1955), *Collected Poems,* 1954
Wallace Stevens, *Opus Posthumous,* ed. Samuel French Morse, 1957
William Carlos Williams (1883–1963), *Collected Later Poems,* 1950, revised edition, 1963
William Carlos Williams, *Collected Earlier Poems,* 1951
William Carlos Williams, *Pictures from Breughel and Other Poems,* 1962
William Carlos Williams, *Paterson,* 1963 (the first edition of the complete collected poem, originally published in five separate parts)

28 · *The Fictional Attack on "Puritanism"*

Skepticism about the social fabric of American life quickly appeared in fiction. The formula of business life seemed to many novelists to produce only a smothered dissatisfaction, inasmuch as economic success was no guarantee of individual happiness. The commonly accepted pattern of bourgeois respectability came to be dubbed "Puritanism." Already under attack in other categories of fiction, "Puritanism" was identified with social hypocrisy—marriage and a happy ending were no longer the climax of the novel. In some novels it was assumed that the ordinary American belief that class distinction was unknown in this country was a fallacy, and in others the identification of felicity with materialistic comfort was exposed as hypocritical. Still others led a crusade for a return to old-fashioned idealism and the rights of man, particularly in the Sacco-Vanzetti case, and against the crushing pressures of city life.

Bernard De Voto (1897–1955), *We Accept with Pleasure*, 1934 (turns on the Sacco-Vanzetti case)

John Dos Passos (1896–1970), *Manhattan Transfer*, 1925

John Dos Passos, *USA*, 1937 (comprises *The 42nd Parallel*, 1930; *1919*, 1932; *The Big Money*, 1936)

F. Scott Fitzgerald (1896–1940), *The Great Gatsby*, 1925

F. Scott Fitzgerald, *The Last Tycoon*, 1941 (unfinished; published in an edition including *The Great Gatsby* and *Selected Stories*)

Sinclair Lewis (1885–1951), *Main Street*, 1920

Sinclair Lewis, *Babbit*, 1922

Sinclair Lewis, *Arrowsmith*, 1925

Sinclair Lewis, *Elmer Gantry*, 1927

Sinclair Lewis, *Dodsworth*, 1929

Sinclair Lewis, *It Can't Happen Here*, 1935 (against incipient Fascism)

John P. Marquand (1893–1960), *The Late George Apley*, 1937

John P. Marquand, *Wickford Point*, 1939

John P. Marquand, *H. M. Pulham, Esq.*, 1941

John P. Marquand, *Sincerely, Willis Wayde*, 1955

Edmund Wilson (1895–1972), *I Thought of Daisy*, 1929

29 · *The Revaluation of American Culture*

The tremendous shock given to traditional mores by the forces outlined in the three foregoing sections disturbed complacency and necessitated a reassessment of American values. Some of this reassessment appears in the books in lists 26 and 27. Deeper problems were raised than could be solved in fiction or poetry alone. Were the traditional religious and philosophic assumptions of the national culture no longer viable? Ought the bases of modern life to be shifted to some new set of postulates more in keeping with twentieth-century science? Or should the thoughtful citizen simply assume that the error originated in the nineteenth century with its romantic belief in human goodness? If so, was not the solution of the modern problem a return to a more ancient wisdom—the traditional humanism of the West? During World War I, the twenties and thirties, and on into World War II and its aftermath, the discussion continued—if indeed it has ever ceased. Characteristic documents are here listed:

Robert M. Hutchins (1899–   ), *The Higher Learning in America*, 1936
Matthew Josephson (1899–   ), *Portrait of the Artist as an American*, 1930
Joseph Wood Krutch (1893–1970), *The Modern Temper*, 1929
Joseph Wood Krutch, *The Twelve Seasons*, 1949
Walter Lippmann (1899–   ), *A Preface to Politics*, 1913
Walter Lippmann, *A Preface to Morals*, 1929
Henry L. Mencken (1880–1956), *The American Credo*, 1920 (with George Jean Nathan)
Henry L. Mencken, *Notes on Democracy*, 1926
Henry L. Mencken, *Treatise on Right and Wrong*, 1934
James Harvey Robinson (1863–1936), *The Mind in the Making*, 1921
Harold E. Stearns (1891–1943), *America and the Young Intellectual*, 1921

The conservative position tended to be that of either the Neo-

Humanists or the Neo-Confederates. Representative books by the Neo-Humanists are these:

Irving Babbitt (1865–1933), *Rousseau and Romanticism*, 1919
Irving Babbitt, *Democracy and Leadership*, 1924
William C. Brownell (1851–1928), *Standards*, 1917
William C. Brownell, *Democratic Distinction in America*, 1927
John Jay Chapman (1862–1933), *Learning and Other Essays*, 1910
John Jay Chapman, *Greek Genius and Other Essays*, 1915
Paul Elmer More (1864–1937), *The Drift of Romanticism*, 1913
Paul Elmer More, *Aristocracy and Justice*, 1915
Paul Elmer More, *The Demon of the Absolute*, 1928
Albert Jay Nock (1872?–1945), *The Theory of Education in the United States*, 1932
Stuart Pratt Sherman (1881–1926), *On Contemporary Literature*, 1917
Stuart Pratt Sherman, *The Main Stream*, 1927

Two representative books in the Neo-Confederate or Neo-Agrarian formula, out of which was to come an important movement in criticism, follow:

Donald Davidson (1893–1968), *The Attack on Leviathan*, 1938
[Twelve Southerners], *I'll Take My Stand*, 1930

Following World War II, the reassessment of American culture concentrated less on ancient wisdom than on survival in "one world," political debates, urban ills, and minority rights. Some observers, however, were able to stand apart from immediate issues, or at least to discuss these issues in a larger framework. Their commentary is frequently more harsh than the criticism of the twenties but none the less valuable as a reflection of the times.

James Baldwin (1924–   ), *Notes of a Native Son*, 1955
James Baldwin, *Nobody Knows My Name: More Notes of a Native Son*, 1961
Francis Biddle (1886–1968), *The Fear of Freedom*, 1952
William O. Douglas (1898–   ), *America Challenged*, 1960

Leslie A. Fiedler (1917–   ), *An End to Innocence: Essays on Culture and Politics,* 1955

Eli Ginzberg (1911–   ), *The Optimistic Tradition and American Youth,* 1962

Herbert Gold (1924–   ), *The Age of Happy Problems,* 1962

Sidney Hook (1902–   ), *Heresy, Yes—Conspiracy, No!* 1953

Sidney Hook, *The Paradoxes of Freedom,* 1962

Dwight Macdonald (1906–   ), *Against the American Grain,* 1962

Marya Mannes (1904–   ), *More in Anger,* 1958

Richard Rovere (1915–   ), *The American Establishment and Other Reports, Opinions, and Speculations,* 1962

Philip Wylie (1902–1971), *Generation of Vipers,* 1942

30 · The Search for a Usable Past

Van Wyck Brooks's famous phrase, "the search for a usable past," may be taken to describe another turn in the cultural revolution that began in the second decade of the century. Merely to find fault with the present state of American culture because of a supposedly bad tradition was insufficient; it was necessary, paradoxically enough, to find a new tradition, or to reinterpret an old one so that it could lend support to the new valuations, hazy as those valuations might be. American history, especially American cultural history, was critically viewed in the light of suppositions agreeable to the postwar world. Among the results was the dethronement of many "classic" American authors (like Longfellow, Whittier, and Lowell), an enlarged sense of the importance of others (Melville, Thoreau, and Henry James), and a search for relevant values in the fine arts (including architecture) as these had developed in the New World, in politics, and in cultural history. History ceased to be political or military in the older sense, and was rewritten in social terms; biography came to dwell on the humanizing imperfections of the subject no less than on his achievements. A kind of amused tolerance for human weakness was for a time characteristic of much exploration of the past.

Carl Becker (1873–1945), *The Declaration of Independence,* 1922 (a distinguished example of the history of ideas)

Gamaliel Bradford (1863–1932), *American Portraits,* 1922

Gamaliel Bradford, *Damaged Souls,* 1923 (These two books represent the method known as "psychography.")

Van Wyck Brooks (1886–1962), *The Wine of the Puritans,* 1908

Van Wyck Brooks, *America's Coming-of-Age,* 1915

Van Wyck Brooks, *Letters and Leadership,* 1918

Van Wyck Brooks, *The Ordeal of Mark Twain,* 1920

Van Wyck Brooks, *The Pilgrimage of Henry James,* 1925 (The general thesis of the last two volumes is that these authors were frustrated by forces in American culture analyzed in the three preceding volumes.)

Ludwig Lewisohn (1882–1955), *Expression in America,* 1932 (a survey of American literature in terms of emotional and psychic energy and frustration)

Alfred Lief, ed., *The Dissenting Opinions of Mr. Justice Holmes,* 1929 (Because he interpreted the law in terms of social development rather than of metaphysical absolutes, Holmes was highly satisfactory to this group, which did not realize he was a conservative at heart.)

John Macy (1877–1932), *The Spirit of American Literature,* 1913 (the earliest of the "debunking" literary histories)

Lewis Mumford (1895–   ), *Sticks and Stones,* 1924 (a history of architecture in America in its social and cultural context)

Lewis Mumford, *The Golden Day,* 1926 (on American literature in the early nineteenth century)

Lewis Mumford, *The Brown Decades,* 1931 (a reinterpretation of the culture of the brownstone-front period)

Vernon L. Parrington (1871–1929), *Main Currents in American Thought,* 3 vols., 1927–1930 (the most influential of the histories of ideas, despite its tendentiousness)

James Harvey Robinson (1863–1936), *The New History,* 1912 (a plea for social history)

Constance Rourke (1885–1941), *American Humor,* 1931 (cultural history from an unorthodox point of view)

31 · *The New Method in the Historical Novel*

Even after the success of *The Red Badge of Courage* (1895) the American historical novel clung to the formula of romance. The hero was at the right hand of some great figure during an important historical crisis and helped to bring about the victory of righteousness in American terms; the villain was invariably on the losing side; the heroine, unsoiled, fell into the hero's arms in the last chapter, where wedding bells brought history and fiction to a successful climax.

In the new novel of history, events were not seen in pattern but as they must have appeared to an ordinary human being only vaguely aware of their outcome and far from aware of their historical significance. This central character is, moreover, filled with human frailty, comes into contact with greatness only casually and not always comprehendingly, and at the end does not necessarily succeed in either his own purposes or the historical mission he is supposed to further. In one sense the new method was dedicated to determinism, since it assumed that human nature does not change; in another sense it showed the American past as the free creation of countless forgotten human beings.

James Boyd (1888–1944), *Drums*, 1925
James Boyd, *Marching On*, 1927
James Boyd, *Long Hunt*, 1930
Walter Van Tilburg Clark (1909–1971), *The Ox-Bow Incident*, 1940
Paul Corey (1903–   ), *Three Miles Square*, 1937
Paul Corey, *The Road Returns*, 1940
Clifford Dowdey (1904–   ), *Bugles Blow No More*, 1939
Walter D. Edmonds (1903–   ), *Rome Haul*, 1929
Howard Fast (1914–   ), *The Unvanquished*, 1942
Esther Forbes (1894?–1967), *O Genteel Lady!* 1926
Esther Forbes, *A Mirror for Witches*, 1928
Esther Forbes, *Paradise*, 1937
Michael Foster (1904–   ), *American Dream*, 1937
A. B. Guthrie, Jr. (1901–   ), *The Big Sky*, 1947
Emerson Hough (1857–1923), *The Covered Wagon*, 1922

MacKinlay Kantor (1904–   ), *Long Remember,* 1934
MacKinlay Kantor, *Andersonville,* 1955
Joseph Stanley Pennell (1908–   ), *The History of Rome Hanks and Kindred Matters,* 1944
Kenneth Roberts (1885–1957), *Arundel,* 1930
Kenneth Roberts, *Rabble in Arms,* 1933
Kenneth Roberts, *Northwest Passage,* 1937
O. E. Rölvaag (1876–1931), *Giants in the Earth,* 1927
Mari Sandoz (1901–1966), *Slogum House,* 1937
Evelyn Scott (1893–   ), *The Wave,* 1929
Wallace Stegner (1909–   ), *The Big Rock Candy Mountain,* 1943
Wallace Stegner, *Angle of Repose,* 1971
Robert Penn Warren (1905–   ), *Brother to Dragons,* 1953 (verse)
Robert Penn Warren, *Band of Angels,* 1955
Glenway Wescott (1901–   ), *The Grandmothers,* 1927

H · THE TWENTIES

32 · *The Revival of the Exotic*

The twenties have become fabulous, but in addition to being the decade of H. L. Mencken, F. Scott Fitzgerald, Edna St. Vincent Millay, and other writers thought to represent rebellion against the mores inherited from the previous century, they also continued a tradition of the nineties—the mood and manner of the esoteric writing of the *fin de siècle* group. This approach to literature emphasized manner, liked to be knowledgeable about persons and places not revealed to the multitude, pretended to accept sex as an amusing game, and determined at all costs to enjoy an existence rescued from tediousness by an incessant parade of novelty, snobbery, and the recherché. Not all the authors listed below exhibit all these qualities, but they have in common what is known as "manner"—that is, an unusual or excessive interest either in style for its own sake, in novelties in literary construction for their own sake, or in a dandiacal attitude toward art, human beings, or life in general.

James Branch Cabell (1879-1958), *The Soul of Melicent,* 1913 (revised and republished as *Domnei,* 1920)
James Branch Cabell, *The Rivet in Grandfather's Neck,* 1915
James Branch Cabell, *The Cream of the Jest,* 1917
James Branch Cabell, *Beyond Life,* 1919
James Branch Cabell, *Jurgen,* 1919
James Branch Cabell, *Figures of Earth,* 1921
John Erskine (1879–1951), *The Private Life of Helen of Troy,* 1925
Joseph Hergesheimer (1880-1954), *The Three Black Pennys,* 1917
Joseph Hergesheimer, *Java Head,* 1919
Joseph Hergesheimer, *Linda Condon,* 1919
Joseph Hergesheimer, *The Bright Shawl,* 1922
Joseph Hergesheimer, *Cytherea,* 1922
Joseph Hergesheimer, *Balisand,* 1924
Robert Nathan (1894–   ), *The Bishop's Wife,* 1928

Robert Nathan, *One More Spring*, 1933
Robert Nathan, *Journey of Tapiola*, 1938
Robert Nathan, *Winter in April*, 1938
Robert Nathan, *Portrait of Jennie*, 1940
Carl Van Vechten (1880–1964), *Peter Whiffle*, 1922
Carl Van Vechten, *The Tattooed Countess*, 1924
Thornton Wilder (1897–   ), *The Cabala*, 1926
Thornton Wilder, *The Bridge of San Luis Rey*, 1927
Thornton Wilder, *The Woman of Andros*, 1930
Thornton Wilder, *The Ides of March*, 1948
Elinor Wylie (1885–1928), *The Venetian Glass Nephew*, 1925
Elinor Wylie, *The Orphan Angel*, 1926
Elinor Wylie, *Mr. Hodge and Mr. Hazard*, 1928

33 · *Drama in the Twenties and After*

Eugene O'Neill continued to build his reputation during the twenties and thirties (see list 22), but he was not alone in producing work of literary merit. The theater had progressed technically for almost a century; now the playwrights were catching up and growing up. Outspoken on social, political, and marital issues, they educated as well as entertained their audiences. They borrowed techniques from German expressionists and American vaudeville for satire. They abandoned the illusion of the fourth wall by extending the stage over the footlights; and by incorporating masks and music into serious drama, they reinforced symbolic action. The temptation to classify their work is great, but it is wiser simply to list major successful playwrights and some of their representative plays. To illustrate the development of drama, the plays are listed in chronological order.

Elmer Rice (1892–1967), *The Adding Machine*, 1923
Owen Davis (1874–1956), *Icebound*, 1923
Maxwell Anderson (1888–1959), *What Price Glory?* 1924 (with Laurence Stallings)
Maxwell Anderson, *Winterset*, 1935
George Kaufman (1889–1961), *Beggar on Horseback*, 1924 (with Marc Connelly)
George Kaufman, *You Can't Take It with You*, 1936 (with Moss Hart)
George Kelly (1887–   ), *The Show-Off*, 1924
Sidney Howard (1891–1939), *They Knew What They Wanted*, 1924
Sidney Howard, *The Silver Cord*, 1926
John Howard Lawson (1895–   ), *Processional*, 1925
Paul Green (1894–   ), *In Abraham's Bosom*, 1927
Philip Barry (1896–1949), *Holiday*, 1929
Philip Barry, *Hotel Universe*, 1930
Marc Connelly (1890–   ), *The Green Pastures*, 1930
S. N. Behrman (1893–   ), *Biography*, 1932
Robert E. Sherwood (1896–1955), *The Petrified Forest*, 1935
Robert E. Sherwood, *Idiot's Delight*, 1936

Robert E. Sherwood, *There Shall Be No Night,* 1940
Sidney Kingsley (1906–   ), *Dead End,* 1935
Clifford Odets (1906–1963), *Waiting for Lefty,* 1935
Clifford Odets, *Awake and Sing!,* 1935
Thornton Wilder (1897–   ), *Our Town,* 1938
Thornton Wilder, *The Skin of Our Teeth,* 1942
Lillian Hellman (1905–   ), *The Little Foxes,* 1939
Lillian Hellman, *Another Part of the Forest,* 1946
Lillian Hellman, *Toys in the Attic,* 1960

34 · *Poetry in the Twenties and After*

Under the impetus of T. S. Eliot and of the issues raised by the war and the postwar world, the writers of the Poetic Renaissance (see lists 23 and 24) ceased to be novel. American poetry began a slow drift away from verse possessing formality of pattern, a "public" style, and acceptance of the traditional vocabulary. The new movement produced verse characterized by a growing difficulty of style, an extreme use of allusion, private symbolism, and the loosening of stanza structure within the patterns of regular meter. The influence of seventeenth-century English verse, particularly that of the metaphysicals, was strongly felt; and toward the end of the phase, some of the verse of this order was written by the "New Critics." In the present list of titles, older or more conservative poets are named under I, and representatives of the newer phase appear under II.

I

Léonie Adams (See list 27.)
Conrad Aiken (See list 27.)
Witter Bynner (1881–1968), *Selected Poems*, 1936
Robert P. Tristram Coffin (1892–1955), *Collected Poems*, new and enlarged edition, 1948
Robert S. Hillyer (1895–1961), *Collected Verse*, 1933
Edna St. Vincent Millay (See list 27.)
John G. Neihardt (1881–   ), *Collected Poems*, 1926
Lizette Woodworth Reese (1856–1935), *Selected Poems*, 1926
George Santayana (1863–1952), *Poems*, collected and revised edition, 1923
Ridgely Torrence (1875–1950), *Poems*, 1941
Mark Van Doren (1894–   ), *Collected and New Poems, 1924–1963*, 1963
William Carlos Williams (See list 27.)

II

John Peale Bishop (1892–1944), *Selected Poems*, 1941
E. E. Cummings (See list 27.)

1920–1972

Kenneth Fearing (1902–1961), *New and Selected Poems,* 1956
Robinson Jeffers (1887–1962), *Selected Poetry,* 1938
Archibald MacLeish (1892–   ), *Collected Poems, 1917–1952,*
   1952
Marianne Moore (1887–1972), *Complete Poems,* 1967
John Crowe Ransom (1888–   ), *Selected Poems,* third edi-
   tion, 1969
Allen Tate (1899–   ), *Poems, 1922–1947,* 1948, revised under
   the title *Poems,* 1960
Robert Penn Warren (1905–   ), *Selected Poems: New and
   Old: 1923–1966,* 1966
Elinor Wylie (1885–1928), *Collected Poems,* 1932

I · THE THIRTIES

35 · *The New Criticism*

Like any other fecund literary movement, the "New Criticism" is difficult to define. It shared with the movement of Neo-Humanism, which was one of its roots, a belief in the moral integrity of the work of art in its own right, but differed from that movement by insisting that the act of moral judgment was not synchronous with the creative act. The creative act (that is, art) is a serious human activity, to be judged in its own right and in its own light. Therefore the New Critics repudiated the sociological interpretation of literature, subordinated historical scholarship to the scanning of the text, adopted many of the tenets of irrational psychology, and insisted that the meaning of a work of art lies in the text of the work of art. If the New Critics thus returned criticism to a proper function, they made reading more difficult for the average reader who, when he was led by the New Criticism to discover so many latent difficulties in comprehending poetry, tended to turn elsewhere for good reading. The movement was strongly influenced by T. S. Eliot and I. A. Richards, began in the twenties, flowered in the thirties, and has now apparently made its contribution and is on the wane.

Mark Schorer, Josephine Miles, and Gordon McKenzie, eds., *Criticism: The Foundations of Modern Literary Judgment*, revised edition, 1958 (a good general introduction to the critical situation, the later selections in Part Two, "Form," being especially relevant)

Lawrence I. Lipking and A. Walton Litz, eds., *Modern Literary Criticism: 1900–1970*, 1972 (concentrates on Pound, Eliot, Richards, and Frye, but also contains sections on problems and methods, poet-critics, and continental criticism)

Conrad Aiken (1889–   ), *Scepticisms*, 1919 (an important predecessor of the New Criticism)

R. P. Blackmur (1904–1965), *The Double Agent*, 1935

R. P. Blackmur, *The Expense of Greatness*, 1940

R. P. Blackmur, *Language and Gesture*, 1952
Cleanth Brooks (1906–   ), *Modern Poetry and the Tradition*, 1939
Cleanth Brooks, *The Well-Wrought Urn*, 1947
Kenneth Burke (1897–   ), *Counter-Statement*, 1931
Kenneth Burke, *The Philosophy of Literary Form*, 1941
Kenneth Burke, *A Grammar of Motives*, 1945
Kenneth Burke, *A Rhetoric of Motives*, 1950
T. S. Eliot (1888–1965), *Selected Essays*, 1932
T. S. Eliot, *The Use of Poetry and the Use of Criticism*, 1933
William Empson (1906–   ), *Seven Types of Ambiguity*, 1930
Ezra Pound (1885–   ), *ABC of Reading*, 1934
Ezra Pound, *Literary Essays*, ed. T. S. Eliot, 1954
John Crowe Ransom (1888–   ), *The World's Body*, 1938
John Crowe Ransom, *The New Criticism*, 1941
I. A. Richards (1893–   ), *Principles of Literary Criticism*, 1924
I. A. Richards, *Practical Criticism: A Study of Literary Judgment*, 1929
Allen Tate (1899–   ), *Reactionary Essays*, 1936
Allen Tate, *Reason in Madness*, 1941
Allen Tate, *Essays of Four Decades*, 1968
Yvor Winters (1900–1968), *Primitivism and Decadence*, 1937
Yvor Winters, *Maule's Curse*, 1939
Yvor Winters, *In Defense of Reason*, 1947 (includes above two titles)

36 · *The Proletarian Movement in the Thirties*

The Great Depression and the New Deal turned the thirties into a period that at times seemed to forebode revolutionary change, and at other times promised a great fulfillment of American life through managed capitalism. There has always been a tradition of social radicalism in American literature; in the thirties this kind of writing tended to take shape as Marxian writing. American Marxist writing was devoted either to criticism or to proletarian fiction. By Marxist criticism, American literary development was reinterpreted. Whenever possible all American literary classics were listed on the side of left-wing change. Proletarian fiction, however, tended to make a member of the laboring class the hero-victim of class war. By the forties the Marxist critics had lost their vogue or changed their views, and the proletarian novelists, by dint of reiterating the same theme, had lost their following. The critics are listed under I, the novelists under II.

I

Victor F. Calverton (1900–1940), *The Newer Spirit: A Sociological Criticism of Literature*, 1925
Victor F. Calverton, *The Liberation of American Literature*, 1932
James T. Farrell (1904–   ), *A Note on Literary Criticism*, 1936
Joseph Freeman (1897–   ), *An American Testament*, 1936
Granville Hicks (1901–   ), *The Great Tradition*, 1933
Granville Hicks and others, eds., *Proletarian Literature in the United States*, 1935
Bernard Smith (1906–   ), *Forces in American Criticism*, 1939

II

Robert Cantwell (1908–   ), *Laugh and Lie Down*, 1931
Robert Cantwell, *Land of Plenty*, 1934
John Dos Passos (See lists 26 and 28.)
"Michael Gold" (Irving Granich, 1894–1967), *Jews Without Money*, 1930

Albert Halper (1904–   ), *Union Square*, 1933
Josephine Herbst (1897–1969), *Pity Is Not Enough*, 1933
Josephine Herbst, *The Executioner Waits*, 1934
Josephine Herbst, *Rope of Gold*, 1939
Meyer Levin (1905–   ), *The Old Bunch*, 1937
Grace Lumpkin (?–   ), *To Make My Bread*, 1932
John Steinbeck (1902–1968), *In Dubious Battle*, 1936
John Steinbeck, *The Grapes of Wrath*, 1939

37 · Neo-Naturalism in the Thirties and After

Scarcely to be distinguished from much proletarian fiction was the neo-naturalistic novel developed in the thirties and after. Emphasis was placed on environment. It was useless to struggle against social conditions, especially if one were a "little man." Even at higher levels freedom of the will was felt to be illusory. An especially grim phase of Neo-Naturalism was a small library of novels exposing the plight of the Negro in American life, hemmed in as he was not only by a crippling economic environment but also by racial tensions. It was felt to be inevitable, therefore, that the Negro should retaliate by an outburst of hatred against the white man, which became the subject of some of this fiction.

Nelson Algren (1909–   ), *Never Come Morning*, 1942
Nelson Algren, *The Man with the Golden Arm*, 1949
John Peale Bishop (1892–1944), *Act of Darkness*, 1935
James M. Cain (1892–   ), *The Postman Always Rings Twice*, 1934
Erskine Caldwell (1903–   ), *Tobacco Road*, 1932
Erskine Caldwell, *God's Little Acre*, 1933
Erskine Caldwell, *Journeyman*, 1935
Erskine Caldwell, *Trouble in July*, 1940
Erskine Caldwell, *Georgia Boy*, 1943
John Dos Passos (See lists 28 and 42.)
James T. Farrell (1904–   ), *Studs Lonigan*, 1935 (comprises *Young Lonigan*, 1932; *The Young Manhood of Studs Lonigan*, 1934; *Judgment Day*, 1935)
William Faulkner (See lists 27 and 42.)
John O'Hara (1905–1970), *Appointment in Samarra*, 1934
John O'Hara, *A Rage To Live*, 1949
Budd Schulberg (1914–   ), *What Makes Sammy Run*, 1941
Budd Schulberg, *The Disenchanted*, 1950 (a fictional life of F. Scott Fitzgerald)
Lillian Smith (1897–1966), *Strange Fruit*, 1944
Robert Penn Warren, *All the King's Men*, 1946
Jerome Weidman (1913–   ), *I Can Get It for You Wholesale*, 1937

1920–1972

Nathanael West (1904–1940), *Miss Lonelyhearts*, 1933
Nathanael West, *The Day of the Locust*, 1939
Ira Wolfert (1908–   ), *Tucker's People*, 1943
Maritta Wolff (1918–   ), *Night Shift*, 1942
Richard Wright (1908–1961), *Native Son*, 1940
Richard Wright, *The Outsider*, 1953
Richard Wright, *Lawd Today*, 1963

38 · *Prelude to World War II*

As in the case of World War I (see list 25), the understanding of a vast cultural convulsion takes the student beyond the realm of belles-lettres into an area in which intelligent writing is important, although the book in question may lack the stigmata of literature. Perhaps the best way to solve the dilemma is to confront it boldly.

The outbreak of World War II and subsequent American participation in the conflict found the nation far more aware of intellectual, cultural, and spiritual issues than was true in 1914. Warnings addressed to the American public by poets, novelists, and foreign correspondents, no less than by public men, were responsible for this awareness. Probably no serious American writing about public affairs since about 1935 has not been conditioned, to some degree, by the world issues of fascism, communism, and democracy; of the dictator state versus the democratic state; of materialism, agnosticism, or atheism versus religious faith, spiritual values, or faith in immaterial things. Sides are chosen under emotional pressures, and points of view are attacked with venom.

The following list, chronologically arranged, mingles both the prose of information and the prose of imagination to suggest the vast library devoted to the nature of the world struggle up to the time that World War II was transformed into the Cold War. Books are listed by a kind of rule-of-thumb process. Partisans of no point of view will be satisfied with the list, but here, as elsewhere, the intention is to suggest trends and movements rather than to be definitive.

Louis Adamic (1899–1951), *The Native's Return*, 1934
Walter Duranty (1884–1957), *I Write As I Please*, 1935
Frederic Prokosch (1908–   ), *The Asiatics*, 1935
Frederic Prokosch, *The Seven Who Fled*, 1937
Frederic Prokosch, *The Skies of Europe*, 1941
George Seldes (1890–   ), *Sawdust Caesar*, 1935

John Gunther (1910–   ), *Inside Europe*, 1936
Marvin Lowenthal (1890–   ), *The Jews of Germany*, 1936
Elliot Paul (1891–1958), *The Life and Death of a Spanish Town*, 1937
Stephen H. Roberts (1901–   ), *The House That Hitler Built*, 1937
Herbert L. Matthews (1900–   ), *Two Wars and More To Come*, 1938
Edgar Snow (1905–1972), *Red Star over China*, 1938
Edgar Snow, *The Battle for Asia*, 1941
Vincent Sheean (1899–   ), *Not Peace but a Sword*, 1939
Nora Waln (1895–   ), *Reaching for the Stars*, 1939
Ernest Hemingway (1899–1961), *For Whom the Bell Tolls*, 1940
Edmund Wilson (1895   ), *To the Finland Station*, 1940
William E. Dodd (1869–1940), *Ambassador Dodd's Diary*, 1941
Emily Hahn (1905–   ), *The Soong Sisters*, 1941
Joseph C. Harsch (1905   ), *Pattern for Conquest*, 1941
Douglas P. Miller (1892–   ), *You Can't Do Business with Hitler*, 1941
William L. Shirer (1904–   ), *Berlin Diary*, 1941
Howard K. Smith (1914–   ), *Last Train from Berlin*, 1942
Alexander Werth (1901–   ), *Moscow War Diary*, 1942
Joseph C. Grew (1880–1965), *Ten Years in Japan*, 1944
Sumner Welles (1892–1961), *The Time for Decision*, 1944

39 · The Literature of World War II

An enormous library of printed material was produced and is still being produced about American participation in World War II. This library is at once too vast and too recent to be evaluated. If, however, one confines oneself to selecting records of combat that seem to have directly influenced the American reading public, the task, although still insoluble, becomes smaller. Two varieties of battle report had influence: (i) nonimaginative work by participants or reporters, or by those in charge of great actions in the war; and (ii) imaginative reports, usually in the form of fiction. The following lists represent these two divisions; and each could of course be indefinitely extended.

I

Vannevar Bush (1890–   ), *Modern Arms and Free Men*, 1949
Dwight D. Eisenhower (1890–1969), *Crusade in Europe*, 1948
John Hersey (1914–   ), *Into the Valley*, 1943
John Hersey, *Hiroshima*, 1946
Ralph Ingersoll (1900–   ), *The Battle Is the Pay-Off*, 1943
George C. Marshall (1880–1959), *General Marshall's Report*, 1945
Samuel Eliot Morison (1887–   ), *History of U.S. Naval Operations in World War II*, Vol. I. *The Battle of the Atlantic, 1939–1943*, 1947 (the first of fifteen volumes)
"Ernie" (Ernest T.) Pyle (1900–1945), *Here Is Your War*, 1943
Robert E. Sherwood (1896–1955), *Roosevelt and Hopkins*, 1948
Edgar Snow (1905–1972), *The Pattern of Soviet Power*, 1945
William L. White (1900–   ), *Report on the Russians*, 1945

II

Lester Atwell (1908–   ), *Private*, 1958
Robert O. Bowen (1920–   ), *The Weight of the Cross*, 1951
Harry Brown (1917–   ), *A Walk in the Sun*, 1944
John Horne Burns (1916–1953), *The Gallery*, 1947
James Gould Cozzens (1903–   ), *Guard of Honor*, 1948

William Wister Haines (1908–   ), *Command Decision*, 1947
Alfred Hayes (1911–   ), *The Girl on the Via Flaminia*, 1949
Thomas Heggen (1919–1949), *Mr. Roberts*, 1946
Joseph Heller (1923–   ), *Catch-22*, 1955
John Hersey, *A Bell for Adano*, 1944
James Jones (1921–   ), *From Here to Eternity*, 1951
E. J. Kahn, Jr. (1916–   ), *The Peculiar War: Impressions of a Reporter in Korea*, 1952 (not fiction, but creates an atmosphere not unlike war fiction)
Norman Mailer (1923–   ), *The Naked and the Dead*, 1948
John P. Marquand (1893–1960), *So Little Time*, 1943
Carson McCullers (1917–1967), *Reflections in a Golden Eye*, 1941 (concerns the "peacetime" army)
James A. Michener (1907–   ), *Tales of the South Pacific*, 1947
Edward Newhouse (1912–   ), *The Iron Chain*, 1946
Lionel Shapiro (1908–   ), *The Sixth of June*, 1955
Irwin Shaw (1913–   ), *The Young Lions*, 1948
William Styron (1925–   ), *The Long March*, 1952
Herman Wouk (1915–   ), *The Caine Mutiny*, 1951

40 · *The Cold War and the Political Problem*

No victory ever left a nation less at ease than did victory in Asia and Europe. The problems remaining or newly appearing after VE-Day and VJ-Day seem in retrospect more complex than those before 1945. The evil of Fascism and Nazism was patent; so, too, was the sneak attack on Pearl Harbor. But the use of the atom bomb raised questions not only of power politics, espionage, and other problems of policy but also of morality. What good was science if it led the human race to destruction? What, moreover, was the nature of man if his latest performances were so doubtful or so evil? What was the nature of the democratic state if, on the one hand, it lay open to communist penetration and, on the other, produced the weak governments of France or the Labor government in Great Britain? And, above all, what was man's place in what seemed to be a hostile universe?

These philosophical or general questions were crisscrossed by problems growing out of investigation into "un-American" activities. Many investigators were more interested in publicity than in truth, and in questions centering on loyalty oaths, loyalty checks, and similar dubious modes of securing loyalty. Was loyalty the same as patriotism? Was patriotism inimical to or sympathetic with the United Nations? Could free men survive in a liberal state when the manipulation of "suspicion" proved to be politically possible? Such were some of the puzzles of the Cold War. The following lists of books are, again, suggestive only. But beginning with these as a base, the student can go further in almost any direction, finding a vast library in which to read.

I · THE PROBLEM OF SCIENCE

Vannevar Bush (1890–   ), *Science, the Endless Frontier,* 1945

Rachel L. Carson (1907–1964), *The Sea Around Us,* 1951

James B. Conant (1893–   ), *On Understanding Science,* 1947 (revised in 1951 under the title *Science and Common Sense*)

Fairfield Osborn (1887–   ), *Our Plundered Plant,* 1948

Hans Zinsser (1878–1940), *Rats, Lice and History,* 1935

II · THE PROBLEM OF POLITICS AND DIPLOMACY

Herbert Agar (1897–   ), *A Time for Greatness*, 1942
Alan Barth (1906–   ), *The Loyalty of Free Men*, 1951
Elmer Davis (1890–1958), *But We Were Born Free*, 1954
George F. Kennan (1904–   ), *American Diplomacy, 1900–1950*, 1951
Owen Lattimore (1900–   ), *Ordeal by Slander*, 1950
Walter Lippmann (1889–   ), *Essays in the Public Philosophy*, 1955
Edgar A. Mowrer (1892–   ), *The Nightmare of American Foreign Policy*, 1948
Henry A. Wallace (1888–1965), *The Century of the Common Man*, 1943
Wendell Willkie (1892–1944), *One World*, 1943

III · THE NEW NATIONALISM

Duncan Aikman (1889–1955), *The Turning Stream*, 1948
Stephen Vincent Benét (1898–1943), *John Brown's Body*, 1928 (included here because its general influence came much later than its date of publication)
Jonathan Daniels (1902–   ), *A Southerner Discovers the South*, 1938
Marshall B. Davidson (1907–   ), *Life in America*, 2 vols., 1951 (a pictorial history)
Paul Engle (1908–   ), *American Song*, 1934
John Gunther (1901–   ), *Inside USA*, 1947
Oscar Handlin (1915–   ), *The Uprooted*, 1951
Archibald MacLeish (1892–   ), *The Irresponsibles*, 1940
Ralph Barton Perry (1876–1954), *Characterisically American*, 1949
"Ernie" (Ernest T.) Pyle (1900–1945), *Home Country*, 1947

41 · *The Cold War and the Moral Problem*

See the preceding discussion in list 40.

Stringfellow Barr (1897–   ), *The Pilgrimage of Western Man*, 1949

Stringfellow Barr, *Let's Join the Human Race*, 1950

James Burnham (1905–   ), *The Managerial Revolution*, 1941

Norman Cousins (1912–   ), *Modern Man Is Obsolete*, 1945

Joseph Wood Krutch (1893–1970), *The Measure of Man*, 1954

Joshua Loth Liebman (1907–1948), *Peace of Mind*, 1946

Henry C. Link (1889–1952), *The Rediscovery of Morals*, 1947

Lewis Mumford (1895–   ), *The Condition of Man*, 1944

Lewis Mumford, *In the Name of Sanity*, 1954

Reinhold Niebuhr (1892–1971), *Moral Man and Immoral Society*, 1932

Reinhold Niebuhr, *The Nature and Destiny of Man*, 2 vols., 1941–1943

Reinhold Niebuhr, *The Children of Light and the Children of Darkness*, 1944

F. S. C. Northrop (1893–   ), *The Meeting of East and West*, 1946

Fulton J. Sheen (1895–   ), *Peace of Soul*, 1949

Walter Terence Stace (1886–1967), *Religion and the Modern Mind*, 1952

Paul Tillich (1886–1965), *The Courage To Be*, 1952

42 · *The Novel: Latest Phases*

Nothing is more difficult than to follow trends in fiction during the last few years. Readers eager for more detailed accounts than this one should consult the annual surveys of American literature in the *Britannica Book of the Year* and the *Americana Annual.* Many novels appearing in the last decade have, for one reason or another, been placed in other categories in this handbook. Some novels that appeared before Pearl Harbor have been included here because they seem to indicate interests characteristic of the last thirty years. It is at least possible that the present list may be suggestive of what is happening in the most elusive of literary forms.

Some established novelists seemed to take a new turn in certain instances:

John Dos Passos (1896–1970), *District of Columbia,* 1952 (composed of *Adventures of a Young Man,* 1939; *Number One,* 1943; and *The Grand Design,* 1949)
John Dos Passos, *Mid-Century,* 1961
William Faulkner (1897–1962), *Intruder in the Dust,* 1948
William Faulkner, *Requiem for a Nun,* 1951
William Faulkner, *A Fable,* 1954
William Faulkner, *The Town,* 1957 (With *The Hamlet,* 1940, and *The Mansion,* 1959, it forms the Snopes trilogy.)
William Faulkner, *The Reivers,* 1962
Ernest Hemingway (1899–1961), *The Old Man and the Sea,* 1952

The "hard-boiled" school continued to produce novels:

Nelson Algren (1909–   ), *A Walk on the Wild Side,* 1956
John Kerouac (1922–1969), *On the Road,* 1957
Norman Mailer (1923–   ), *The Deer Park,* 1955
Norman Mailer, *An American Dream,* 1965
Willard Motley (1912–   ), *Knock on Any Door,* 1947

One or another aspect of the psychological novel is exemplified in such titles as these:

James Baldwin (1924–   ), *Go Tell It on the Mountain*, 1953
John Barth (1930–   ), *The Floating Opera*, 1956
John Barth, *The End of the Road*, 1958
Donald Barthelme (1931–   ), *Snow White*, 1967
Saul Bellow (1915–   ), *The Adventures of Augie March*, 1953
Saul Bellow, *Herzog*, 1964
Saul Bellow, *Mr. Sammler's Planet*, 1970
Vance Bourjaily (1922–   ), *Confessions of a Spent Youth*, 1960
Paul Bowles (1911–   ), *The Sheltering Sky*, 1949
William Burroughs (1914–   ), *Naked Lunch*, 1959
Truman Capote (1924–   ), *Other Voices, Other Rooms*, 1948
John Cheever (1912–   ), *Bullet Park*, 1969
James Gould Cozzens, *By Love Possessed*, 1957
J. P. Donleavy (1926–   ), *The Ginger Man*, 1955 (revised edition, 1958; complete and unexpurgated edition, 1965)
George Garrett (1929–   ), *Which Ones Are the Enemy?* 1961
Caroline Gordon (1895–   ), *The Strange Children*, 1951
William Goyen (1915–   ), *The House of Breath*, 1950
John Hawkes (1925–   ), *The Cannibal*, 1948
John Hawkes, *The Blood Oranges*, 1971
Shirley Jackson (1919–1965), *The Haunting of Hill House*, 1959
Ken Kesey (1935–   ), *One Flew over the Cuckoo's Nest*, 1962
John Knowles (1926–   ), *A Separate Peace*, 1960
Jerzy Kosinski (1933–   ), *Steps*, 1968
William Maxwell (1908–   ), *The Château*, 1961
Carson McCullers (1917–1967), *The Heart Is a Lonely Hunter*, 1940
Wright Morris (1910–   ), *The Field of Vision*, 1956
Vladimir Nabokov (1899–   ), *Lolita*, 1955
Vladimir Nabokov, *Pale Fire*, 1962
Flannery O'Connor (1925–1965), *The Violent Bear It Away*, 1960
Sylvia Plath (1932–1963), *The Bell Jar*, 1966 (first published in 1963 under the pseudonym Victoria Lucas)
James Purdy (1923–   ), *Cabot Wright Begins*, 1964
Thomas Pynchon (? –   ), *V*, 1963

1920–1972

J. D. Salinger (1919–   ), *The Catcher in the Rye*, 1951
Jean Stafford (1915–   ), *The Mountain Lion*, 1947
William Styron (1925–   ), *Lie Down in Darkness*, 1951
John Updike (1932–   ), *Rabbit, Run*, 1960
John Updike, *Rabbit Redux*, 1971

Novels of social comment have been listed earlier. Other more recent titles are:

Evan Connell (1924–   ), *Mrs. Bridge*, 1958
Joan Didion (1934–   ), *Play It As It Lays*, 1970
Ralph Ellison (1914–   ), *Invisible Man*, 1952
Herbert Gold (1924–   ), *The Prospect Before Us*, 1954
John Hersey (1914–   ), *The Wall*, 1950
Laura Z. Hobson (1896–   ), *Gentleman's Agreement*, 1947
Randall Jarrell (1914–1965), *Pictures from an Institution*, 1954
Bernard Malamud (1914–   ), *The Assistant*, 1957
Mary McCarthy (1912–   ), *The Groves of Academe*, 1952
Arthur Miller (1915–   ), *Focus*, 1945
Joyce Carol Oates (1938–   ), *Them*, 1969
Marge Piercy (? –   ), *Going Down Fast*, 1969
Philip Roth (1933–   ), *Letting Go*, 1962
Philip Roth, *Portnoy's Complaint*, 1969
Hubert Selby (1924–   ), *Last Exit to Brooklyn*, 1964
Elizabeth Spencer (1921–   ), *The Voice at the Back Door*, 1956
Jean Stafford, *Boston Adventure*, 1944
William Styron, *Set This House on Fire*, 1960
Harvey Swados (1920–   ), *Out Went the Candle*, 1951
Kurt Vonnegut, Jr. (1922–   ), *Slaughterhouse-Five; or, The Children's Crusade*, 1969
Dan Wakefield (1932–   ), *Going All the Way*, 1970
Charles Webb (1939–   ), *The Graduate*, 1964

43 · *Drama: Latest Phases*

After the brilliance of the American drama between the years 1920 and 1940, a decline was inevitable. Only three playwrights of distinction emerged during the decade following World War II. Television has made obvious inroads, and economic problems seem forever incurable; yet drama survives and shows signs of new life in the little theaters off Broadway and in the college and community theaters across the country.

These playwrights showed staying power as well as talent between 1945 and 1955, and made for themselves international reputations:

Tennessee Williams (1914–   ), *The Glass Menagerie*, 1945
Tennessee Williams, *A Streetcar Named Desire*, 1947
Tennessee Williams, *Cat on a Hot Tin Roof*, 1955
Arthur Miller (1915–   ), *Death of a Salesman*, 1949
Arthur Miller, *The Crucible*, 1953
Arthur Miller, *The Price*, 1967
William Inge (1913–   ), *Come Back, Little Sheba*, 1950
William Inge, *Picnic*, 1953
William Inge, *The Dark at the Top of the Stairs*, 1957

A still younger generation of playwrights emerged in the fifties, some of them trained in television, all of them intent on commenting on American mores:

Robert Anderson (1917–   ), *Tea and Sympathy*, 1953
Paddy Chayefsky (1923–   ), *The Middle of the Night*, 1956
Gore Vidal (1925–   ), *Visit to a Small Planet*, 1957
Lorraine Hansberry (1930–1965), *A Raisin in the Sun*, 1959
Jack Gelber (1932–   ), *The Connection*, 1959

In the sixties, one playwright moved from off-Broadway, where he had instant success, to the Broadway theaters, where his meteoric career now shows signs of waning:

Edward Albee (1928–   ), *The Zoo Story*, 1959
Edward Albee, *The American Dream*, 1960
Edward Albee, *Who's Afraid of Virginia Woolf?* 1962
Edward Albee, *Tiny Alice*, 1964

The following playwrights (with the exception of Neil Simon, prolific and highly successful writer of Broadway comedies) have made their reputations in off-Broadway theaters. Most of them are, above all, experimental and polemical. The list is chronological to indicate trends.

Jack Richardson (1934–   ), *The Prodigal*, 1960
Arthur Kopit (1937–   ), *Oh Dad, Poor Dad, Mama's Hung You in the Closet and I'm Feelin' So Sad*, 1960
Murray Schisgal (1926–   ), *Luv*, 1963
LeRoi Jones (1934–   ), *Dutchman*, 1964
James Baldwin (1924–   ), *Blues for Mister Charlie*, 1964
William Hanley (1931–   ), *Slow Dance on the Killing Ground*, 1964
Neil Simon (1927–   ), *Barefoot in the Park*, 1964
Paul Zindel (1936–   ), *The Effect of Gamma Rays on Man-in-the-Moon Marigolds*, 1965
Jean-Claude van Itallie (1935–   ), *America Hurrah*, 1967
Jules Feiffer (1929–   ), *Little Murders*, 1967
Israel Horovitz (1939–   ), *The Indian Wants the Bronx*, 1968
Lonne Elder (? –   ), *Ceremonies in Dark Old Men*, 1969
Terence McNally (1940–   ), *Next*, 1969
Charles Gordone (1925–   ), *No Place To Be Somebody*, 1969
David Rabe (1940–   ), *The Basic Training of Pavlo Hummel*, 1971

44 · Poetry: Latest Phases

Generally speaking, the movement in poetry during the last two decades has been a movement away from the elliptic verse of T. S. Eliot and his contemporaries. Under the influence of W. H. Auden, Stephen Spender, and other British poets, verse has been restored to the duty of immediate communication in terms of living language; and though more difficult of apprehension than was true of the generation of Robert Frost, verse now tends to avoid the studied difficulties of Ezra Pound and his admirers. The later movements seem to endorse the practice of the Poetic Renaissance (see lists 23 and 24) in believing that public communication is part of the nature of literature. The following list is suggestive and concentrates on poets who began publishing before World War II:

W. H. Auden (1907–   ), *Collected Poetry*, 1945
W. H. Auden, *The Age of Anxiety*, 1947
W. H. Auden, *Homage to Clio*, 1960
W. H. Auden, *About the House*, 1965
Richard Eberhart (1904–   ), *Collected Poems, 1930–1960*, 1960
Robert Fitzgerald (1910–   ), *In the Rose of Time: Poems 1931–1956*, 1956
Stanley Kunitz (1905–   ), *Selected Poems: 1928–1958*, 1959
Theodore Morrison (1901–   ), *The Dream of Alcestis*, 1950
Muriel Rukeyser (1913–   ), *Poems 1935–1961*, 1961
Delmore Schwartz (1913–1966), *Summer Knowledge: New and Selected Poems, 1938–1958*, 1959
Winfield Townley Scott (1910–   ), *Collected Poems*, 1962

A younger group of poets earned their reputations through volumes published during the late forties and fifties:

John Berryman (1914–1972), *Homage to Mistress Bradstreet*, 1956
John Berryman, *His Toy, His Dream, His Rest: 308 Dream Songs*, 1968
Elizabeth Bishop (1911–   ), *Poems: North and South, A Cold Spring*, 1955

1920–1972

John Malcolm Brinnin (1916–   ), *The Sorrows of Cold Stone: Poems 1940–1950*, 1951

John Ciardi (1916–   ), *As If: Poems New and Selected*, 1955

Louis Coxe (1918–   ), *The Wilderness and Other Poems*, 1958

Jean Garrigue (1914–   ), *The Monument Rose*, 1953

Anthony Hecht (1923–   ), *The Summoning of Stones*, 1954

Randall Jarrell (1914–1965), *Selected Poems*, 1955

Robert Lowell (1917–   ), *Poems, 1938–1949*, 1950

Robert Lowell, *Life Studies*, 1959

William Meredith (1919–   ), *The Open Sea*, 1958

Howard Moss (1921–   ), *A Winter Come, A Summer Gone: Poems 1946–1960*, 1960

Howard Nemerov (1920–   ), *New and Selected Poems*, 1960

Charles Olson (1910–1970), *The Maximus Poems*, 1960

Kenneth Patchen (1911–   ), *Selected Poems*, 1947

Theodore Roethke (1908–1963), *Words for the Wind*, 1959

Karl Shapiro (1913–   ), *Poems, 1940–1953*, 1953

Peter Viereck (1916–   ), *Terror and Decorum: Poems, 1940–1948*, 1948

Theodore Weiss (1916–   ), *The Catch*, 1951

Reed Whittemore (1917–   ), *An American Takes a Walk and Other Poems*, 1956

Richard Wilbur (1921–   ), *Poems, 1943–1956*, 1957

A still younger group of poets who came to prominence in the late fifties and sixties can be sampled in two paperback collections, both of which claim to be the "new" poetry. The more academic group appears in *New Poets of England and America: Second Selection*, edited by Donald Hall and Robert Pack (Cleveland and New York, Meridian Books, 1962). The best experimental poets are collected in *The New American Poetry: 1945–1960*, edited by Donald M. Allen (New York, Grove Press, 1960). For more recent work, see *Poems of Our Moment*, edited by John Hollander (New York, Pegasus, 1968), and *Naked Poetry*, edited by Stephen Berg and Robert Mezey (Indianapolis, Bobbs-Merrill, 1969). The following list, representative of both groups, could easily be expanded:

A. R. Ammons (1926–   ), *Selected Poems*, 1968

John Ashbery (1927–   ), *The Tennis Court Oath*, 1962
Robert Creeley (1926–   ), *For Love—Poems 1950–1960*, 1962
Peter Davison (1928–   ), *The Breaking of the Day*, 1964
James Dickey (1923–   ), *Poems 1957–1967*, 1967
Alan Dugan (1923–   ), *Poems*, 1961
Robert Duncan (1919–   ), *Selected Poems*, 1959
Lawrence Ferlinghetti (1919–   ), *A Coney Island of the Mind*, 1958
Allen Ginsberg (1926–   ), *Howl and Other Poems*, 1956
Donald Hall (1928–   ), *Exiles and Marriages*, 1955
Daryl Hine (1936–   ), *The Wooden Horse*, 1965
Daniel Hoffman (1923–   ), *A Little Geste and Other Poems*, 1960
John Hollander (1929–   ), *A Crackling of Thorns*, 1958
Richard Howard (1929–   ), *Untitled Subjects*, 1969
LeRoi Jones (1934–   ), *Black Magic: Collected Poetry, 1961–1967*, 1969
Donald Justice (1925–   ), *Night Light*, 1967
Galway Kinnell (1927–   ), *What a Kingdom It Was*, 1960
Kenneth Koch (1925–   ), *The Pleasures of Peace and Other Poems*, 1969
Denise Levertov (1923–   ), *With Eyes at the Back of Our Heads*, 1959
John Logan (1923–   ), *The Zigzag Walk: Poems 1963–1968*, 1969
James Merrill (1926–   ), *Selected Poems*, 1961
W. S. Merwin (1927–   ), *The Moving Target*, 1963
Frank O'Hara (1926–1966), *Meditations in an Emergency*, 1957
George Oppen (1908–   ), *Of Being Numerous*, 1968
Sylvia Plath (1932–1966), *Ariel*, 1966
Adrienne Rich (1929–   ), *The Will To Change: Poems 1968–1970*, 1971
Anne Sexton (1928–   ), *Live or Die*, 1967
Louis Simpson (1923–   ), *Selected Poems*, 1965
William Jay Smith (1918–   ), *Poems, 1947–1957*, 1957
W. D. Snodgrass (1926–   ), *Heart's Needle*, 1959
Gary Snyder (1930–   ), *The Back Country*, 1968
William Stafford (1914–   ), *Traveling Through the Dark*, 1962

Mark Strand (1934–   ), *Reasons for Moving*, 1968
May Swenson (1927–   ), *To Mix with Time: New and Se-
lected Poems*, 1963
James Wright (1927–   ), *Collected Poems*, 1971

45 · *Criticism: Latest Phases*

Literary criticism in America seems to be still under the influence of the "New Criticism," no later school having arisen seriously to challenge its supremacy. Volumes in which American literature is made to relate more closely to American cultural history than the New Criticism allows for have, indeed, appeared; and some of these are listed below. Moreover, the pursuit of myth and symbol has occupied a number of the following interpreters of poetry and fiction.

Conrad Aiken (1889–   ), *Collected Criticism from 1916 to the Present: A Reviewer's ABC*, 1958

Quentin Anderson (1912–   ), *The Imperial Self: An Essay in American Literary and Cultural History*, 1971

R. P. Blackmur (1904–1965), *The Lion and the Honeycomb*, 1955

R. P. Blackmur, *A Primer of Ignorance*, ed. Joseph Frank, 1967

Louise Bogan (1897–   ), *Selected Criticism*, 1955

Wayne C. Booth (1921–   ), *The Rhetoric of Fiction*, 1961

Cleanth Brooks (1906–   ), *The Hidden God: Studies in Hemingway, Faulkner, Yeats, Eliot, and Warren*, 1963

Kenneth Burke (1897–   ), *Language As Symbolic Action: Essays on Life, Literature and Method*, 1966

R. S. Crane (1886–1967), *The Idea of the Humanities and Other Essays Critical and Historical*, 2 vols., 1967

Ralph Ellison (1914–   ), *Shadow and Act*, 1964

Charles Feidelson, Jr. (1918–   ), *Symbolism and American Literature*, 1953

Francis Fergusson (1904–   ), *The Idea of a Theater*, 1949

Leslie A. Fiedler (1917–   ), *Collected Essays*, 2 vols., 1971

E. D. Hirsch, Jr., (1928–   ), *Validity in Interpretation*, 1967

Stanley Edgar Hyman (1919–1970), *The Armed Vision*, 1948

Randall Jarrell (1914–1965), *Poetry and the Age*, 1953

Alfred Kazin (1915–   ), *Contemporaries*, 1962

Harry Levin (1912–   ), *The Power of Blackness*, 1958

R. W. B. Lewis (1917–   ), *The American Adam*, 1955

John F. Lynen (1924–   ), *The Design of the Present*, 1969

Wright Morris (1910–), *The Territory Ahead*, 1958
Norman Podhoretz (1930–), *Doings and Undoings*, 1964
Richard Poirier (1925–), *The Performing Self: Compositions and Decompositions in the Languages of Contemporary Life*, 1971
Philip Rahv (1908–), *Image and Idea*, 1940 (revised and enlarged in 1957)
Robert Scholes (1929–) and Robert Kellogg (1928–), *The Nature of Narrative*, 1966
Karl Shapiro (1913–), *In Defense of Ignorance*, 1960
Wilfrid Sheed (1930–), *The Morning After: Selected Essays and Reviews*, 1971
Lionel Trilling (1905–), *The Liberal Imagination*, 1950
Lionel Trilling, *The Opposing Self*, 1955
Lionel Trilling, *Beyond Culture*, 1965
Ray B. West, Jr. (1908–), *The Writer in the Room*, 1968
Edmund Wilson (1895–1972), *Axel's Castle*, 1931
Edmund Wilson, *The Triple Thinkers*, 1938
Edmund Wilson, *The Wound and the Bow*, 1941
Edmund Wilson, *The Boys in the Back Room*, 1941
Edmund Wilson, *Patriotic Gore*, 1962
W. K. Wimsatt, Jr. (1907–), *The Verbal Icon: Studies in the Meaning of Poetry*, 1954
Yvor Winters (1900–1968), *Forms of Discovery*, 1967

III · SOME CONTINUING ELEMENTS

46 · *The Short Story in the Twentieth Century*

Basic changes in the concept of literary art, in the nature and costs of American magazines, and in the interests and caliber of the reading public affected the short story, which is sometimes thought to be a particularly American contribution to literary form. The "slick" story continued in the popular magazines, whether as a love story, a tale of adventure or mystery, or a story of humor; but as the century advanced, the formula story tended to recede among serious writers in favor of the "unfinished" or slice-of-life story, often pessimistic, sometimes confined to a single inconclusive episode, and occasionally twisted in the direction of an enigmatic or ironical ending. The distinction between the "long short story" and the "short story" seemed more and more to break down, what Henry James might have called a short novel or novella being difficult to distinguish from the short story (for example, in the books by William Faulkner listed below); and equally, the short narrative tended more and more to fade into the single-line narrative and even into the personal essay. The arrangement of titles in this section is not alphabetical by authors, but is in a general sense chronological, the stories of O. Henry serving as a base line. Other volumes of short stories are of course to be found on other lists in this guide.

"O. Henry" (William Sydney Porter, 1862–1910), *The Four Million*, 1906

Ring Lardner (1885–1933), *Gullible's Travels*, 1917

Ring Lardner, *How To Write Short Stories (with Samples)*, 1924

Ring Lardner, *The Love Nest and Other Stories*, 1926

Sherwood Anderson (1876–1941), *The Triumph of the Egg*, 1921

Ruth Suckow (1892–1960), *Iowa Interiors*, 1926

Wilbur Daniel Steele (1886–1970), *The Man Who Saw Through Heaven*, 1927

Katherine Anne Porter (1894–   ), *Flowering Judas*, 1930

Katherine Anne Porter, *Pale Horse, Pale Rider*, 1939

CONTINUING ELEMENTS

Katherine Anne Porter, *The Leaning Tower*, 1944
William Faulkner (1897–1962), *Doctor Martino and Other Stories*, 1934
William Faulkner, *Go Down, Moses, and Other Stories*, 1942
William Faulkner, *Knight's Gambit*, 1949
Erskine Caldwell (1903–   ), *Kneel to the Rising Sun*, 1935
Kay Boyle (1903–   ), *The White Horses of Vienna and Other Stories*, 1936
Ernest Hemingway (1898–1961), *The Fifth Column and the First Forty-Nine Stories*, 1938
William Saroyan (1908–   ), *My Name is Aram*, 1940
Eudora Welty (1909–   ), *The Wide Net*, 1943
Caroline Gordon (1895–   ), *The Forest of the South*, 1945
John O'Hara (1905–1970), *Pipe Night*, 1945
J. F. Powers (1917–   ), *The Prince of Darkness and Other Stories*, 1947
Peter Taylor (1917–   ), *The Long Fourth and Other Stories*, 1948
Truman Capote (1924–   ), *A Tree of Night*, 1949
Shirley Jackson (1919–1965), *The Lottery; or, The Adventures of James Harris*, 1949
Wallace Stegner (1909–   ), *The Women on the Wall*, 1950
Hortense Calisher (1911–   ), *In the Absence of Angels*, 1951
Carson McCullers (1917–1967), *The Ballad of the Sad Café*, 1951
Jean Stafford (1915–   ), *Children Are Bored on Sunday*, 1953
John Cheever (1912–   ), *The Enormous Radio and Other Stories*, 1953
J. D. Salinger (1919–   ), *Nine Stories*, 1953
Shirley Ann Grau (1929–   ), *The Black Prince and Other Stories*, 1955
Flannery O'Connor (1925–1965), *A Good Man Is Hard To Find*, 1955
Flannery O'Connor, *Everything That Rises Must Converge*, 1965
James Purdy (1923–   ), *The Color of Darkness*, 1957
George Garrett (1929–   ), *King of the Mountain*, 1958
Bernard Malamud (1914–   ), *The Magic Barrel*, 1958
Bernard Malamud, *Idiots First*, 1964

Grace Paley (1922–   ), *The Little Disturbances of Man,* 1959
Philip Roth (1933–   ), *Goodbye, Columbus,* 1959
Herbert Gold (1924–   ), *Love and Like,* 1960
John Updike (1932–   ), *Pigeon Feathers,* 1962
William H. Gass (1924–   ), *In the Heart of the Heart of the Country,* 1968
Donald Barthelme (1931–   ), *Unspeakable Practices, Unnatural Acts,* 1968
John Barth (1930–   ), *Lost in the Funhouse,* 1968

CONTINUING ELEMENTS

47 · *Conventional Fiction in the Twentieth Century*

Not all writers of talent yielded to the mood of experimentation that characterized much fiction in the second quarter of the present century. Many were content to keep the usual conventions of the novel, borrowing from the experimenters a wider range of topics, a deeper richness of psychology, a distrust of classifying human beings into types, and a greater flexibility of style. They retained some of the older concepts of novel-writing, namely, that fiction has a primary duty of story-telling and another duty of pleasing the intelligent reader. Literary histories are commonly unkind to novels of this sort, which in another era might have drawn to themselves a greater degree of critical attention. It is a mark of critical imperceptivity to assume, because a writer produces a "conventional" novel, that he is therefore an inferior writer. The following titles vary greatly in literary art, but the best of them are quite as excellent as the "advanced" or "experimental" fiction.

James Agee (1909-1955), *A Death in the Family*, 1957
Hervey Allen (1889–1949), *Anthony Adverse*, 1933
Louis Auchincloss (1917–   ), *The Great World and Timothy Colt*, 1956
Louis Auchincloss, *The Rector of Justin*, 1964
Gerald Warner Brace (1901–   ), *The Garretson Chronicle*, 1947
Louis Bromfield (1896–1956), *The Green Bay Tree*, 1924
Louis Bromfield, *The Strange Case of Miss Annie Spragg*, 1928
John Brooks (1920–   ), *A Pride of Lions*, 1954
Pearl Buck (1892–   ), *The Good Earth*, 1931 (the first of a trilogy, followed by *Sons*, 1932, and *A House Divided*, 1935)
Mary Ellen Chase (1887–   ), *Mary Peters*, 1934
John Cheever (1912–   ), *The Wapshot Chronicle*, 1957
Peter DeVries (1910–   ), *The Tunnel of Love*, 1954
Edna Ferber (1887–1968), *Show Boat*, 1926
Dorothy Canfield Fisher (1879-1958), *The Bent Twig*, 1915
Leonard Gardner (? –   ), *Fat City*, 1969
George Garrett (1929–   ), *Death of the Fox*, 1971

Paul Horgan (1903–   ), *Everything To Live For,* 1968
Charles Jackson (1903–1968), *The Lost Weekend,* 1944
Elizabeth Janeway (1913–   ), *The Walsh Girls,* 1943
Victoria Lincoln (1904–   ), *February Hill,* 1934
Helen MacInnes (1907–   ), *Above Suspicion,* 1941
Margaret Mitchell (1900–1949), *Gone with the Wind,* 1936
Christopher Morley (1890–1957), *Kitty Foyle,* 1939
Theodore Morrison (1901–   ), *The Stones of the House,* 1953
Edwin O'Connor (1918–1968), *The Last Hurrah,* 1956
Walker Percy (1916–   ), *The Moviegoer,* 1961
William Saroyan (1908–   ), *The Human Comedy,* 1942
Budd Schulberg (1914–   ), *The Disenchanted,* 1950
Betty Smith (1904–   ), *A Tree Grows in Brooklyn,* 1943
John Steinbeck (1902–1968), *Tortilla Flat,* 1935
John Steinbeck, *Of Mice and Men,* 1937
Robert Lewis Taylor (1912–   ), *The Travels of Jamie McPheeters,* 1958
Lionel Trilling (1905–   ), *The Middle of the Journey,* 1947
Gore Vidal (1925–   ), *Washington, D.C.,* 1967
Jessamyn West (1907–   ), *The Friendly Persuasion,* 1945
Sloan Wilson (1920–   ), *The Man in the Gray Flannel Suit,* 1955

CONTINUING ELEMENTS

48 · The Twentieth-Century Regional Novel

After 1920, the regional novel also benefited from experimentation in other fields, particularly in the writing of historical fiction and in a renewed interest in the psychology of uneducated persons. The tendency to lyricism in the style of regional fiction already evident in earlier examples (see list 3) did not vanish, but character became more credible in twentieth-century terms, the happy ending disappeared, and the enforced comparison between the supposed superiority of city ways and that of country folk tended to vanish. The Negro was treated with tenderness vaguely recalling some of the "Yes, massa" fiction, and the same mixture of envy and condescension was sometimes felt; but on the whole, regional fiction after 1920 is better art than was regional fiction in the 1890s. Again it is difficult to distinguish regional fiction from other sorts (is J. P. Marquand, for example, a regional writer because he is chiefly concerned with New England?), but the following list is suggestive. Additional novelists who might be classed as regional may be found in almost any other list containing fiction titles in this guide.

Gladys Hasty Carroll (1904–   ), *As the Earth Turns,* 1933
Homer Croy (1883–1965), *West of the Water Tower,* 1923
August Derleth (1909–   ), *Still Is the Summer Night,* 1937
(the first of four novels concerning the Prairie du Sac region of Wisconsin)
Rachel Field (1894–1942), *All This and Heaven, Too,* 1938
Dorothy Canfield Fisher (1879–1958), *The Brimming Cup,* 1921
Berry Fleming (1899–   ), *Siesta,* 1935
Shelby Foote (1916–   ), *Shiloh,* 1952
Daniel Fuchs (1909–   ), *Summer in Williamsburg,* 1934
Shirley Ann Grau (1929–   ), *The Keepers of the House,* 1964
Paul Green (1894–   ), *This Body the Earth,* 1935
DuBose Heyward (1885–1940), *Porgy,* 1925
Paul Horgan (1903–   ), *A Distant Trumpet,* 1960
Oliver La Farge (1901–1963), *Laughing Boy,* 1929
Rose Wilder Lane (1887–   ), *Free Land,* 1938
Harper Lee (1926–   ), *To Kill a Mockingbird,* 1960

Ross Lockridge (1914–1948), *Raintree County*, 1948

Andrew Lytle (1902–   ), *The Velvet Horn*, 1957

Wright Morris (1910–   ), *The Home Place*, 1948

Julia Peterkin (1880–1961), *Black April*, 1927

James Purdy (1923–   ), *The Nephew*, 1960

Marjorie Kinnan Rawlings (1896–1954), *The Yearling*, 1938

Conrad Richter (1890–1968), *The Awakening Land* (a trilogy, comprising *The Trees*, 1940; *The Fields*, 1946; *The Town*, 1950)

Elizabeth Madox Roberts (1886–1941), *The Time of Man*, 1926

Elsie Singmaster (1879–1958), *Ellen Levis*, 1921

Elizabeth Spencer (1921–   ), *Fire in the Morning*, 1948

Jesse Stuart (1907–   ), *Taps for Private Tussie*, 1943

William Styron (1925–   ), *The Confessions of Nat Turner*, 1967

Robert Penn Warren (1905–   ), *Night Rider*, 1939

Robert Penn Warren, *Meet Me in the Green Glen*, 1971

Eudora Welty (1909–   ), *Delta Wedding*, 1946

Eudora Welty, *Losing Battles*, 1970

CONTINUING ELEMENTS

49 · *Autobiography in the Twentieth Century*

Although autobiographies were occasionally written in the nineteenth century, they did not constitute an important literary genre, the *Memoirs* of Ulysses S. Grant being one of the few that aspired to literary merit. In the twentieth century, however, perhaps because of a change in publishing conditions, perhaps because of an alteration of the reading public, but above all because of the devouring interest of the twentieth century in personality, the autobiography has become an important mode of literary expression. Where formerly a public figure expected to have an official biography written by someone else, he now anticipates this by publishing his own account of himself. These books, which picture all kinds of human beings in all sorts of situations, are of varying literary merit. The following titles are suggestive of an endless field.

Dean Acheson (1893–1971), *Present at the Creation: My Years in the State Department,* 1969
Henry Adams (1838–1918), *The Education of Henry Adams,* 1907 (published in 1918)
Conrad Aiken (1899–   ), *Ushant,* 1952
Margaret Anderson (? –   ), *My Thirty Years' War,* 1930
Margaret Anderson, *The Strange Necessity,* 1969
Sherwood Anderson (1876–1934), *Memoirs,* 1942
Michael J. Arlen (? –   ), *Exiles,* 1970
Mary Austin (1868–1934), *Earth Horizon,* 1932
S. N. Behrman (1893–   ), *The Worcester Account,* 1954
S. N. Behrman, *People in a Diary: A Memoir,* 1972
Henry Seidel Canby (1878–1961), *American Memoir,* 1947 (comprises *The Age of Confidence,* 1934; *Alma Mater,* 1936; and later material)
Hodding Carter (1907–1972), *Where Main Street Meets the River,* 1953
Eldridge Cleaver (1935–   ), *Soul on Ice,* 1968
David L. Cohn (1897–1961), *Where I Was Born and Raised,* 1948
Frank Conroy (1936–   ), *Stop-time,* 1967

Malcolm Cowley (1898–   ), *Exile's Return*, 1934 (revised edition, 1951)

Wilbur L. Cross (1862–1948), *Connecticut Yankee*, 1943

W. E. B. Du Bois (1868–1963), *Autobiography*, 1968

Edna Ferber (1887–1968), *A Peculiar Treasure*, 1939

Joseph Freeman (1897–   ), *An American Testament*, 1936

Hamlin Garland (1860–1940), *A Son of the Middle Border* 1917

Hamlin Garland, *A Daughter of the Middle Border*, 1921

Hamlin Garland, *Trailmakers of the Middle Border*, 1926

Hamlin Garland, *Backtrailers of the Middle Border*, 1928 (followed a second series of four books, running from *Roadside Meetings*, 1930, to *Afternoon Neighbors*, 1934)

Ellen Glasgow (1874–1945), *The Woman Within*, 1954

Woody Guthrie (1912–1967), *Bound for Glory*, 1943

Moss Hart (1904–1961), *Act One*, 1959

Lillian Hellman (1905–   ), *An Unfinished Woman*, 1969

Henry James (1843–1916), *A Small Boy and Others*, 1913

Henry James, *Notes of a Son and Brother*, 1914

Henry James, *The Middle Years*, 1917

Alfred Kazin (1915–   ), *A Walker in the City*, 1951

Charles A. Lindbergh (1902–   ), *The Spirit of St. Louis*, 1953

Mabel Dodge Luhan (1879–1962), *Intimate Memories*, 1933–1937 (comprises *Background*, 1933; *European Experiences*, 1935; *Movers and Shakers*, 1936; *Edge of Taos Desert*, 1937)

Norman Mailer (1923–   ), *Advertisements for Myself*, 1959

"Malcolm X" (Malcolm Little, 1925–1965), *Autobiography*, 1965

H. L. Mencken (1880–1956), *The Days of Henry L. Mencken*, 1947 (comprises *Happy Days*, 1940; *Newspaper Days*, 1941; *Heathen Days*, 1943)

Albert Jay Nock (1872?–1945), *Memoirs of a Superfluous Man*, 1943

William Alexander Percy (1885–1942), *Lanterns on the Levee*, 1941

Bliss Perry (1860–1954), *And Gladly Teach*, 1935

William Lyon Phelps (1865–1943), *Autobiography and Letters*, 1939

CONTINUING ELEMENTS

Kenneth Rexroth (1905–), *An Autobiographical Novel*, 1966
Eleanor Roosevelt (1884–1962), *This Is My Story*, 1937
Carl Sandburg (1878–1967), *Always the Young Strangers*, 1952
George Santayana (1867–1952), *Persons and Places*, 1944–1953 (comprises *The Background of My Life*, 1944; *The Middle Span*, 1945; *My Host the World*, 1953)
Vincent Sheean (1899–), *Personal History*, 1935
Gertrude Stein (1874–1946), *The Autobiography of Alice B. Toklas*, 1933
Carl Van Doren (1885–1950), *Three Worlds*, 1936
Edith Wharton (1862–1937), *A Backward Glance*, 1934
Hans Zinsser (1878–1940), *As I Remember Him*, 1940

50 · *Biography in the Twentieth Century*

One of the oldest forms of writing in what was to become the United States, American biography dates from 1658, when the Reverend John Norton published in Cambridge a brief life of the Reverend John Cotton. In the eighteenth and nineteenth centuries biography wavered between two poles: the popular book, teaching by example, of which the most famous is probably Mason L. Weems's life of Washington (1800), and stately public memorials of the life-and-times or life-and-letters category. James Parton (1822–1891) combined scholarship with literary skills in biographies of Aaron Burr, Andrew Jackson, Benjamin Franklin, and Thomas Jefferson that still have primary value. The creation of the "American Men of Letters" series under Charles Dudley Warner in 1881 and of the "American Statesmen" series under John T. Morse, Jr., in 1882 marked a firm union of historical scholarship and literary skill, but did nothing for the intimate lives of the subjects. But in the 1920s, as part of the drive toward "liberation" and under the influence of Lytton Strachey in England and Gamaliel Bradford in America, informality and exposure became the rule. A spate of "debunking" biographies appeared at the same time that the influence of theories of irrational psychology altered the conventional view of motives. In the last twenty or thirty years, biography has tended to return to more responsible notions of scholarship; it has also developed the multivolume biography of great figures.

What is "good" biography from the point of view of historical scholarship may not be a work of literary art; and contrariwise, a biography that ranks high as literature because it persuasively sets forth a character may require constant correction as fact. The following list tries to select representative biographies appearing since 1890 that keep a good balance between art and information. Although American biographers have ranged widely, the list includes only lives of American subjects by American writers.

Since only important figures attract biographies, and since these figures are likely to be complex personalities, biographers will vary in their approaches to the truth of a life. Some of these titles have been superseded, in an historical sense; some have aroused controversy; and some are as characteristic of the biographer as they are of the subjects chosen. Should anyone have the time to read all the list, however, he would gain considerable insight into biographical methodology and its changes since the 1890s. The titles are arranged chronologically to indicate trends.

Moncure D. Conway (1832–1907), *The Life of Thomas Paine,* 1892

Henry James (1843–1916), *William Wetmore Story and His Friends,* 2 vols., 1903

George Edward Woodberry (1855–1930), *Ralph Waldo Emerson,* 1907

William Dean Howells (1837–1920), *My Mark Twain,* 1910

Albert Bigelow Paine (1861–1937), *Mark Twain: A Biography,* 3 vols., 1912

Herbert Croly (1869–1930), *Marcus Alonzo Hanna: His Life and Work,* 1912

Gamaliel Bradford (1863–1932), *Lee, the American,* 1912

Harvey Cushing (1869–1939), *The Life of Sir William Osler,* 2 vols., 1925

Kenneth B. Murdock (1895–   ), *Increase Mather: The Foremost American Puritan,* 1925

Hervey Allen (1889–1949), *Israfel· The Life and Times of Edgar Allan Poe,* 1926

Carl Sandburg (1878–1967), *Abraham Lincoln: The Prairie Years,* 2 vols., 1926 (followed by *Abraham Lincoln: The War Years,* 4 vols., 1939)

Rupert Hughes (1872–1956), *George Washington,* 3 vols., 1926–1930 (never completed)

Paxton Hibben (1880–1928), *Henry Ward Beecher: An American Portrait,* 1927

Robert H. Fuller (1865–1927), *Jubilee Jim: The Life of Colonel James Fisk,* 1928

Allan Nevins (1890–1971), *Frémont: The West's Greatest Adventurer,* 2 vols., 1928

Emanie Louise Nahm Sachs (? –   ), *"The Terrible Siren": Victoria Woodhull, 1838–1927,* 1928

Edwin F. Dakin (1898–   ), *Mrs. Eddy: The Biography of a Virginal Mind,* 1929

Marquis James (1891–1955), *The Raven: A Biography of Sam Houston,* 1929

Lloyd Paul Stryker (1885–1955), *Andrew Jackson: A Study in Courage,* 1929

Claude M. Fuess (1885–1963), *Daniel Webster,* 2 vols., 1930

John K. Winkler (1891–   ), *Morgan the Magnificent: The Life of J. Pierpont Morgan (1837–1913),* 1930

Burton J. Hendrick (1870–1949), *The Life of Andrew Carnegie,* 2 vols., 1932

Gilbert Chinard (1881–1972), *Honest John Adams,* 1933

Parker Morell (1906–1943), *Diamond Jim: The Life and Times of James Buchanan Brady,* 1934

Douglas Southall Freeman (1866–1953), *R. E. Lee: A Biography,* 4 vols., 1935

Mari Sandoz (1907–1966), *Old Jules,* 1935

Odell Shepard (1884–1967), *Pedlar's Progress: The Life of Bronson Alcott,* 1937

Carl Van Doren (1885–1950), *Benjamin Franklin,* 1938

Henry Seidel Canby (1878–1961), *Thoreau,* 1939

Allan Nevins, *John D. Rockefeller: The Heroic Age of American Enterprise,* 2 vols., 1940

Wheaton J. Lane (1902–   ), *Commodore Vanderbilt: An Epic of the Steam Age,* 1942

Muriel Rukeyser (1913–   ), *Willard Gibbs,* 1942

DeLancey Ferguson (1888–   ), *Mark Twain: Man and Legend,* 1943

Russel B. Nye (1913–   ), *George Bancroft: Brahmin Rebel,* 1944

Fawn McKay Brodie (1915–   ), *No Man Knows My History: The Life of Joseph Smith, the Mormon Prophet,* 1945

Stanley Vestal (1887–   ), *Jim Bridger: Mountain Man,* 1946

Alpheus T. Mason (1899–   ), *Brandeis: A Free Man's Life,* 1946

Arthur S. Link (1920–   ), *Wilson,* 1947–(in progress, 5 vols. published)

Morris Bishop (1893–   ), *Champlain: The Life of Fortitude,* 1948

CONTINUING ELEMENTS

Dumas Malone (1892–   ), *Jefferson and His Times,* 1948–
(in progress, 4 vols. published)

Ernest Samuels (1903–   ), *The Young Henry Adams,* 1948
(followed in 1958 by *Henry Adams: The Middle Years,* and
in 1964 by *Henry Adams: The Major Phase*)

Thomas Coulson (1886–   ), *Joseph Henry: His Life and
Work,* 1950

Arthur Mizener (1907–   ), *The Far Side of Paradise: A
Biography of F. Scott Fitzgerald,* 1951

Leon Edel (1907–   ), *Henry James,* 5 vols., 1953–1972

Wallace Stegner (1909–   ), *Beyond the Hundredth Meridian: John Wesley Powell and the Second Opening of the
West,* 1954

Talbot Hamlin (1889–1956), *Benjamin Henry Latrobe,* 1955

Mark DeWolfe Howe (1906–1967), *Justice Oliver Wendell
Holmes,* 2 vols., 1957–1963 (never completed)

Mark Schorer (1908–   ), *Sinclair Lewis: An American Life,*
1961

Arnold Schwab (1922–   ), *James Gibbons Huneker: Critic
of the Seven Arts,* 1963

Helen Huntington Howe (1905–   ), *The Gentle Americans,
1864–1960: The Biography of a Breed,* 1965

Edward Chase Kirkland (1894–   ), *Charles Francis Adams,
Jr., 1835–1915: The Patrician at Bay,* 1965

Justin Kaplan (1925–   ), *Mr. Clemens and Mark Twain,*
1966

Martin B. Duberman (1930–   ), *James Russell Lowell,* 1966

Lawrance Thompson (1906–   ), *Robert Frost,* 1966– (in
progress, 2 vols. published)

Gay Wilson Allen (1903–   ), *William James,* 1967

Edward C. Wagenknecht (1900–   ), *John Greenleaf Whittier: A Portrait in Paradox,* 1967

Andrew Turnbull (1921–1970), *Thomas Wolfe,* 1967

Louis Sheaffer (? –   ), *O'Neill, Son and Playwright,* 1968–
(in progress, 1 vol. published)

Thomas J. Fleming (1927–   ), *The Man from Monticello:
An Intimate Life of Thomas Jefferson,* 1969

Carlos Baker (1909–   ), *Ernest Hemingway: A Life Story,*
1969

Jay Martin (1930–   ), *Nathanael West: The Art of His Life,*
1970
Kenneth S. Lynn (1923–   ), *William Dean Howells: An
American Life,* 1971
Joseph P. Lash (1909–   ), *Eleanor and Franklin: The Story
of Their Relationship Based on Eleanor Roosevelt's Private
Papers,* 1971

CONTINUING ELEMENTS

51 · *Humor and Satire in the Twentieth Century*

Somewhat apart from the shocks of world conflict and intellectual battles over the nature of art, morals, and society, certain traditional forms of American writing went forward, absorbing only so much of the novel and the controversial as readers would accept. Humor is not a literary genre but a mode of interpretation; nevertheless, in American literature the humorist is a sufficiently well-known type, skilled in light verse, in brief essay or comic story, or in whimsical or sardonic commentary on human folly. After World War I, folk humor became the possession of the folklorist; and under the aegis of the immensely successful *New Yorker*, the twentieth-century American humorist has become increasingly urbane and "sophisticated." Undoubtedly the twenties set a fashion, yet the fashion for urbane humor is old (see list 8); and in recent decades the humorist has quietly yet sturdily asserted an intellectual independence of cult and fashion, especially in satire.

But the sixties saw the development of "sick" humor, especially in the so-called underground culture, though not exclusively there. "Sick" humor is hard to define; it exaggerates the grotesque (long an element in humor), it seeks to give a humorous twist to frightening or forbidden thought and activity, and it represents a nonintellectual rebellion against the "Establishment." In addition, it consciously avoids "literary" expression, since literature is thought to be a mode of the "Establishment."

F. P. Adams (1881–1960), *The Conning Tower Book*, 1926
Fred Allen (1894–1956), *Treadmill to Oblivion*, 1954
Russell Baker (1925–   ), *No Cause for Panic*, 1964
Russell Baker, *All Things Considered*, 1965
Robert C. Benchley (1889–1945), *20,000 Leagues under the Sea; or, David Copperfield*, 1928
Robert C. Benchley, *The Treasurer's Report*, 1930
A Benchley Round-up, ed. Nathaniel Benchley, 1962
Morris Bishop (1893–   ), *A Bowl of Bishop*, 1954
"Art" (Arthur) Buchwald (1925–   ), *How Much Is That in Dollars?* 1961

"Art" Buchwald, *The Establishment Is Alive and Well in Washington,* 1969

Clarence Day (1874–1935), *This Simian World,* 1920

Clarence Day, *Life with Father,* 1935

Peter DeVries (1910–   ), *The Mackerel Plaza,* 1958

Bruce Jay Friedman, (1930–   ), *A Mother's Kisses,* 1964

Marion Hargrove (1919–   ), *See Here, Private Hargrove,* 1942

Samuel Hoffenstein (1890–1947), *Poems in Praise of Practically Nothing,* 1928

Jean Kerr (1923–   ), *Please Don't Eat the Daisies,* 1957

Ring Lardner (1885–1933), *The Ring Lardner Reader,* ed. Maxwell Geismar, 1963

Don Marquis (1878–1937), *Hermione and Her Little Group of Serious Thinkers,* 1916

Don Marquis, *archy and mehitabel,* 1927

Groucho Marx (1891–   ), *Memoirs of a Mangy Lover,* 1963

David McCord (1897–   ), *And What's More,* 1941

Phyllis McGinley, (1905–   ), *Times Three: Selected Verse from Three Decades,* 1960

Ruth McKenney (1911–1972), *My Sister Eileen,* 1938

Ogden Nash (1902–1971), *Free Wheeling,* 1931

Ogden Nash, *Verses from 1929 On,* 1959

Dorothy Parker (1893–1967), *The Portable Dorothy Parker,* 1944

S. J. Perelman (1904–   ), *Perelman's Home Companion,* 1955

S. J. Perelman, *The Road to Miltown; or, Under the Spreading Atrophy,* 1957

Will Rogers (1879–1935), *The Autobiography of Will Rogers,* 1949 (essentially a chronology of his quips)

"Leonard Q. Ross" (Leo C. Rosten, 1908–   ), *The Education of Hyman Kaplan,* 1937

Leo C. Rosten, *The Joys of Yiddish,* 1968

Damon Runyon (1884–1946), *Guys and Dolls,* 1932

Damon Runyon, *The Best of Runyon,* 1938

Neil Simon (1927–   ), *The Odd Couple,* 1966

Cornelia Otis Skinner (1901–   ) and Emily Kimbrough 1899–   ), *Our Hearts Were Young and Gay,* 1942

CONTINUING ELEMENTS

H. Allen Smith (1907–   ), *Low Man on a Totem Pole*, 1941
Frank Sullivan, (1892–   ), *A Pearl in Every Oyster*, 1938
James Thurber (1894–1961), with E. B. White (1899–   ), *Is Sex Necessary?* 1929
James Thurber, *My Life and Hard Times*, 1933
James Thurber, *Let Your Mind Alone!* 1937
James Thurber, *The Thurber Carnival*, 1945
E. B. White, *One Man's Meat*, 1942
E. B. White, *The Second Tree from the Corner*, 1953
William K. Zinsser (1922–   ), *The Haircurl Papers and Other Searches for the Lost Individual*, 1964
William K. Zinsser, *The Lunacy Boom*, 1970

52 · *Fantasy, Murder, Science, Escape*

In the literary histories the detective story and science fiction seem to begin and end with Edgar Allan Poe. Since the late nineteenth century and increasingly in the twentieth century, however, science fiction and mystery stories have drawn larger and larger audiences. The whodunits fill the paperback libraries; and science fiction, whether straight science or fantasy, not only appears in paperback books but is also the stock in trade of a number of magazines. In both categories there is much trash, an enormous amount of hack-writing, and the overworking of stereotypes of plot, character, and motif. In the highly moral world of the detective story, virtue always wins, if sometimes by outrageously mechanical means. Nor is the world of science fiction less moral, for if distant planets or the remote future are now and then populous with supermen capable of crushing out the odious little race of little men, evil nevertheless vanishes either by some trick of fantastic discovery or by virtue of the superior strength of goodness. For no clear reason, both branches of fiction are considered to be beneath the dignity of literary history; yet both branches have their passionate aficionados; and the rules of the game are as scrupulously maintained between writer and public as are the rules of baseball.

The background for understanding the cult of the detective story is provided in Howard Haycraft, *Murder for Pleasure: The Life and Times of the Detective Story* (1941), and Alma Elizabeth Murch, *The Development of the Detective Novel* (1958). Good general sources for understanding science fiction are J. O. Bailey, *Pilgrims Through Space and Time* (1947); Kingsley Amis, *New Maps of Hell: A Survey of Science Fiction* (1960); and H. Bruce Franklin, *Future Perfect: American Science Fiction of the Nineteenth Century* (1966). For understanding the use of supernatural elements in the fantasy story, see Peter Penzoldt, *The Supernatural in Fiction* (1952). The supernatural in Penzoldt's sense of the word, however, is mostly absent from science fiction proper, though it may appear in science fantasy. The following lists are (i) detective stories of literary merit by American authors, arranged in the order of publication to illustrate development;

CONTINUING ELEMENTS

and (ii) science fiction, *not* in chronological order but chosen for its superior intellectual appeal.

I · THE DETECTIVE STORY

Anna Katharine Green (1846–1935), *The Leavenworth Case*, 1878 (listed despite its date because it marks the resumption of the writing of detective fiction after Poe and because it stands at the headwaters of the contemporary American detective story)

Jacques Futrelle (1875–1912), *The Thinking Machine*, 1907 (reissued in 1918 as *The Problem of Cell 13*)

Mary Roberts Rinehart (1876–1958), *The Circular Staircase*, 1908

Mary Roberts Rinehart, *The Man in Lower Ten*, 1909 (written earlier and serialized, but not published in book form until 1909)

Earl Derr Biggers (1884–1933), *The House Without a Key*, 1925

"S. S. Van Dine" (Willard Huntington Wright, 1888–1939), *The Benson Murder Case*, 1926

Frances Noyes Hart (1890–1943), *The Bellamy Trial*, 1927

"Ellery Queen" (Frederic Dannay, 1905–   , and Manfred B. Lee, 1905–1971), *The Roman Hat Mystery*, 1929

Dashiell Hammett (1894–1961), *The Maltese Falcon*, 1930

Dashiell Hammett, *The Thin Man*, 1932

John Dickson Carr (1906–   ), *Hag's Nook*, 1933

John Dickson Carr, *To Wake the Dead*, 1938

Erle Stanley Gardner (1889–   ), *The Case of the Sulky Girl*, 1933

Richard (1898–   ) and Frances (1896–1963) Lockridge, *Mr. and Mrs. North*, 1936

Richard and Frances Lockridge, *Death of a Tall Man*, 1946

Rex Stout (1886–   ), *Some Buried Caesar*, 1939

Rex Stout, *The Black Mountain*, 1954

Raymond Chandler (1888–1959), *Farewell, My Lovely*, 1940

Raymond Chandler, *The Long Goodbye*, 1954

Elizabeth Daly (1878–1967), *Evidence of Things Seen*, 1943

Phoebe Atwood Taylor (1909–   ), *Proof of the Pudding*, 1945

Mabel Seeley (1903–   ), *The Whistling Shadow,* 1954
John H. MacDonald (1916–   ), *Murder in the Wind,* 1956
Mignon Eberhart (1899–   ), *Jury of One,* 1960
"Ross MacDonald" (Kenneth Millar, 1915–   ), *The Ferguson Affair,* 1960
"Ross MacDonald," *The Underground Man,* 1971
Harry Kemelman (1908–   ), *Friday the Rabbi Slept Late,* 1964
Aaron Marc Stein (1906–   ), *Deadly Delight,* 1967
Helen MacInnes (1907–   ), *The Salzburg Connection,* 1968
"Emma Lathen" (? –   ), *Murder To Go,* 1969
"Ed McBain" (Evan Hunter, 1926–   ), *Jigsaw,* 1970

II · SCIENCE FICTION

Isaac Asimov, ed., *The Hugo Winners,* 2 vols., 1962, 1971
Groff Conklin, ed., *The Best of Science Fiction,* 1946
Groff Conklin, ed., *The Treasury of Science Fiction,* 1948
Groff Conklin, ed., *The Big Book of Science Fiction,* 1950
H. L. Gold, ed., *Galaxy Reader of Science Fiction,* 1952
Damon Knight, ed., *A Century of Science Fiction,* 1952
Robert Silverberg, ed., *Science Fiction Hall of Fame,* 1970
Donald A. Wollheim, ed., *Flight into Space: Great Science Fiction Stories of Interplanetary Travel,* 1950

Poul Anderson (1926–   ), *Tau Zero,* 1971
Isaac Asimov (1920–   ), *I, Robot,* 1950
Isaac Asimov, *The Caves of Steel,* 1953
Edwin Balmer (1883–1959) and Philip Wylie (1902–1971), *When Worlds Collide,* 1932
Edwin Balmer and Philip Wylie, *After Worlds Collide,* 1934
Herbert Best (1894–   ), *The Twenty-fifth Hour,* 1940
Alfred Bester (1913–   ), *The Demolished Man,* 1953
Ray Bradbury (1920–   ), *The Martian Chronicles,* 1950
Ray Bradbury, *The Golden Apples of the Sun,* 1953
Algirdas Budrys (1931–   ), *Rogue Moon,* 1960
"Hal Clement" (Harry C. Stubbs, ? –   ), *Mission of Gravity,* 1954

CONTINUING ELEMENTS

Robert A. Heinlein (1907–   ), *Rocket Ship Galileo*, 1947
Robert A. Heinlein, *Stranger in a Strange Land*, 1968
H. P. Lovecraft (1890–1937), *The Shadow out of Time*, 1939
F. Wright Moxley (1889–   ), *Red Snow*, 1930
"Larry" (Laurence V.) Niven (1938–   ), *Ringworld*, 1970
Alexei Panshin (1940–   ), *Rite of Passage*, 1969
Frederik Pohl (1919?–   ) and Cyril Kornbluth (1923–1958),
    The Space Merchants, 1953
"Akkad Pseudoman" (Edwin Fitch Northrup, 1866–1940), *Zero
    to Eighty*, 1937
Robert Silverberg (? –   ), *Tower of Glass*, 1970
Clifford D. Simak (1904–   ), *The City*, 1952
Edward Elmer Smith (1890–1965), *The Skylark of Space*, 1946
A. E. van Vogt (1912–   ), *Slan*, 1946 (reissued, 1951)
Kurt Vonnegut, Jr. (1922–   ), *The Sirens of Titan*, 1961
Stanley Waterloo (1846–1913), *The Story of Ab*, 1897

Index of Authors

245

INDEX

INDEX

INDEX

INDEX

INDEX

257

INDEX

259

INDEX

INDEX